# Rural Child Welfare Practice

# Rural Child Welfare Practice

*Stories from "the Field"*

Edited by Joanne Riebschleger

and

Barbara J. Pierce

OXFORD
UNIVERSITY PRESS

# OXFORD
UNIVERSITY PRESS

Oxford University Press is a department of the University of Oxford. It furthers
the University's objective of excellence in research, scholarship, and education
by publishing worldwide. Oxford is a registered trade mark of Oxford University
Press in the UK and certain other countries.

Published in the United States of America by Oxford University Press
198 Madison Avenue, New York, NY 10016, United States of America.

Library of Congress Cataloging-in-Publication Data
Names: Riebschleger, Joanne, editor. | Pierce, Barbara J., 1956– editor.
Title: Rural child welfare practice : stories from the field /
edited by Joanne Riebschleger, Barbara J. Pierce.
Description: New York, NY : Oxford University Press, [2018] |
Includes bibliographical references and index.
Identifiers: LCCN 2017035655 (print) | LCCN 2017045918 (ebook) |
ISBN 9780190870430 (updf) | ISBN 9780190870447 (epub) |
ISBN 9780190870423 (alk. paper)
Subjects: LCSH: Rural children—Services for. | Child welfare. | Social work with children.
Classification: LCC HV713 (ebook) | LCC HV713 .R789 2018 (print) |
DDC 362.709173/4—dc23
LC record available at https://lccn.loc.gov/2017035655

1 3 5 7 9 8 6 4 2

Printed by Webcom, Inc., Canada

For my "up north" clients and colleagues who taught me so much about rural social work practice. I still feel like I'm there with you. JLR

For Jim, Ian, and Peter with love and gratitude and for my rural clients, students, and colleagues who helped me to learn and grow. BJP

# CONTENTS

# ACKNOWLEDGMENTS

We are grateful for the mentoring and nurturing from so many people over the years. We thank the National Rural Social Work Caucus and the National Child Welfare Workforce Institute for providing a forum for us not only to meet but also grow as our ideas. We also thank our schools, Michigan State University School of Social Work (Joanne) and Indiana University School of Social Work (Barb), for their kind support. We are so grateful to have wonderful colleagues who contributed chapters to this book. Thanks to those who provided photographs for the casebook. Special thanks are offered to David Follmer at Lyceum Press, now a consultant for Oxford University Press, for taking us under his wing even when we had no experience and helping our project come to be. In addition, we thank Dr. James Cruise for his expert and painstaking editorial assistance. Last, we thank our spouses and children who made time to do the domestic chores necessary to keep the family afloat and for providing loving support while we worked on "the book." We could not have completed this project if all of these pieces had not fallen into place.

# ABOUT THE EDITORS

**Joanne Riebschleger**, PhD, LMSW, ACSW, is an associate professor at the School of Social Work at Michigan State University. She grew up in northern Michigan in a town of 3,000 residents. She worked in social work practice with children and families for over two decades in the forested rural areas of lower central Michigan. Her research focuses on rural mental health, health, and child welfare practice with at-risk children and families. A lifetime passion includes developing mental health knowledge and resources for children who have a parent with a mental illness such as anxiety and depression. She was past vice president of the National Rural Social Work Caucus.

**Barbara J. Pierce**, PhD, LCSW, ACSW, is an associate professor at the Indiana University School of Social Work. Despite having grown up and having been educated in two large US cities, she has over 35 years of experience in social work, most of the time serving children, youth, and families in small towns and rural communities in various parts of the United States. Her major research interests include trauma-informed social work education, child welfare workforce issues, strengthening university-agency partnerships, and professional development of child welfare professionals.

# ABOUT THE AUTHORS

**Richard Brandon-Friedman**, MSW, LCSW, LCAC, is a doctoral student at the Indiana University School of Social Work. His professional work has focused on youth and families involved in the child welfare and juvenile justice systems. His primary areas of research include the development of sexual identities among LGBTQ+-identified individuals, adolescent experiences in the child welfare system, the intersection of sociology and social work, and the ways in which childhood socialization affects adolescent and adult interactions.

**Katharine Cahn**, PhD, MSW, is on the faculty at Portland State University's School of Social Work where she directs the Child Welfare Partnership, a research and training center focused on child welfare and children's services in Oregon and beyond. A long-time child welfare trainer, researcher, and systems consultant, she is dedicated to tapping the strengths of family and community to keep children safe and help them realize their full potential.

**Susie T. Cashwell**, PhD, MSW, is an associate professor at Saint Leo University. Dr. Cashwell has practiced in the field of child welfare, community development, student support and advising, working with individuals with disabilities, healthcare, and education as a social worker for 20 years. She is a past president of the National Rural Social Work Caucus.

**Heather Craig-Oldsen**, MSW, began working with children and families in 1970 at the line level, then as a supervisor and eventually as an administrator of child protection and foster family care programs in two different states. By 1980 she had begun providing training, consultation, and curriculum design services in over half of the states in the United States, as well as in several other countries. In 2004 Heather began working at Briar Cliff University as director of the social work program. She retired from academia in 2016 and currently serves as a child welfare consultant and trainer when she is not busy as a city councilwoman in Ponca, Nebraska.

**Angelique Day**, PhD, MSW, is an assistant professor at the University of Washington. She was awarded a Congressional Fellowship with the Society for Research on Child Development in May 2016 where she worked with the US Senate Caucus on Foster Youth to promote public policy reform in the field of child welfare. Angelique is a former child protective services worker and was a ward of the court when she was growing up.

**Gail Folaron**, MSW, PhD, is a professor at Indiana University School of Social Work. She has an extensive history in the field of child welfare with practice experience in both urban and rural areas. Dr. Folaron currently teaches a trauma-informed approach to working with children and families.

**Toni Hail**, MSW, LCSW, is an instructor of social work at Northeastern State university in Tahlequah, Oklahoma. She is an ABD student at Oklahoma State University researching foster alumni in college. She is a member of the Chickasaw nation. She has child welfare practice experience working with tribal families in Oklahoma.

**Rochelle Hine** is a PhD candidate at Monash University in Australia. She has worked with Aboriginal people in South Western Victoria over the past 16 years. She wishes to acknowledge consultation with Roslyn Pevitt, a Gilgar Gunditj woman and Traditional Owner with a wealth of experience in working with rural families in an education context. She also acknowledges the support of Monash University School of Rural Health.

**Steven M. Hyer** is an active duty major, US Air Force, and a LCSW social worker. He has served on active duty since 2010. He successfully completed social work residency at Andrews AFB, Maryland, and was then assigned as the family advocacy officer at Mountain Home AFB, Idaho, for three years. While in Idaho, Capt. Hyer was awarded an Air Force fellowship to complete a PhD in social work at Indiana University. His research interests are in military social work.

**Andrea Kephart** is a LMSW actively pursuing the LCSW. Andrea is married to a retired soldier and has a passion for giving back to the military community. Andrea has worked as a case manager for a military nonprofit and as a clinician in a behavioral healthcare hospital with adults and adolescents.

**Khadija Khaja**, PhD, grew up in Africa but has worked in Canada and the United States. She received her BA, BSW, and MSW degrees in Canada and her PhD in the United States. Her interests include international social work practice and curriculum development, Islamic social service delivery, the impact of terrorism on minority communities, peace building, human rights, ethnographic qualitative research, and culturally competent child welfare practice. She works as an associate professor at the Indiana University School of Social Work.

**Debra Norris**, EdD, MSW, is the director of the BSSW program at the University of South Dakota. Her experience includes residential care for children, rural community mental health, intergenerational family practice, and medical social work. She is involved in initiatives in the areas of interprofessional education, trauma-informed social work practice, and rural intergenerational practice. She worked with the John Hartford Foundation Gero-rich program and directed the South Dakota Child Welfare Traineeship Project.

**Michelle Warden**, MSW, worked in the field of child welfare for more than 20 years and has resided in a rural community for more than 40 years. Throughout her career, she has been a voice for the Indian Child Welfare Act, a liaison to local tribes, and an advocate for supporting and educating others about rural social work. Her personal and professional dedication is that all voices be honored and included in planning for children. Michelle is currently a training specialist with Oregon's Child Welfare Partnership at Portland State University's School of Social Work.

**Charlie Wellenstein**, MSW, is an adjunct assistant professor with the Center for Children, Families and Workforce Development housed in the School of Social Work at the University of Montana. He has developed innovative curriculum for preparing social work students for child welfare practice in the frontier regions of rural Montana.

# INTRODUCTION

## JOANNE RIEBSCHLEGER

*Rural Child Welfare Practice: Stories from "the Field"* is a collage of contemporary case vignettes drawn from the real world of practice experienced by the authors and their rural child welfare colleagues. The overarching aim of the text is to provide students and professionals insider views of child welfare practice in rural areas of the United States, Australia, and Canada. The insider views can be used to help prepare the reader for rural practice, child welfare practice in general, and child welfare practice in rural areas.

Each chapter contains learning objectives, rural social work background information, an applied case vignette drawn from lived experience, teaching suggestions, resource lists, discussion questions, and references. Some chapter authors, including Joanne Riebschleger and especially Barb Pierce, have tested many of the vignettes, teaching exercises, and recommended resources within social work education courses. Student feedback was used to make modifications in the learning materials. In every vignette, the names of the people, as well as any identifying details about them, have been changed to protect confidentiality.

The stories themselves have been written with mindful attention to the complexities social workers face in working with a child welfare clientele with few resources and many problems. The authors do not sugarcoat anything. The cases are challenging and messy. The descriptions in the casebook reveal the nitty-gritty actions and discussions that happen in the field but rarely appear in textbooks or journal articles. The text content recognizes systems of care models of today's child welfare practice by including cases that illustrate children in the child welfare system who are served by child welfare community partner agencies, such as health, mental health, and veterans' services agencies. Regardless of agency setting, the authors take care to provide a balance of strength and challenge information about rural child welfare practice so that readers get a true-to-life, balanced perspective. Additionally, the text emphasizes "rural" as a cultural influence on human development. This means that workers need to learn how to engage in culturally sensitive practice with rural people. This kind of content, unfortunately, is often overlooked in professional education programs (Chipp et al., 2011). It is hoped this casebook can begin to address that gap.

The idea of building a child welfare casebook with rural practice examples was originally proposed by members of the Bachelor of Social Work Peer Network of the National Child Welfare Workforce Initiative (NCWWI). This peer network comprised a group of social work educators who collaborated regularly to share information about child welfare courses, field education/internships, research studies, policies, and systems of care. This particularly pertained to how to prepare, recruit, and retain social work students for the child welfare workforce. Support for the group came from a federal workforce grant funded by the US Department of Health and Human Services, Children's Bureau. The idea for the casebook, accordingly, grew out of the group's involvement with its multiple NCWWI activities. More than anything, the authors hope that this book will contribute to rural child welfare workforce development.

As it stands, this casebook should prove useful in the training of new child welfare workers or those workers with limited rural practice experience. It also provides applied practice examples suited to the education of health and human services professionals. Educators may find the textbook content particularly useful for demonstrating applied practice within a rural practice course, a child welfare practice course, or other courses with content on generalist practice and cultural diversity. Finally, rural people are a diverse minority group, so the case construction format offered here lends itself to easy integration into class assignments describing client system diversity. Given its scope and applications, *Rural Child Welfare Practice* has been crafted to contribute to better rural child welfare practices and policies for at-risk rural children and families across the globe.

## REFERENCE

Chipp, C., Dewane, S., Brems, C., Johnson, M., Warner, T., & Roberts, L. (2011). "If only someone had told me . . .": Lessons from rural providers. *The Journal of Rural Health, 27*, 122–130. http://dx.doi.org/10.1111/j.1748-0361.2010.00314.x

# Rural Child Welfare Practice

# CHAPTER 1

⌀

# Rural Child Welfare Practice

## JOANNE RIEBSCHLEGER AND BARBARA J. PIERCE

Best Friends. This small town child has a comforting best friend.
David G. Riebschleger

## LEARNING OBJECTIVES

- Articulate the complex factors of defining "rural"
- Engage in self-awareness about one's assumptions about rural and urban people

- Describe the three R's of rural child welfare practice: remoteness, resources, and relationships
- State rationales for striving toward cultural competency pertaining to rural areas

## THE CALL TO RURAL PRACTICE

This chapter introduces some of the main constructs in rural social work practice drawn from the professional literature. It begins with an illustrative "call to service" from our chapter 3 author, Deb Norris:

> Professionals called to rural service are people who enjoy long rides, rough weather, marginal coffee, and a warm slice of pie. They are the professionals who make no apology for having a fishing pole and tackle box loaded before their laptop. They are the professionals who know every geographic region of their state has its own distinct lay of the land and that the lay of the land is not just topography; it includes the history, politics, economy, weather, culture, and the ways of living within the environment that Herder referred to as 'local genius' (Herder, 1968). [They] delight in the discovery of their rural areas.

Norris' call to service provides a glimpse into rural practice that seems to fit with experiential methods of understanding rural culture, services, and communities. Often "practice wisdom" about rural practice is best communicated by descriptions of lived experiences (Maidment & Bay, 2012). Norris points out that some of the practice behaviors for effective rural practice include overcoming large geographic distances, finding recreation in natural environments, and knowing the histories and cultures of the people.

This aligns with the work of Riebschleger (2007) who asked rural social work experts to describe what one needs to know to engage in best practices in rural areas. Participants identified that it was important to learn about *communities* including engaging in community-based practice assessments and interventions, dealing with high rates of poverty and scare resources, using abundant informal resources, and adjusting to a slower pace of community and change. The rural social work experts also said that there is a need to understand rural *connections*, including realizing that in rural areas nearly everything is connected; managing intersecting personal-professional roles; using closer, connected relationships to affect change; and knowing how to span broad geographic distances and professional isolation. The need for working with *diverse groups* was highlighted; they recommended including using cultural competency skills, seeking "insider" status (becoming a trusted person by cultural group members), identifying the impacts of rural stigma, and advocating for social justice for rural areas. Finally, the experts reported that workers who engage in good social work practice in rural areas are adept at using *generalist practice skills* and are not afraid to be flexible, creative, and innovative. They advocate for more rural content in social work education. According to the experts in this study, it is important to consider the challenges and rewards of rural practice. While much of the literature of rural practice tends to emphasize the challenges, especially fewer resources and rural isolation, many rewards of rural professional practice were identified. Examples included more practice autonomy, less bureaucracy, more professional respect, the ability to be influential in the community, quicker career advancement, and better quality of life. These constructs will be further explored across this casebook.

## HISTORICAL CONSIDERATIONS

### Rural Communities

Locke and Winship (2005) report that rural context is not new to the profession of social work. Rural communities have emerged and changed in response to greater social forces such agrarianism, industrialization, urbanization, the rise of technology, and, increasingly, globalization. Theodore Roosevelt's "Country Life Movement" began to examine what led rural to urban migration in the early part of the 20th century. Although controversial in its deficit-focused view of country life, it did begin to focus attention on the rural regions of the country. This movement was happening close to the time that Jane Addams, Mary Richmond, and others worked to identify social work as a profession (Locke & Winship, 2005, p. 4). Of particular note is a book written by Josephine Brown in 1933 called *The Rural Community and Social Casework* that argued for educating social workers to engage in practice customized to rural communities.

Practice wisdom leads child welfare professionals to understand that it is important to know the history of rural areas, many of which were founded on agricultural and extraction economies, such as oil, gas, lumber, fish, soil, rock, water, coal, and ore. A sense of community can be in decline when these industries falter in today's world economy. For example, Bell (2009) reported that the coal mining decline in West Virginia has led to "There ain't no bond in town like there used to be" (p. 1). The expectation for professionals to contribute to the community good is often derived from the value of banding together to ensure survival in new territories. At the same

time, community members can be proud of their independence as historical or contemporary "pioneers" in new lands.

In contrast, those who lived on the lands before historical and contemporary settlers may experience cultural erosion and unwanted community
changes associated with suburban outreach, urban migration, extraction
economy booms, and tourism. For example, child welfare workers need to
understand that Native American people have a long history of children
being removed from their care via the pretense that if one is to "save the
man," one must first "kill the Indian." Children as young as three years
old were removed from their families by religious organizations and white
settler policies to be "Christianized" and "civilized" in boarding homes
that are now known for their horrendous physical, sexual, emotional, and
cultural abuses (Hirshberg & Sharp, 2005). Rising concerns about boarding home costs and revelations of widespread child abuse and neglect in
boarding homes preceded the passage of the Indian Child Welfare Act
of 1978. The Indian Child Welfare Act is also tied to the status of Indian
tribes as sovereign nations in treaty legal decisions. This act requires child
welfare workers to show cause for removal of children from their homes. If
removed, the children are expected to be placed within their Native communities, preferably in kinship care. The worker is expected to work with
tribal leaders for child welfare placements. The idea is to prevent the cultural erosion of Native communities and to allow children the opportunity
to grow up within their own culture. But this is not just a cultural matter;
it is a *legal* compliance phenomenon based on the rights of a sovereign
nation to act on behalf of its people. The Child Welfare Act also expects
Native families to be supported long before home removal is considered.
Unfortunately, professionals in rural and urban communities have been
particularly lax in carrying out the actions prescribed in the Indian Child
Welfare Act. This a major policy noncompliance issue for much of child
welfare practice.

## Child Welfare

Social workers who are prepared to work in rural child welfare should know
the history of child welfare services. Up to and through the 19th century,
children were considered "little adults." Many of the ideas we have today
about children did not exist. For example, today it is expected that children will be closely nurtured as developing beings who are not yet fully
grown cognitively, emotionally, and physically. That was not the view of
children through most of human history. Children were often expected to

work more than to play; they were expected to behave politely so as to be "seen and not heard."

Many children from destitute families lived in poor houses, orphanages, and households of families to be used as indentured servants (DiNitto & Johnson, 2016). Orphaned children were put on trains to western rural regions to be raised by families seeking low-cost farm labor. Even children who did live with their birth or kinship families labored long hours in inner-city factories. The first American child abuse cases commencing about 1874 were tried with laws prohibiting animal abuse such as horse-whipping, since protection against the abuse of animals was established in the law. The plaintiffs argued that children were animals and thus should be provided the same protection from abuse and neglect as farm animals.

As awareness of child abuse and neglect rose, new federal laws were implemented. Lindenmeyer (1997) described the broad social changes that followed as policymakers appeared to support the idea that children had "a right to a childhood" (p. 1). As concerns for children and families began to rise among American citizens, their needs began to be addressed with emerging public policy:

> On April 9, 1912, President William Howard Taft signed the Children's Bureau into law and created the first government agency in the world focused solely on the needs of children. Over the next 100 years, the Children's Bureau played a critical role in improving the lives of children and their families. (Children's Bureau Centennial, n.d.)

The Children's Bureau recently celebrated 100 years of guiding practice, programs, and policies to help children and families across the nation (Briar-Lawson, McCarthy, & Dickinson, 2013). For example, Children's Bureau staff and their university and community collaborators have helped to advance family-driven and community-based systems of care, trauma-informed child welfare practice, and child welfare workforce development.

Today child welfare is much more than a federal government child protective services response to child abuse and neglect, particularly one emphasizing removing children from their families. Both public and private child welfare organizations exist at local, state, and federal levels that oversee prevention, child abuse, child neglect, adoption, kinship care, family preservation, foster care, and other services intended to help assist at-risk, struggling children and families. More attention is being paid to family empowerment. Child welfare approaches used today are intended to help families stay together whenever possible. Services that support families in their homes, such as family preservation programs, are commonplace.

Institutional care for children continues to decrease, and kinship care (placement with family members) is rising. Cultural considerations are now part and parcel of child welfare practice, and these are set within interagency collaborative, community-inclusive systems of care. Emerging ventures include more emphases on stakeholder voice in program and policy development and evaluation; evidence-promising and evidence-based practices in child welfare settings; university-community research collaboration; workforce preparation and retention, including organizational changes such as supportive supervision; children's human rights; and transition from foster care to independent living.

## WHAT IS RURAL?

Before social workers and other professionals consider child welfare services in rural areas, it is important to ask: "What is rural"? It is common for rural literature to point out that defining rural areas is a complex endeavor. An area may be considered rural, or not rural, depending on the definition applied. Further, the definitions have changed over time. Daley and Avant (2014) explain that prior to 1991 rural meant an incorporated or unincorporated community with 2,500 or fewer residents. After 1991, the US Census Bureau developed a rural-to-urban continuum with a benchmark of 50,000 residents. Specifically, the Census Bureau dropped the terms "rural" and "urban" and began to use "metropolitan" and "nonmetropolitan" areas. A metropolitan area was defined as a place with a central city population of 50,000 or more (Reynellis, 2008). This definition included the entire "bedroom community" or county surrounding the central city as part of the metropolitan area. It also encapsulated social mobility, as many people worked in the city but chose to live in the surrounding suburbs and outlying areas. With this city-plus-suburbs metropolitan designation, anything else was considered nonmetropolitan. In the United States, nonmetropolitan is often presumed to be rural. In Canada, the Census office uses a population total-plus-density definition, or "an area with fewer than 1,000 inhabitants and a population density below 400 people per square kilometer" (Canada Census, 2011, p. 1). Australia uses a World Bank mathematic formula of "the difference between total population and urban population" with urban considered to be "agglomerations of more than one million [people]" (Trading Economics, n.d.).

But rural definition questions linger. How does one classify a central city of 50,000 or more people who are located six or more hours away from another central city? It is a metropolitan area, but it is also geographically isolated. Daley and Avant (2014) cite Olaveson, Conway, and Shaver (2004) who assert that "some classification models use population density, commuting patterns, the economy, and 'open country' as identifiers of rurality" (p. 7). Olaveson et al. also identify political boundaries such as state lines as boundaries for specific rural areas. And some rural scholars recommend adding the concept of social inclusion or exclusion as a construct within the definition of rural areas (Brown & Shafft, 2011).

No matter what definition is used, it is clear that there are a lot of rural people, and they are dispersed across vast areas of the United States and other countries. In the United States, rural people comprise about 19% of the population and they live on 80% of the land. In a country of 330 million people, this means about 65 million people live in rural areas (US Census Bureau, n.d.). In Canada, 18.9% of the population, or approximately 6.3 million people, lived on over 90% of the land in 2011 (Canada Census, 2011). As of 2010, nearly 2.5 million Australians were categorized as rural, with the majority of the population living in a few coastal cities (Trading Economics, n.d., p. 3).

## WHY STUDY RURAL OR EVEN MAKE A DISTINCTION?

Some social workers believe that making a distinction between clients based on geography is unnecessary. Pugh (2003) describes having to make a "case for the countryside" in order to convince policymakers and services planners that rural practice requires specialized knowledge and practice modifications. While it is true that social work generalist practice techniques include working with diverse groups, social workers are also expected to adapt practice interventions to the needs of clients in their cultural and community contexts. For example, Barclay (2000) discusses the utilization of resources "behind the pine curtain" of rural east Texas; and Jacobsen (2002) describes dealing with the "local realities" of child protection in a frontier region. Each person and community is different and may require small, but important, changes within a generalist practice frame. For example, a worker practicing in one rural community may be dealing with clients or consumers for whom English is a second language. This means that the worker will have to speak the language as well or find certified translators who are trained in confidentiality. The worker will need to learn how to work appropriately in communicating with the client, including looking at the client instead of the translator while conversing and knowing they should avoid using children as the family interpreters (thus setting up the potential to disempower parents).

Generalist practice is the most common kind of approach to practice used in rural settings. Generalist practice as a descriptive label is a bit misguiding, since engaging in generalist practice means that one will begin "where the client is" within a specific service agency but then must consider a wide array of person-in-environment levels, factors, and stages of practice. For example, a worker will need to consider the *levels* of individuals, families, organizations, communities, and social policies, including their strengths, resources challenges, and stressors. They must also consider the structure of the client or consumer system (the target they are trying to help). In trying to understand what is going on, they will need to pay attention how the client or consumer system, others, and their environment includes *factors* of structure, power, rules, myths, communication, and decision-making. It is particularly critical to examine the history of the client system and their environments as well as person-in-environment factors that may be biological, psychological, sociological, cultural, and spiritual in nature. All of these layers and factors (as well as many others) are examined across a progressive series of *stages* of practice that include engagement, assessment, planning, intervention, evaluation, termination/transition, and follow-up. During these stages workers may help to connect people and resources as well as to build new resources through creative local innovation, such as pooling agencies' resources or tweaking access to resources for a particular child and family. More formal processes such as grant writing and program development are also part of linking and brokering activities common to generalist practice.

Thus generalist practice means that the worker considers the client or consumer within the layers of the world that surround him or her. The worker will assess the child, parents, family (including siblings and extended family), and local community resources. The ability to implement and the need to advocate for state and federal policies within a particular setting must also be considered. Each rural area and the people who live there should be assessed as a diverse group.

When rural people are considered a diverse group, there are expected adaptations that should be considered within social work practice in rural child welfare (Templeman & Mitchell, 2001). Graham, Brownlee, Shier, and Doucette (2008) specifically describe the need for rural community knowledge to guide practitioners in northern Ontario and the Northwest Territories of Canada. For example, social workers may have to talk to clients *in advance* about how to interact (or not interact) when they see them in community locations such as a church, grocery store, or park. Urban state office policies may not fit local cultures or resources and may require some modifications. Osburn described a mandatory meeting requirement for clients that could not be implemented in a rural setting when the only bridge into town was washed out (personal communication, R. Osburn, 2007). This is a good example of a time when a worker may need to advocate for policy exceptions and/or changes.

*Informal* sources of help may become more critical in rural communities with limited resources. For example, when there are no homeless shelters in the area, a social worker may need to call a local pastor on Friday evening to help find temporary client housing for the weekend. It is not unusual for workers in rural areas to look for resources from the business and religious community, and it is often routine to combine agency resources to meet the needs of a particular child and family.

Some of the "What's different about rural practice?" debate focuses on comparing inner-city poor people to rural poor people. Generalist practice actions for working with inner-city clients who are poor are similar in many ways to working with rural clients who are poor. However, poor rural clients are also likely to be living some distance away from health and human services agencies. In addition, rural areas have regional socialization processes for residents that may differ from those in urban areas.

Professionals familiar with the delivery of services in rural areas report that working in rural areas requires a good deal of independent decision-making, innovation in developing access to services, and interdependence among service providers. Professionals may need to build community capital in order to acquire resources for a client. For example, health, mental health, and child welfare providers may need to pool resources to find help for children and families at risk. In rural communities, this can involve the engagement of local service clubs, schools, churches/temples/mosques, schools, and businesses.

One recommended distinction in assessing the study of rural and urban areas is to acknowledge that it is not urban *versus* rural; the concepts are not dichotomous. Rather, they form a continuum. Similar social problems can extend to urban and rural areas. Rural people can move to cities and city people can move to rural areas. It is common to exclude or pay inadequate attention to suburban areas in examining urban services. While poor suburbs do exist, there is evidence that, taken as a whole, suburban areas are more likely to have increased wealth and resources than urban or rural areas (Dreier, Mollenkopf, & Swanson, 2005).

It is important for people from a rural area not to fall into the trap of assuming that all urban areas overflow with resources or that all metropolitan areas are alike. Conversely, people from suburban and urban areas must exercise caution to avoid constructing sweeping generalizations about rural areas. Effective practice requires professionals to maintain objective perspectives of communities. Their views should not include constructions of rural areas using overly idealistic pastoral myths or overly deficit-focused views, such as paying attention only to rural poverty or resource deficiencies (Ginsberg, 2011). A pastoral myth is an expression used to illustrate that some people may speak only of rural areas in a positive light often associated with the idea of clean environments and beautiful, peaceful scenery. Social workers and other professionals may find that acquiring background information about rural people, child welfare agencies, and rural child welfare services facilitates objectivity.

## RURAL CHILD WELFARE

Brown proposed rural social work practice considerations in 1933 and the Children's Bureau was signed into law in 1912. However, the Child Welfare League of America (2011) reported: "Rural children and families are overlooked in the current CFSR [Child and Family Services Reviews] methodology and as a result little is known about how rural children fare in the child welfare system" (p. 2). Rural child welfare remains an underdeveloped educational and training content area in social work education and child welfare practice today. There is much to be done to work toward adequate preparation of child welfare workers. Avertt, Carawan, and Burroughs (2012) describe the words used by social work students (to explain their learning outcomes of placement in rural agency internship sites) as "getting tillerized." One example of "getting tillerized" could include learning how rural cultures and child welfare services intersect in order to work toward community and culturally effective practice. Every social worker at some point will interact with rural clients. For example, a major issue in many states currently is the lack of foster families in each community, causing rural children to be placed where an open slot exists in a foster family anywhere in the state, whether urban or rural. This necessary practice can lead to substantial culture shock for children and youth; and social workers in rural and urban areas must learn how to respond competently.

But where does one begin this learning process? What *is* important to know to engage in effective social work practice with the 73.8 million rural people in the United States, Canada, and Australia, plus many millions of more people across the world? Some of the social work generalist practice skill sets are the same regardless of the practice setting: social workers and other providers should engage in strength-based, person-in-environment perspectives. They should use warmth, genuineness, and empathy in communication with people at risk for or those in need of social work services. Mackie, Zammitt, and Alvarez (2016) recommend that social workers be competent in working with systems that are micro (individuals), meso (families and small groups), and macro (large groups, organizations, and communities). Continual striving for cultural competency is an important skill for helping the plethora of diverse people living within communities and regions of any size.

Experienced rural practitioners are able to identify the major tenets of rural practice such as using abundant informal rural resources, having professional autonomy, being part of multidisciplinary collaborations, and having other community members' respect their profession (Riebschleger, 2007). They are also likely to expect to face professional challenges such as living with the "fishbowl" effect (where community members know a good deal about the professionals and their families), driving long distances—often in inclement weather—and avoiding or managing dual relationship encounters with clients (Halverson & Brownlee, 2010; Pugh, 2007). It is even possible that Norris's "warm piece of pie" is a part of rural practice, since experts in rural social work practice identified "homecooked food" as a practice benefit (Riebschleger, 2007).

Portland State University researchers studied rural Alaskan communities and determined that the three areas of practice for social work concentration within rural child welfare practice are the three R's: remoteness, resources, and relationships (Cahn, 2007). The authors endorse the three R's, while adding practicing cultural competence and humility within a framework of self-reflection, to insure sound rural social work practice.

## Remoteness

Rural child welfare workers often deliver services in isolated places with insufficient access to services. Much of the rural social work literature discusses isolation and remoteness as factors in rural living. All too often remote areas lack sufficient health and human services, including sufficient access to social work supervision and continuing education. Remote areas tend to have either no Internet service or spotty service, making it difficult to use agency and other online resources. Practitioners in remote areas must learn also to cope with extensive travel to and from client homes or foster homes, as well as when facilitating family visits for foster children. They travel alone in all kinds of weather. Long commutes for home visits or court appearances can stretch the resources of a single worker. Remoteness and lack of resources also put a strain on the workforce as a whole. Sometimes there just are not enough workers in rural areas or child welfare, and it can be difficult to recruit and retain well-trained rural child welfare workers. There are fewer applicants in rural areas since not as many people reside in these areas. Further, not everyone who is available for rural social work and rural child welfare jobs is interested in these positions. If a worker leaves a child welfare agency, the burden of replacing that person is not only borne by the agency but also by the families on the worker's caseload. Other workers must add cases to their already heavy loads, which stretches the workforce even thinner.

Mackie and Lips (2010) claim that for every additional 10 miles of distance from a metropolitan area, it is 3% more difficult to hire a social worker. The workforce shortage for rural child welfare workers can be influenced by numerous factors. Some people do not want to live in a rural area or have family members who do not want to live there. People who grew up in a rural area are more likely to want to live in a rural area.

To support increased access to practitioners in rural areas, the federal government created the National Health Services Corps to provide incentives for healthcare professionals who work in rural areas. These professionals work in underserved rural areas in exchange for reductions in their federal student loans. The National Child Welfare Workforce Institute (2013) and Title IV-E programs are government-sponsored programs that provide incentives for educating social work students who study for child welfare agencies. Similar to the National Health Services Corps, these child welfare workforce enhancement programs are designed to help pay for the education of social work students in exchange for postgraduation practice in child welfare services. The National Association of Social Workers' (2013) policy on social work in rural areas recommends stronger and more frequent education to increase worker skills for engaging in rural social work. Members of the National Rural Social Work Caucus originally drafted the policy. This is a grassroots organization that hosts an annual conference in a rural location once a year. Recently the group expanded to sponsor the *Journal of Contemporary Rural Social Work,* an open access, double-blinded peer-reviewed journal available at http://journal.und.edu/crsw/.

## Rural Resources

Insufficient resources are a major issue in rural communities. The services that are available may be a hundred miles or more away from where the rural people live. This can be partially explained by the fact that government policymakers and administrators tend to distribute services by defined population clusters. For example, an agency might be required to deliver services to 250,000 people. A rural, or especially a frontier services, area would likely be serving 250,000 people spread out across a large geographic area. Hence, many rural communities tend not to have federally or state-funded clinics, hospitals, or substance abuse treatment facilities. Domestic violence shelters may be nonexistent or far away, as illustrated by Sheperd's (2001) aptly titled article, "Where Do You Go When It's 40 Below?" about a lack of domestic violence shelters for Native Alaskan women in the heart of winter. Even if clients live near the child welfare office, helping them access services may mean either arranging for transportation or driving them to one or more faraway resources, which can be extremely time consuming. Services such as in-home family preservation may not be available at all. If these services are available, preservation workers may only be able to visit one family per day given the vast distance to travel between client homes.

### Relationships

The National Association of Social Workers (2013) has developed a policy statement that guides rural social work practice. The rural social work policy states clearly the need for social workers to develop good relationships with rural people, since rural communities often are formed upon long-standing relationships among their members. The ideas of Gemeinschaft and Gesellshaft as explained by Tönnies (1887) are relevant here. Gemeinschaft communities are built on affective bonds and tradition, not necessarily commercial contracts or business concepts (Gesellschaft). Rural community residents tend to emphasize "multiple, mutually reinforcing roles which produce a clear sense of commitments, obligations, and social boundaries" (Brown & Schafft, 2011, p. 37). In other words, rural people tend to value people and traditions over rationality and business-only connections.

People and relationships are important in rural communities, and social capital becomes quite important. Things get done in these communities based on trusting relationships with others in the community, while lack of trust, especially of new people, can lead rural residents to be wary of working with them. Social workers in rural areas must establish and keep the trust of clients, other professionals, and community leaders if they are to be successful and achieve positive results for their clients. These trust-based relationship bonds are central to accessing informal and formal community resources that can be used to assist and support clients.

## RURAL PEOPLE AS A CULTURAL MINORITY

In order to engage in effective social work practice in rural areas, it is important to consider the person-in-environment and the historic and cultural differences of people living in rural environments. Rural people may have experienced and/or continue to experience trauma, social stigma, and oppression. They may face communication barriers, especially since there continues to be an influx of immigrants who speak other languages and little or no English. There may be differences in rural people's expectations related to help-seeking behaviors, self-disclosure, and body language. Similarly, events and interactions can be interpreted differently from one cultural/ethnic group to another. Further, there is a tremendous amount of diversity within each rural area or group (Yahn, 2011). This means that "the people on one side of the mountain can be different than the people on the other side of the mountain" (Riebschleger, 2007, p. 210). In addition, culture is often intersectional when one considers the multiple possible developmental influences of country of origin, region, religion, sexual orientation, and race/ethnicity (Ortega & Faller, 2011). For example, people who are rural and Latino may come from many countries. Within those countries, they may come from different regions that engage in different customs. They may speak different languages and dialects.

It is important for social workers to demonstrate respect and cultural humility when interacting with people from minority groups. Social workers need to cultivate a practice of intense self-reflection with regard to their feelings and biases. Self-reflection helps the worker to remain as humble as possible in the face of working with the rich diversity demonstrated by clients. This self-reflection also applies to feelings or biases about rural communities.

Rural people *are* a diverse group who are often ascribed a minority status by the dominant culture. Not only are their numbers smaller and their resources often fewer, but they may report experiencing historical and ongoing social stigma directed toward rural people. Wendell (2002) talks about the "prejudice against country people," and Murray (2013) purports that television provides "skewed views" of rural people as slower and less intelligent with less social status. Several social work students told one of the authors that their college roommates tease them about coming from a farm background. One described a roommate asking her questions about milking cows, followed by gales of laughter from others in the room. Michigan State University has a 150-year strong land grant agricultural background; it is not unusual to hear it referred to as "Moo U." *The Beverly Hillbillies* sitcom shows the rural Clampett family referring to a swimming pool as the "cee-ment" pond, implying that the family members do not recognize a swimming pool. Some Americans make jokes about rural people lacking teeth, wearing large belt buckles, and marrying their siblings and cousins. There is even discriminatory language when some Americans talk about US presidents. For example, President Bill Clinton was a Rhodes Scholar, but there were a rash of Arkansas jokes during his presidential tenure. President Jimmy Carter was a graduate of Annapolis and a Navy nuclear engineer, but many jokes about him centered on his Georgia peanut farming background. It is important to understand that rural people may experience oppressive and discriminatory treatment due to their rural environment.

The salient point is that all social workers need to cultivate a sense of cultural humility and a learning stance with regard to working with rural residents. They need to advocate for social inclusion of rural residents and the end of rural stigma. Tackle box or no tackle box, social workers who choose to respond to the call for rural service are likely to be particularly challenged and rewarded in their career-long journeys toward cultural humility and competency.

## CASE VIGNETTE

Diana Izzo, a senior social work student at a large, inner-city university, was placed in a public child welfare agency for her field experience. She grew up in the same city in which her university was located and had no experience with life or practice in any area but her big, urban city. She loved that inner-city "vibe." She was shadowing a caseworker, her field instructor, when they received a case that was being transferred to them. In reviewing the case records, she realized that the child involved was placed three hours away in a rural town upstate. The child, Tamira, was a seven-year-old, African American child. She had been in foster care for two years with Mr. and Mrs. Miller and their children, Thomas, age 9, and Anne, age 11. The Miller family was Caucasian and of German descent. Mr. and Mrs. Miller had expressed an interest in adopting Tamira since parental rights had just been terminated. Tamira was in foster care because her mother suffered from heroin addiction and she had been unable to stay "clean." Tamira had not seen her mother at all for visits since her mother had not kept any of the visitation appointments. Further, there were no family members willing to have Tamira placed with them, and family members also refused visitation offers. Tamira's mother refused to give any information about Tamira's father.

Diana and her field instructor were required to make a visit to check on Tamira's well-being and to discuss how the placement had been going. Tamira was lucky in that this had been her only placement and she had, to this point, done very well in the Miller home. One summer Tuesday morning at 7 AM, Diana and her field instructor set out for the visit upstate. They took the interstate as far as they could and got off on a less traveled road, which, after 20 miles, led to the town where the Millers lived. Diana was quite interested in the scenery along the way. She had never really seen a working farm or cows in a field before. Driving along she noticed homes that were spread far apart and a few churches along the way. There was one fast-food restaurant at the interstate exchange but no other stores until they arrived at the little town where Diana noticed a small restaurant, a hardware store, a pharmacy, and a doctor's office.

As they drove the long three hours, Diana's field instructor engaged her in conversation about rural practice. She noted that it was hard to find services for families "up here," but they did their best. Diana stated that she found it almost inconceivable that children who live in rural areas do not have access to services that other children have. Further, she was concerned that Tamira, an African American child, was placed with a Caucasian family. They discussed the lack of foster homes and the necessity of finding safe, loving homes. Diana's field instructor asked her to think about how she might plan for services in case Tamira needed them.

When they arrived, they found the Miller family picking cucumbers and tomatoes in the garden. The Millers were a lively, fun-loving family, and Tamira seemed to fit right in. Tamira appeared to be a typical seven-year-old. She loved to read, play video games, run around the yard playing "tag," and swim in the family's above-ground pool. She seemed very comfortable with her "siblings" and her "parents." She called Mr. and Mrs. Miller "Dad" and "Mom." Mrs. Miller noted that Tamira did well mostly but she did have nightmares at times. Mrs. Miller disclosed that Tamira talked sometimes about a man with a gun trying to hurt her mom. Mrs. Miller thinks Tamira was about 4½ when this happened. She was placed with the family soon afterward. Diana and her field instructor explored other signs of trauma with Mrs. Miller who noted that she had not observed any other signs. The family said that they would like to adopt Tamira and were interested in exploring what needed to happen next.

On the ride home, Diana expressed surprise that the Miller family seemed just like any other middle-class family she had met. Her field instructor asked her to reflect on what that meant to her and said they would talk about it in supervision the following week.

## Practice Application

In this vignette, Diana has the new experience of being in a rural environment for the first time and interacting with a rural family. She also experiences an interracial foster placement. She must confront many of her own biases about rural families and about race. It is important to understand that social workers experience all kinds of families over the course of their careers, and they must be mindful and reflective about pre-existing notions and biases about families.

## DISCUSSION QUESTIONS

1. What are your experiences with rural communities or people who live in rural places?
2. How do the three R's relate to a rural community that you are familiar with?
3. Think of the people of a rural community that you know about. In what ways might the people of this community be different from each other?
4. What are some words that people might use to refer to rural people? What do you think of these words?
5. What are your honest feelings and biases about rural communities and people? About urban communities and people? About suburban communities and people?
6. What did Diana mean when she told her field instructor that the Miller family seemed like any other middle-class family she had met? What biases does that statement imply?
7. How often and how do you engage in self-reflection about social work practice?
8. What are ways that you can strive to develop stronger skills in rural cultural competence and humility? Be specific.

## LEARNING ACTIVITIES

1. *Country Boys*: Video and Discussion
   a. The film *Country Boys* shows two boys living in severe poverty and without family support while coming of age in a rural area. It follows their lives over a number of years. The instructor can use this for an assessment of the risks and resiliencies of the two teenagers and the influence of poverty and a rural environment on their lives. Participants can apply what they are learning about rural child welfare to the real examples of two young men in risky environments.
2. *The Appalachians*: Video and Discussion
   a. The film series *The Appalachians* tells a history of rural people. It comes with suggested educator lessons plans about the importance of oral storytelling in rural Appalachian culture, including people

from the Cherokee nation. It is possible to find shorter snippets of the series on YouTube and within the main website: http://appala-chiafilm.org/.

3. Interactive Rural Post-It Note Exercise
   a. Participants can explore social constructions of rural within a 30-minute class exercise. The instructor gives participants two or three large post-it notes of varying colors. They are asked to use black markers to write down words that can be associated with rural areas (one word for each post-it note).
   b. One by one participants come to the front of the class, place the post-it on a flip chart paper, and explain the words they chose. This exercise elicits stereotypes, pastoral myths, risks, and resiliencies. The power of language and metaphors can help learners identify the possible impacts of rural stereotypes on people. It also can help them identify their own biases about rural areas and how to use a strength and empowerment focus in rural practice.

## SUGGESTED READING

Belanger, K., & Brooks, S. (2009). *Guidelines for cultural competence in rural child welfare.* Arlington, VA: Child Welfare League of America.

Brown, D. L., & Schafft, D. A. (2011). *Rural people and communities in the 21st century.* Cambridge, MA: Polity Press.

Daley, M. R. (2015). *Rural social work in the 21st century.* Chicago, IL: Lyceum.

Davey, R. & Woman, Y.T. (Producers & Directors). (2010). *The canary effect: Kill the Indian, save the man* [CD]. Retrieved from: http://topdocumentaryfilms.com/canary-effect/

Ginsberg, L. (2011). *Social work in rural communities* (5th ed.). Alexandria, VA: Council on Social Work Education.

National Child Welfare Workforce Initiative. (2011). *Issues in rural child welfare.* Webinar featuring Barbara Pierce and Debra Norris. Retrieved from http://ncwwi.org/index.php/resource-library-search/resource-topics/community-context/item/1106-issues-in-rural-child-welfare

National Rural Social Work Caucus. (n.d.). *Home page.* Retrieved from http://www.ruralsocialwork.org/

Riebschleger, J., Norris, D., Pierce, B., Pond, D., & Cummins, C. (2015). Preparing social work students for rural child welfare practice: Emerging curriculum competencies. *Journal of Social Work Education, 51*(+Suppl. 2), S209–S224. doi:10.1080/10437797.2015.1072422

Ross, J., & Spears, R. (Producers & Directors). (2005). *The Appalachians: A history of mountains and people.* James Agee Film Product. http://appalachiafilm.org/

Sutherland, D. (Producer & Director). *Country boys.* PBS and Frontline affiliated video. http://davidsutherland.com/films/country-boys

US Department of Health and Human Services, Administration on Children and Families, Children's Bureau, National Child Welfare Workforce Institute. (2012).

*Rural child welfare practice.* Child Welfare Information Gateway. Issue Briefs. Retrieved from https://www.childwelfare.gov/pubs/issue-briefs/rural/

# REFERENCES

Averett, P., Carawan, L., & Burroughs, C. (2012). Getting "tillerized": Traits and outcomes of students in a rural community field placement. *Journal of Social Work Education, 48*(1), 75–91. http://dx.doi.org/10.5175/JSWE.2012.201000016

Barclay, V. A. (2000). *Behind the pine curtain: A look at Child Protective Services' utilization of resources in rural east Texas.* Nacogdoches, TX:. Stephen F. Austin State University.

Bell, S. E. (2009). "There ain't no bond in town like there used to be": The destruction of social capital in the West Virginia coal fields. *Sociological Forum, 24,* 631–657. doi: 10.1111/j.1573-.7861.2009.01123x

Briar-Lawson, K., McCarthy, M., & Dickinson, N. (Eds.). *The Children's Bureau: Shaping a century of child welfare practices, programs, and policies.* Washington, DC: NASW Press.

Brown, D. L., & Schafft, D. A. (2011). *Rural people and communities in the 21st century: Resilience and transformation.* Cambridge, UK: Polity Press.

Brown, J. (1933). The *rural community and social casework.* New York, NY: Little and Ives.

Cahn, K. (2007). *The three R's of child welfare practice.* Portland: Center for the Improvement of Children and Family Services. Retrieved from http://www.rtg.pdx.edu/newsletter/newsletter0507finalweb.pdf

Canada Census. (2011). *Census in brief: Canadian rural population since 1851.* Retrieved from www12.statcan.gc.ca/census-recensement/2011/as-sa/98-310-x/98-310-x2011003_2-eng.cfm

Child Welfare League of America. (2011). *Federal monitoring of the Child and Family Services Review.* Washington, DC: Author. Retrieved from http://www.cwla.org/wp-content/uploads/2014/05/2011CFSRcommentsfinal.pdf

Children's Bureau Centennial. (n.d.). *The story of the Children's Bureau.* US Department of Health and Human Services, Administration for Children and Families. Retrieved from cb100.acf.hhs.gov/CB_ebrochure

Daley, M. R., & Avant, F. L. (2014). Down-home social work: A strengths-based model for rural practice. In T. L. Scales, C. L. Streeter, & H. S. Cooper (Eds.), *Rural social work: Building and sustaining community capacity* (2nd ed., pp. 5–18). Hoboken, NJ: Wiley.

DiNitto, D. M., & Johnson, D. H. (2016). *Social welfare: Politics and public policy* (8th ed.). New York, NY: Pearson.

Dreier, P., Mollenkopf, J., & Swanstrom, J. (2005). Metropolitics for the twenty-first century. In J. Lin & C. Mele (Eds.), *The urban sociology reader* (2nd ed., pp. 157–166). New York, NY: Routledge.

Ginsberg, L. (Ed.). (2011). Introduction to basic concepts of rural social work. In L. Ginsberg (Ed.), *Social work in rural communities* (5th ed., pp. 5–20). Alexandria, VA: Council on Social Work Education.

Graham, J. R., Brownlee, K., Shier, M., & Doucette, E. (2008). Localization of social work knowledge through practitioner adaptations in Northern Ontario and the Northwest Territories, Canada. *Arctic, 61*(4), 399–406. http://dx.doi.org/10.14430/arctic48

Halverson, G., & Brownlee, K. (2010). Managing ethical considerations around dual relationships in small rural and remote Canadian communities. *International Social Work, 53*(2), 247–260. http://dx.doi.org/10.1177/0020872809055386

Herder, J. G. (1968). *Reflections on the philosophy of the history of mankind.* Chicago, IL: University of Chicago Press.

Hirshberg, D., & Sharp, S. (2005). *Thirty years later: The long-term effect of boarding schools on Alaskan Natives and their communities.* Anchorage: University of Alaska Anchorage.

Jacobsen, M. (2002). Local realities: A frontier perspective on child protection team practice. *Child Welfare, 81,* 737–755.

Lindenmeyer, K. (1997). *"A right to childhood": The U.S. Children's Bureau and child welfare, 1912–46.* Chicago, IL: University of Illinois.

Locke, B. L., & Winship, J. (2005). Social work in rural America: Lessons from the past and trends for the future. In N. Lohmann & R. A. Lohmann (Eds.), *Rural social work practice* (pp. 3–24). New York, NY: Columbia University Press.

Mackie, P. F. E., & Lips, R. A. (2010). Is there really a problem with hiring rural social service staff? An exploratory study among social service supervisors in rural Minnesota. *Families in Society: The Journal of Contemporary Social Services, 91*(4), 433–439. http://dx.doi.org/10.1606/1044-3894.4035

Mackie, P. F., Zammitt, K., & Alvarez, M. (2016). *Practicing rural social work.* Chicago, IL: Lyceum.

Maidment, J., & Bay, U. (Eds.). (2012). *Social work in rural Australia: Enabling practice.* Sydney, Australia: Allen & Unwin.

Murray, J. D. (2013). Op-ed: Rural stereotypes in reality TV serve up skewed views. http://www.pennlive.com/opinion/2013/01/op-ed_rural_stereotypes_in_reality_tv_serve_up_skewed_views.html

National Association of Social Workers. (2013). Rural social work. In *Social work speaks: National Association of Social Workers' policy statements, 2012–2014* (pp. 296–301). Washington, DC: NASW Press.

National Child Welfare Workforce Institute. (2013). *Twelve NCWWI traineeship programs: Comprehensive summary of legacies and lessons learned.* Albany, NY: Author. Retrieved from: http://ncwwi.org

Olaveson, J., Conway, P., & Shaver, C. (2004). Defining rural for social work practice and research. In T. L. Scales & C. L. Streeter (Eds.), *Rural social work: Building and sustaining community assets* (pp. 9–33). Belmont, CA: Brooks/Cole.

Ortega, R., & Faller, K. C. (2011). Training child welfare workers from an intersectional cultural humility perspective: A paradigm shift. *Child Welfare, 90*(5), 27–49. Retrieved from http://www.cwla.org/child-welfare-journal/

Pugh, R. (2007). Dual relationships: Personal and professional boundaries in rural social work. *British Journal of Social Work, 37,* 1405–1423. http://dx.doi.org/10.1093/bjsw/bcl088

Pugh, R. (2003). Considering the countryside: Is there a case for rural social work? *British Journal of Social Work, 33,* 67–85.

Riebschleger, J. (2007). Social workers' suggestions for effective rural practice. *Families in Society, 88,* 203–213. doi:www.ce4alliance.com/articles/101109/riebschleger.pdf

Reynellis, L. (2008, September). *What is rural?* US Department of Agriculture. Retrieved from www.nal.usda.gov/ric/ricpubs/what_is_rural.shtml

Sheperd, J. (2001). Where do you go when it's 40 below? Domestic violence among rural Alaska Native women. *Affilia, 16*(4), 468–510.

Templeman, S. B., & Mitchell, L. (2001). Challenging the one-size-fits-all myth: Findings and solutions from a statewide focus group of rural social workers. *Child Welfare, 81*(5), 757–772. Retrieved from http://www.cwla.org/child-welfare-journal/

Tönnies, F. (1887). *Gemeinschaft und Gesellschaft.* Leipzig: Fues's Verlag. Translated by Charles Price Loomis as *Community and Society* (East Lansing: Michigan State University Press, 1957).

Trading Economics (n.d.). *Australian rural population.* Retrieved from http://www.tradingeconomics.com/australia/rural-population-percent-of-total-population-wb-data.html

US Census Bureau (n.d.). *2010 census urban and rural classification and urban area criteria.* Retrieved from https://www.census.gov/geo/reference/ua/urban-rural-2010.html

Wendell, B. (2002). The prejudice against country people. *Progressive, 66*(4), 21.

Yahn, J. (2011, November 21). *Appreciate the diversity in rural places.* Teaching tolerance: A project of the Southern Poverty Law Center. Retrieved from www.tolerance.org/blog/appreciate-diversity-rural-places

# CHAPTER 2

✿

# Theories for Rural Child Welfare

## BARBARA J. PIERCE

## LEARNING OBJECTIVES

- Use concepts of ecological-systems theory to explain the idea of "connectedness" in rural child welfare
- Describe the concept of social capital and use it as the basis for forming relationships with others in rural communities
- Give an example of how trauma theory can be used to assess and intervene in the lives of children and families

## INTRODUCTION

The mark of a true professional is the ability to take theoretical knowledge and put it into practice. But, which theories? There are so many of them. While for each family with whom you work you may use many theories to effect change, there are some larger theories that form a lens through which you might view the work that needs to be done. In this chapter we discuss three such theoretical lenses: ecological-systems theory, trauma theory, and social capital theory. Each plays a role in working in child welfare in rural communities.

## ECOLOGICAL SYSTEMS THEORY

The largest or most encompassing theory that most social workers learn is ecological systems theory. This is the notion that everything is connected or affects everything else. As social workers, we identify this idea as person-in-environment and signify that each part of the system is equally important. The system, as laid out by Bronfenbrenner (1979), consists of the micro, meso, exo, macro, and chrono subsystems. While most texts teach micro, meso, and macro subsystems, we include all systems since the chrono sub-system becomes an important part of our understanding of transmission of trauma and further abuse in the ongoing life of a family. (See Table 2.1.)

It is important for child welfare workers to pay attention to all of the subsystems when making assessments, finding strengths, and planning for treatment and services. The intersections of systems can produce stress points for families, and social workers can help to smooth the way sometimes. In rural child welfare, the macro subsystem is quite important, particularly in relation to geography, as the rural community comes with its own set of norms, rules, and relationships that the social worker must navigate.

When we develop genograms and ecomaps with our client families, we are actually using ecological systems theory. When we draw a genogram we are representing generations of a family with all of the people, their relationships, and their patterns, such as whether or not they have addictions or domestic violence issues. When we draw an ecomap we make a

*Table 2.1.* ECOLOGICAL SYSTEMS THEORY: FIVE SUBSYSTEMS

| | |
|---|---|
| Micro | The co-construction of the everyday experience within the life of an individual in relation to family and friends, teachers, pastors, doctors, etc. |
| Meso | Intersectional relationships between micro systems (relationship of home to school or home to church, for example) |
| Exo | Intersections or links between a social setting in which a person has an active role and one in which there is no active role but which produces a consequence (parent goes to prison and there is an effect on the child's behavior) |
| Macro | Cultural contexts including socioeconomic status, ethnicity, geography (rural, for example) |
| Chrono | Incorporation of time such as sociohistorical context and life transitions (transmission of abuse from generation to generation or historical trauma, for example) |

*Source*: Bronfenbrenner (1979).

pictorial representation of all of the community contacts with which the family is involved. We might draw schools, jobs, therapeutic helpers, the child welfare agency, other public programs, church, and extended relatives. In addition, when we use ecomaps we note whether the relationships between and among these contacts are strong and perceived as helpful or if the family deems them conflictual. Of course, different members of the family may have different perceptions of various contacts, and that is also noted.

As you read the case vignettes in this chapter, analyze the subsystems that appear to be salient and think about how you might assess and plan for work with that family. Draw out the genograms and ecomaps for the families presented and think about ways that a family such as the one presented in the case vignette might be served or helped in your own community. Likewise, look for aspects of generational transmission of family violence or historical trauma, which may be expressions of the chrono subsystem.

## SOCIAL CAPITAL

As we learned in chapter 1, rural communities are based on the concept of Gemeinschaft: this is comprised of affective bonds and long-lasting relationships. To work in rural communities, you need to learn how to develop good and trusting relationships with community stakeholders and clients. This is a skill. Becoming a social worker involves learning many skills. Students learn to work with clients by using the therapeutic process of: interviewing, conducting assessments, intervening based on those assessments, and evaluating their practice. The process, though, starts with the development of relationships. In fact, social workers have to learn to form many different kinds of relationships in the course of doing their work. While forming relationships with clients allows clients to form a therapeutic alliance with workers, forming relationships with other professionals helps workers to form professional social networks. The development of social networks is an integral part of developing social capital. The aim is to assist social workers in learning about the concept of social capital and about building social capital in order to help them to work with clients more effectively.

The concept of capital, that is, the amassing of goods and wealth by one group, which was generated by the work of another group, forms the basis of exchange theory. Workers produce products, which are then exchanged for money by the owners of the means of production. As profits grow so do exchanges. In this economic theory, the original forms of capital are financial (the wealth amassed) and physical (the goods produced). Sociologists began to look at exchange theory in light of social relationships, and two new forms of capital, cultural and social capital, were described (Bourdieu, 1972; Coleman, 1988; Jacobs, 1961; Loury, 1977; Portes, 1998; & Putnam, 1993, 1995). Cultural capital is defined as the education, knowledge, skills, and advantages that people have had that help them to get ahead. (Bourdieu, 1972). Social capital, on the other hand, involves the reciprocal social relationships or social networks that people have at their disposal to effect change within a group. These could be variable-sized groups, such as a work group, an organization, a community, or an entire country (Putnam, 1995, 2000; Woolcock, 1998, 2001).

Through social contacts, relationships are built, and social capital can increase if those relationships form in positive and trusting ways. Social workers form social networks with other social workers and other professional colleagues such as lawyers and judges, doctors, and psychologists. Social workers also develop contacts through their own personal lives by belonging to community groups, a worship community, or even the gym. The more people social workers meet and develop relationships with, the more their social networks increase. Also, the more positive civic engagement a worker has, the higher his or her social capital will be (Putnam, 2000). With each new contact, they also potentially have the contacts of all of groups that the new contact has. For example, a contact may ask a social worker to be on an agency board of directors or to join the Kiwanis or other community club. In one's personal life, a social worker could ask the opinion of a friend or social contact about where to get a car repaired or which pediatrician they use for their children. As relationships form in trusting ways, social capital grows. In professional circles, as a social worker gains a reputation for being a competent professional, other professionals begin to trust the social worker and social capital grows. Yet, social capital can also diminish if the social worker acts in untrustworthy ways or against the norms of the community. (See Figure 2.1.)

**Figure 2.1:** Exchange theory and social capital theory.

# TRAUMA

A trauma is a deeply disturbing or distressing experience. It can be in the form of physical trauma such as a serious car accident, physical assault, or sexual assault, or it can be a psychological trauma such as witnessing domestic violence in the home. All children in the child welfare system have, by definition, been traumatized. The public child welfare agency would not be involved in their lives if there had not been some sort of trauma. Even babies abandoned at birth who have no seeming awareness of trauma may exhibit signs of trauma later on in life. In fact, the child welfare system itself often exacerbates trauma in the lives of children and families. For most children and families involved in the child welfare system, trauma is, sadly, a way of life. These families have more domestic violence, community violence, and generational transmission of violence than other families in society. They also often have substance abuse and mental health issues.

Trauma for children comes in many forms: neglect, emotional abuse, physical abuse, and sexual abuse. However, these are not the only forms of trauma for children. Children experience trauma from observing violence against a parent and seeing violence in their neighborhoods. Children are also traumatized by multiple trips to the hospital for say, asthma, where, while experiencing difficulty breathing (scary in itself), they are subjected to invasive medical procedures like intravenous infusions and breathing treatments that can be very frightening to a child. Further, children who grow up in families that have been historically oppressed such as African American, Japanese, or Native American families can experience historical trauma as attitudes are passed generationally.

Felitti et al. (1998) devised the Adverse Childhood Experiences (ACE) study. They studied 17,000 middle-class Americans and discovered that adverse childhood experience (i.e., traumas) are very common. They devised categories of these traumas including child maltreatment, exposure to domestic violence, death of a caregiver, and so on and were able to demonstrate that the more ACEs a person has, the more likely the person is to have long-term social and health consequences such as addictions, depression or anxiety, and even heart disease.

Child maltreatment is a common means of experiencing trauma in childhood. According to the Children's Bureau (2015), a federal agency that collects child maltreatment statistics each year, over 6 million individual children are reported to child welfare agencies as potentially having been maltreated. Of these about 3 million are actually investigated. Of these children, around 702,000 were found to have been substantiated victims of some sort of maltreatment in 2014, the latest year for which statistics are available. This number, sadly, is fairly stable over time. Maltreatment can occur through physical or emotional neglect or an omission of customary care for a child such as not feeding a child, leaving a child unattended, or not providing appropriate medical care; physical abuse in which a child is actually injured through broken bones, bruises, burns, or death; or sexual maltreatment including fondling, exposure, and penetration. In 2014, 1,580 children died as a result of maltreatment, and most of these children were under three years of age.

By far the most common form of maltreatment is neglect (omission of care), which accounted for about 75% of all maltreatment cases in 2014, while 17% were physical abuse cases and 8.3% sexual abuse cases. The majority of children experienced a single type of maltreatment but may have experienced that maltreatment many times (being physically maltreated many times, for example) and also may experience multiple forms of trauma. For example, a child may live in a home with a parent who is addicted to methamphetamines and is a victim of domestic violence; he or she may be neglected as a result. This counts as having had three traumas on the ACE. With regard to sexual abuse (i.e., sexual contact between people of different developmental levels for the gratification of the person of the higher developmental level [adult/child; older child or teen/younger child]), the rates of abuse are higher for boys than girls but the opposite is true as children age. Girls are victimized more often than boys as they age. Risk factors for abuse include young age, disability, language and communication deficits (including being too young to speak yet), and having a caregiver who is addicted to drugs or alcohol.

A traumatic stress reaction can occur after the experience of any of these traumas. Traumatic stress in children and families is expressed as emotional and/or behavioral dysregulation (Saxe, Ellis, & Kaplow, 2009). Children are frightened by traumatic events. During an event, the nervous system attempts to protect the child by way of activating neurochemicals such as cortisol and norepinephrine producing the fight, flight, or freeze response in the body. This response allows people in extreme danger to respond to increased demands to stay safe. After the event, when all is safe, the body returns to its typically calm state.

However, traumatized children in the child welfare system typically have more than one traumatic event in their history and in fact live with high stress levels much of the time. For example, it is quite typical for a child welfare worker to work with children whose parents abuse substances, cannot provide meals for their children, and may physically or sexually abuse their children when they are high or drunk. These children do not learn to expect that their needs for food and safety will be met, so their bodies never return to the typical calm state. Over time, the child's body learns to be on guard all the time, which leads to emotional dysregulation with symptoms such as anxiety and inability to pay attention in school and behavioral dysregulation symptoms such as acting out, bullying, and, in older children, sexual acting out or substance abuse (Saxe et al., 2009). We know that children who have experienced multiple traumas are at much higher risk over their lifetimes for higher rates of substance abuse, anxiety, depression, and physical symptoms of hypertension and heart disease (Felitti et al., 1998). In extreme cases of neglect Makinodan, Rosen, Ito, and Corfas (2012) found alterations in the myelination of nerves and pathological changes to the white matter in the brain, which affect long-term outcomes.

Age and stage of development play strong roles in the expression of trauma in children. For example, infants experiencing trauma may tend to react to lack of the attachment figure or disruption of schedules or usual caregivers, while preschoolers may respond with temper tantrums, regression in development, and excessive fears. Older youth and teens may respond with difficulty concentrating in school, embarrassment at being in the traumatizing situation or not wanting others to know what is happening in their families, aggressive acts with foster parents or in school, eating disorders, or, in extreme situations, delinquent behavior such as harming animals or setting fires. Number and severity of traumas play a part in how a child may react as does caring and support from family and friends. Children who disclose maltreatment and who are supported and receive good care tend to recover more quickly and more fully as well.

All is not lost though, even for children who have little support or are placed in foster care. If the children can obtain appropriate therapy to treat the traumatic stress using evidence-based techniques such as traumafocused cognitive behavioral therapy, motivational interviewing, and mindfulness training, we stand a good chance of helping them to learn to regulate both their emotions and their behaviors.

Every vignette in this casebook involves some sort of traumatic event. Learn to identify those and begin to identify the types of trauma and how the trauma may have affected the child's emotional or behavioral state, then think of ways to ameliorate the traumatic stress.

## CASE VIGNETTE

You become the case in this chapter. Write an assessment of yourself as if you were the client. This may be really difficult for some of you, but as a beginning professional social worker, it is really important to be in touch with those areas of your life that may have been traumatic. It is also important to get in touch with your life context. Who comprises your family? Did you grow up in a rural area? Do you have cultural or social capital? Do you have privilege? When you have finished writing up an intake assessment on yourself applying the theories in this chapter, then do the activities and answer the questions at the end of this chapter.

## Practice Application

The process of self-reflection is an important aspect of professional social work. Unfortunately, every day social workers confront aspects of trauma in the lives of their clients. When social workers have a history of trauma, working with clients can be difficult. Social workers also grow up with biases based on all sorts of aspects of their lives: the urban/rural divide, class, culture, race, gender expression. By learning and practicing reflection and theory/practice integration, social workers can serve their clients in a less biased and more competent manner.

## DISCUSSION QUESTIONS

1. Identify in your own family life aspects of the subsystems of ecological systems theory. How do you negotiate the various intersections?
2. How confident are you in your ability to form professional relationships with others? What sorts of behaviors must you exhibit in order to do so? Can you identify examples of social capital in your own life or community?
3. Have you experience a traumatic event? Can you remember what it felt like and how you reacted? If you experienced multiple traumas over time, have you been able to successfully overcome the emotional dysregulation that is inherent in these situations?

## LEARNING ACTIVITIES

1. Sociograms and Social Capital Assessment
   a. Complete a genogram and ecomap on you and your family. What did you learn? What are your social connections?
   b. Identify your areas of social capital. How do you use your social capital? How can you use your social capital in your field placement or on the job?

2. Trauma History Assessment
   a. Go to https://acestoohigh.com to take the ACEs quiz and the resil-
      iency quiz for yourself. What did you discover? It is not uncommon
      at all for the people who work in child welfare to have had trauma in
      their past. How can you put into place a plan for yourself to care for
      your trauma if you appear to have it? How can you protect yourself
      from secondary traumatic stress that comes from the stressful job of
      child welfare social work?
3. Trauma Content Trainings
   a. Go to www.nctsn.org and/or https://tfcbt.musc.edu to complete
      these trauma trainings online.

## SUGGESTED READING

Centers for Disease Control: http://www.cdc.gov/violenceprevention/childmaltreat-
      ment/index.html
National Child Traumatic Stress Network: http://www.nctsn.org

## REFERENCES

Bourdieu, P. (1972). *Outline of a theory of practice*. Cambridge, UK: Cambridge
      University Press.
Bronfenbrenner, U. (1979). *The ecology of human development: Experiments by nature and
      design*. Cambridge, MA: Harvard University Press.
Children's Bureau. (2015). *Child maltreatment 2014*. Retrieved from http://www.acf.
      hhs.gov/programs/cb/research-data-technology/statistics-research/child-
      maltreatment
Coleman, J. S. (1988). Social capital in the creation of human capital. *The American
      Journal of Sociology*, 94(Suppl.): S95–S120.
Felitti, V. J., Anda, R. F., Nordenberg, D., Williamson, D. F., Spitz, A., Edwards, V.,
      Koss, M. P., & Marks, J. S. (1998). Relationship of childhood abuse and house-
      hold dysfunction to many of the leading causes of death in adults: The Adverse
      Childhood Experiences (ACE) study. *American Journal of Preventive Medicine*,
      14(4), 245–258. doi:10.1016/S0749-3797(98)00017-8
Jacobs, J. (1961). *The death and life of great American cities*. New York, NY: Vintage Books.
Loury, G. (1977). A dynamic theory of racial income differences. In P. A. Wallace &
      A. LeMund (Eds.), *Women, minorities, and employment discrimination* (pp. 153–
      188). Lexington, MA: Lexington Books.

Makinodan, M., Rosen, K. M., Ito, S., & Corfas, G. (2012). A critical period for social experience–dependent oligodendrocyte maturation and myelination. *Science, 337*(6100): 1357–1360. doi:10.1126/science.1220845

Portes, A. (1998). Social capital: Its origins and applications in modern sociology. *Annual Review of Sociology, 24,* 1–24.

Putnam, R. D. (1993). *Making democracy work: Civic tradition in modern Italy.* Princeton, NJ: Princeton University Press.

Putnam, R. D. (1995). Tuning in, tuning out: The strange disappearance of social capital in America. *Political Science and Politics, 28*(4), 664–683.

Putnam, R. D. (2000). *Bowling alone: The collapse and revival of American Community.* New York, NY: Simon & Schuster.

Saxe, G., Ellis, B. H., & Kaplow, J. B. (2009). *Collaborative treatment of traumatized children and teens: The trauma systems therapy approach.* New York, NY: Guilford Press.

Woolcock, M. (1998). Social capital and economic development: Toward a theoretical synthesis and policy framework. *Theory and Society, 27*(2), 151–208. doi:10.1023/A:1006884930135

Woolcock, M. (2001). The place of social capital in understanding social and economic outcomes. *Canadian Journal of Policy Research, 2*(1), 1–27.

# CHAPTER 3

c√/o

# Poverty, Pavement, and Paying Attention

*Rural Child Welfare Practice
in the American Great Plains*

DEBRA NORRIS

Scarecrows in South Dakota. Scare crows made from straw grown on local farms greet visitors every Halloween.

Debra Norris

POVERTY, PAVEMENT, AND PAYING ATTENTION (33)

## LEARNING OBJECTIVES

- Give a specific example of learning from a community "windshield assessment"
- Define two or more concrete ways to increase one's social capital within communities
- List two or more "formal" ways to assess communities and what kind of information that can be gleaned from each source

## RURAL PRACTICE

This chapter offers insight into rural practice distinctions, including ways to gather community and regional information that helps guide effective rural practice. The chapter itself essentially tells a story about an experienced rural child welfare professional who gives advice to those who will be beginning their child welfare career in the American Great Plains. This is the kind of practical advice new workers need for adjusting to, and sustaining, a child welfare career in a particular remote area. Workers in any rural area should look for the "what one really needs to know out there" kinds of advice demonstrated in this real life vignette. It is not unusual for this kind of child welfare practice "navigation" advice to come directly from others in the community as well, for example, business leaders, service club members, and, often, child welfare consumers and clientele.

In addition, the chapter includes a child welfare case vignette that illustrates how to use knowledge of community culture to communicate with a family. The advice for new child welfare providers touches on the following topics: worker temperament for those called to rural service; the need for flexibility in one's use of time; the importance of food in connecting with others; the use of the radio as a weather monitor; the challenges of driving on slick, oiled roads; the need for seasonal survival kits; the use of negotiation skills across levels of service organization (local, regional, state, and federal); and the cultural content of local stories. The aims are to demonstrate how to find data to explore rural community contexts and cultures and ways to apply knowledge of local community cultures in child welfare practice.

## THE GREAT PLAINS: ADVICE VOICED BY
## A PROFESSIONAL COLLEAGUE

In the Great Plains states, the poor condition of roads, distances to services, dangerous weather, and sparse population complicate the lives of the people who live there. The increased stress of poverty is a powerful contributor to the disparities in health, incarceration, and out-of-home placement of children. South Dakota comprised 8 of the 10 poorest counties in the United States in 2010; in fact, some counties in South Dakota include population distributions of one person per square mile (Data Masher, 2008). Other Great Plains states share these same characteristics of poverty and sparse population density.

### Time, Food, and Relationships

The most critical supply is time. Forget the schedule, the watch, or the fruitless attempt of trying to cram five tasks into an hour. For that reason, the different valuation of time in the Great Plains can be maddening for type A people. In practical terms, supervisors in rural areas need to give serious attention to the "time" temperament of those who work under their direction. This different order of time spent between conversations and caring will amount to either an enjoyment or an annoyance, feeling as comfortable as one's favorite shoes for some or the cause of blisters for others. Those rural workers whose time temperament is out of sync with the ethos of time in the Great Plains should prepare themselves for much misery.

In the vast expansion of land with its pockets of extreme persistent poverty, few communities enjoy the structures of population, resources, and agents of social control most social work practice models are based on. Social service offices can be "itinerant" and can be serviced by workers who travel over 120 miles just to get to the office. Some caseworkers work from home. Some communities in the Great Plains are even farther away from medical care, fire and rescue, or law-enforcement services.

### Listening to the Radio

Some claim that an appreciation of country music is another requirement. Radio reception is better than it used to be, but some areas are still limited to AM reception. The good news is that one may be able to hear the local ball games on AM radio. Rural social workers can pay attention to the area by listening to the local radio broadcasts. Keeping an eye on the weather is critical; local stations usually have a local spotter who keeps an eye to the sky. Every year the National Weather Service holds spotter training across the Great Plains states. Even with all of the advancements in Doppler radar and 3D storm prediction, tracking tornados still requires human confirmation of rotation and the movement of a debris cloud. Many an eager spotter has been scolded for buying an emergency vehicle bubble and trying to convince local law enforcement they are agents of the National Oceanic and Atmospheric Administration (NOAA) when they are pulled over for speeding. NOAA takes a dim view of this behavior.

In addition to providing storm confirmation to the local weather station, Great Plains travelers who take long rides across the prairie provide the opportunity to find out what is important to the people who live there. Swap shop programs, by which people call in with items they are willing to sell or trade, reveal evidence of the barter system, which is both alive and well in rural areas. With the recent cutbacks on funding for county-based extension agents, many rural areas now rely on regional offices and limited windows of opportunity for shelter-belt tree distribution, gardening tips, and the latest herbicide programs. Having local information to share is the mark of an engaged rural social worker because rural workers must wear many hats if they hope to be effective.

## Relationships

A rural social worker in the Plains states should be able to identify who knows nearly everyone in the region and how to approach them. If a child welfare worker is told where someone lives and is advised not to attempt a visit that day, it is best to heed the warning unless this is an emergency visit. People may or may not share why one needs to let a visit go, but it is best to thank them for their concern and visit someone else. A rural social worker needs to know who will house a family that just lost their home, who has a backhoe and tractor to pull someone out of the ditch, and who can help execute a commitment order when someone is a threat to themselves or others. A good working relationship with local law enforcement is a must, and dropping off a box of fresh baked goods from the small town bakery is an effective ice-breaker. Many times in rural work it is wise to let local law enforcement know when one is visiting certain families because sometimes they may want them to ride along. The gesture of baked goods conveys a few messages that are most helpful in building a supportive relationship. Bringing baked goods from the best bakery sends the message that (a) one is familiar enough with the area to know where the good bakery is; (b) one cares enough about the relationship to bring a gift; (c) one paid for the gift personally, as no state program will ever reimburse for donuts from the local bakery; and (d) one is willing to make time for a good story and a cup of coffee.

It is important to make friends along the way and listen to stories for the messages. One can let folks know they are friends by dropping off some fresh produce, a chunk of their favorite cheese from the small town dairy, or a sour-cream raisin pie from the little café where three generations still cook together. Food gifts are significant to rural people and especially rural people who persist within areas of relentless poverty and hardship.

## Local Stories

Stories shared by local people carry a message of history, especially a regionalized account of history. Local stories can also serve as coded messages of what one needs to know in order to belong. A professional who "belongs" to the area (as decided by the local people) will be given extra support, respect, and, sometimes, resource access/development assistance. Those who do can become "insiders"—at least to a degree; being an insider comes with a reputation for trustworthiness, which no "outsider" enjoys. It comes with the social capital that helps get work done. Many of the local stories will be shared with the professionals and others while the storytelling residents are helping someone out of a jam. The stories carry a richness of meaning that signifies cultural values and beliefs. They indicate the ways of a region and the survival adaptations of the people who live there.

## Negotiating

Skills for cultivating relationships need to include negotiation skills. A child welfare professional will be expected to negotiate with, and for, troubled families as well as to negotiate with local and state agencies for the provision of services. On the Great Plains, this means that the professional needs to understand state, tribal, and federal jurisdiction. Federally recognized tribes are sovereign nations and those with whom states have negotiated agreements for the delivery of child protection services consistent with the federal mandates of the Indian Child Welfare Act (National Indian Child Welfare Association, n.d.). Whenever a Native American child is in need of out-of-home care, the tribe the child is, or could be, a member of must be contacted. The extent of involvement from the tribe depends upon the state tribal agreements. The agreements may vary, but the adherence to Indian Child Welfare Act (ICWA) guidelines does not. Child protection on the Great Plains requires sensitivity to tribal distinctions, mediation skills when state and tribal relationships are tense, and extraordinary stamina because the days are long and distances to travel even longer. It is not unusual for a worker to spend the day on the road to provide one precious hour of supervised visitation for a child and that child's family.

## On the Road: Pavement, Oil, and Gumbo

With extreme distances to travel, the worker needs survival skills and supplies. Workers need tire replacement supplies, tow straps, a box of rags, a map, and a compass. It is not always possible to access global positioning satellites (GPS) in remote areas. Other practical items to bring include peanut butter, a good thermos, a big stick, a couple gallons of water, and ways to entertain young passengers and friends along the way. In rural areas, it is common to ask for coffee to be put in one's thermos by the person selling coffee. This can even be pretty reasonable. One special note is shared here: summer survival kits should not include chocolate, as experience has demonstrated the near-impossibility of removing a stain left by what use to be a Hershey bar.

Many roads may be oiled and/or not paved, particularly if those roads connect very small communities. An oiled road could mean a road finished with asphalt-tar concoction or just a spread of some petroleum product to keep the dust down during the dry season. Where one is in the state determines the quality of the material used to produce the "oiled" roads. Those new to an area learn that it is best to question the definition of "oiled" and to inquire whether there are breaks in the oil that expose "gumbo." Gumbo in South Dakota is as hard as concrete during the dry season and hosts very limited plant growth. An excellent roadway is one baked hard by the relentless sun. If a full expanse of a road is all gumbo and the sky suggests rain (or there has been a recent rain), one should not take the gumbo because, once wet, it is as treacherous as quicksand and as slippery as axle grease. If you ever hit a patch (the operant word here is patch) less than 1/8 mile long, do not slow down. Throw whatever beverage, snack, or electronic device you may be holding into the passenger seat; grab the wheel with both hands; accept the screaming, wild whooping, or other expressions of terror passengers emit; and remember—do not slow down. A person who slows down is doomed. He or she will experience wild fishtailing and must drive blind because of the adobe splats of mud that cover every window. It is not possible to put the wipers on because letting go of the wheel means spinning into a vortex of mud one can never escape. The driver can clean the windows with the extra rags and two gallons of water (from the summer survival kit) later, but the first goal is to get through the gumbo.

You will know you are back on the oil when the car makes an uncontrollable lunge once it hits dry ground. If you are lucky, you will be facing the appropriate direction on the roadway. It will take a bit to bring the rig to a stop because of the 5" layer of gumbo on the tires. If the vehicle is turned toward the ditch and the wheels hit the dry ground with the gas petal posed to propel the car to 95 mph, you can end the ride by jumping the ditch. Jumping the ditch involves a continuum of success from actually propelling partially airborne over the ditch, landing in a field or pasture, or wedging the car in the fold of the ditch with only one wheel making contact with the ground. The wedging end of the continuum requires a tractor or other form of heavy equipment for recovery of the vehicle. Depending upon the landing and the lay of the land adjacent to the ditch, a Dodge Ram 4 by 4 may do. One may add to the survival kit two good tow straps and a new one never to be used except as a wonderful thank-you gift. Do not buy tow straps from the people that come through town with a semi-tractor trailer full of bargains. These straps are fine for in town and most interstate predicaments but prove worthless in real towing challenges.

In most Plains states, the roads are cut narrow and the ditches deep. Specific dimensions of road-to-ditch ratios depend upon the direction of the road and how important it is in the transportation network. A deep ditch runs alongside important roads that run east to west to catch the snow. Deep ditches reduce drifting and closures. Hence landing in a deep ditch full of snow in the winter requires rescue from a tow truck or an experienced winter-rescue farmer with a heated shop. The heated shop is necessary because removal of the snow now compacted like a cinder block will have to be blasted off the flywheel.

It is best to know where one is while on the road, the distance, say, to the next little community. That means you must know how to track mileage, read a map, and use a compass. Also, it is important to let someone know where you are going and by what time you expect to arrive. Continual contact with your Twitter friends is a pipedream, but safety may depend on someone else being concerned. Cell reception is spotty at best on the Great Plains, so good boots (the winter and nonwinter variety) are a good idea. In the summer, snakes love the hot roadways, and in winter "outsiders" cannot imagine how cold the feet can get while the person attached to them waits for help. In winter, one should always have a survival kit that includes a decent sleeping bag (good to −20°), food, water, coffee can, candles, shovel, flashlight, extra batteries, a change or two of socks, snow pants, good coat, hat, waterproof gloves, and a red flag for the antenna. If desired, one can add a bicycle flag on a pole as a good addition to the survival kit. Regardless of what is in the survival kit—if it is snowing, bitterly cold, or the weather promises to turn bad, stay off the back roads.

In any type of weather, there are few services of convenience, so peanut butter is a staple road-food item. Another survival key is in learning how to change a tire and have a good spare (not a "donut" tire that helps one limp into the tire store). Also make sure that you have a tire iron and jack. It is not a bad idea to have a foot square 1" thick piece of plywood and a wedge or two to level the plywood under the jack. Generous level shoulders along roadways do not exist, and jacks do slip in gravel.

An understanding of how to read the weather is critical to a rural worker in the Plains. For summer safety it is a very good idea to take weather-spotter training. Squall lines with straight-line winds of 80 to 100 miles-an-hour are more frequent and do more damage than tornadoes. Incorrect placement of the vehicle can toss one about like tumbleweed. Place the car perpendicular to the approaching line of storms. Keep a blanket in the car. In storms with large hail and flying debris, it is important to cover up with a blanket while waiting out the hail or squall line. The blanket provides protection from broken window glass. A roll of clear plastic and duct tape are other must-haves in the tool kit; they can be used for many purposes, including piecing together cracked windshields.

Directions are often given in terms of cattle gates. Cattle gates are steel barred contraptions buried at the entrance to a minimum maintenance road (gumbo or petroleum product roadway), lane, or shortcut that prevents cattle from leaving a particular area. Note if cattle guards are in place, fencing may be limited, so be prepared to share the road with a herd. Wait patiently as honking could spook the herd and lead to animal injury. Spooking cattle is always bad form in the Plains states. The compass, mentioned earlier, is a must. Left or right mean nothing in the Plains, only north, south, east, west, or some strange combination of these directions. Traveling the western region often requires following directions like this: "Drive on the southwest path in the shadow of chimney butte until you see (pass) three cattle gates off the oil; cut against the wind and slide hard west until the sun blinds you; stay true and you'll make it."

### Culture, Adaptation, and Practice

The vastness of the land is beautiful, the harshness of the weather is halting, and the resilience of the people is stunning. However, there is a "heaviness" to the people of the Plains that seems to be cloaked in humor and humility. Drawing attention to personal achievement or bragging is not approved, and many a newcomer have "shown their hand" by doing so. Words mean little to the Plains people unless one is giving one's word. Giving one's word to do, or not do, something is as solemn a trust as there is for the rural people of the Plains. Trust is measured by behaviors, not words. Trust is not anything earned as some may understand that phrase. Trust evolves, it grows deeper, and the bonds tighten. There is no greater violation in the lives and minds of rural Plains people than the violation of trust. In the Plains, it is better to "fly below the radar" and not call attention to one's self. It is best not to ponder the cause; to keep one's activities confidential, enjoy a joke, share the sadness, and never brag about one's self. Researching the history of the Great Plains is a good idea. One of the best novels about settling part of the Plains is *Giants in the Earth* (Rölvaag, 1927). Perhaps the heaviness is because of the human cost to settle this huge expanse of land.

For rural Plains people, family and community are central to survival; however, that centrality of family and place has seemingly always been challenged. These fiercely family- and location-bound people find themselves and their ways of living disenfranchised from the larger American society or what many have come to refer to as "mainstream." For many rural Plains people, they are only "whole" when they are home or able to practice the ways of home that makes them whole. The mindset is collective even though one hears much about the rugged individual; for the Plains people, the rugged individual is attached to family and place. Thus, one often hears, "Every outlaw had a mother." It is important to understand that this rugged individual focus with simultaneous attention to helping each other is part of the world of child welfare clients/customers. For example, people living in poverty often have a cadre of strengths and an intra- and interfamily resource sharing-system, especially for emergencies. According to Valladares and Moore (2009), the strengths of people living in poverty should always be considered. They are rugged and collective as they may be part of an infrastructure of exchange that may be invisible when viewed in the context of formal services.

Mainstream social work interventions have historically targeted "fixing a problem" and narrowed the focus to individuals who need help fixing themselves. The fix or intervention too often placed an individual in isolation from his or her ways and community role. Interventions of isolation may sever a people from their collective view of wholeness. In many small towns, especially culturally distinct small towns, a return to wholeness can only be achieved through restoring individuals to their role in the collective by working with the family and community in unison while working with an individual. This may be especially true for many Native American people. Good social work in rural areas requires weaving community- and family-based interventions into the interventions for individuals. Strategies found in restorative justice and systems of care family group decision-making practices provide a wonderful structure.

Many family and community members say that they have no alternative for their children's future but to send them off to college. Jobs that support a family are often scarce. This promise from postsecondary education has complicated community, family, and individual wholeness. Just as Carr and Kefalas (2009) discussed in *Hollowing Out the Middle: The Rural Brain Drain and What It Means to America*, rural youth who enjoyed the resources, accolades, and high school to university connections from their small towns leave for the "promised land" of metropolitan areas. The young adults who stay in small towns are often the youth the small towns invested little in. With brain drain, political neglect, and dwindling resources, many small rural towns empty of their future generation leadership. The small towns that struggle the most are often in the reservation counties. The diminished funding for education and the tendency to locate universities in larger metropolitan areas force community high schools to invest only in the most promising students, while universities troll for the best catches. Many rural students do not fare well at the larger universities. The lack of adequate funding for small schools leaves the graduates with a very steep learning curve. The limited preparation of many rural students can lead to needed remedial coursework, adding time and pressure to the university experience. Some rural students say they feel responsible for their families and share their financial aid money; most struggle with being comfortable in the university environment. The competitive culture of larger universities is particularly hard for students from geographically isolated communities where the culture of cooperation was often more important than individual achievement.

Educational policies and practices that leave rural areas underresourced and stripped of population fuel can yield a "us versus them" mindset. Rural residents are acutely aware of the financial imbalance and subsequent impression of privileges they believe is enjoyed by residents of metropolitan areas. Indeed, rural areas usually do have fewer services, and getting to them can be difficult. Perhaps an unintended consequence of these policies, practices, and imbalances is that they may have contributed to a great distrust of policymakers and service providers among American Indian families and communities. The policies and practices of distrust are far-reaching and deeply rooted. The forced removal of children to attend boarding schools and the disproportional incarceration, health disparities, and over-representation of American Indian children in foster care reinforce distrust and illustrate the continual misunderstanding of what community, family, and wholeness mean to American Indian and rural Plains people. The earlier education policies reinforced the push for the Indian Child Welfare Act. The tension between rural areas and nonrural areas can be further fueled by historical events, as well as a current lack of rural services and economic development. The tension does provide opportunity for some clever innovations and practices of self-sufficiency on the part of folks who live rural. The following story illustrates such an innovation:

A couple embarked on a contract for deed agreement on a piece of property owned by an old farmer in a neighboring state. After moving in, the couple discovered the house did not have a sufficient septic system for waste. To appease the local code enforcement officials, they rented a porta-potty and placed it in the front yard. The gentleman discovered he could apply to be certified in septic installation and inspection. He ordered the materials necessary for certification, and to his delight the test was included in the study material. The couple spent the afternoon filling out the test, and within a month the certificate came in the mail. The couple poured one side of concrete to shore-up the caved in septic, threw two pieces of plywood on top to form a cover, and covered the plywood with dirt. Since the owner was certified to inspect, he smiled and said "Good enough!" The papers were filed, no questions asked, and the story is now a toasted example of "sticking it to the man."

The key to rural social work is to respect the tension, learn the history, enjoy the local genius of the people, and work to change the policies and practices that continue disparities. Some information can be found by "windshield assessment"—simply paying attention to the people and place, taking the time to think about one's observations, and putting ideas to use that emerge within culturally aligning child welfare practice. One can also search for historical and current area data.

## CASE VIGNETTE

Raelyn Dawn was a new child protective services worker in a rural region of a Great Plains state. She was also new to the Great Plains state and found that her rural roots growing up in Kentucky were, and were not, helping her to understand the people and landscape of her employment catchment area. For example, as a rural Kentucky native, she knew that food gifts and relationships with other services providers, and even the business community, were important. However, she did not know exactly where to begin to learn about the region she was now working in. She spoke to her supervisor and work colleagues who began to teach her about local customs, travel, and "survival kits." This information was offered so frequently that she wondered whether this practical information about pavement and paying attention was routinely offered to new workers at her rural agency. It had not been part of the state-level formal training program she had recently completed.

She studied rural social work practice and even attended the summer conference of the National Rural Social Work Caucus. In addition, she began to ask for more specific community/regional information. One of the recommendations of her supervisor was to keep a journal and note observations about the communities and regions she traveled to for her home visits and community meetings. Thus she began her "windshield survey" of the community with a journal, albeit one filled with hastily scrawled notes usually prepared from the front seat of a car. In addition, she studied maps and historical publications about the area that she found on the Internet, the local library, and a Great Plains historical museum located near the state capital. She began to show up at the local coffee shop for breakfast once or twice a week. As time went on, she was invited to join some of the "regulars" who talked about hunting, fishing, hobbies, local events, and local people. An elderly couple who owned a ranch in the area also began to offer helpful advice about ways to get engaged in the community; they helped her meet other ranch and community business leaders. The couple served as "cultural guides" for Ms. Dawn, all of which aided her acclimation and connections across the region.

Ms. Dawn also began to forage for a more thorough knowledge of local history: population demographic data, as well as traditional community events such as rodeos and pow wows. She attended the events and paid attention to the content of conversations and the actions and rituals that took place. She consulted "the community tool kit" of Kansas University (2016); this exploration further strengthened the idea of talking to people about the community. The toolkit suggested engaging in windshield (and walking) assessments, as well as seeking online and local demographic data (often found at the local courthouse building). She joined a local church and the Zonta club. She paid attention to changes in the community and how the connections with a global economy were impacting the ranching world. She listened to the ranchers tell stories about how they needed to adapt their practices to the business environment. It appeared to her that the greater social and economic environments tested traditional culture and that particular regions adapted to those demands according to their region.

Ms. Dawn began to try to use what she was learning in her negotiations with the family members she served. She recently did so when attempting to deal with a mother (Bree Balinger) about the substantiated physical abuse inflicted upon her six-year-old (Jimmy Balinger). His school teacher noted bruises in various stages of healing on the back of his arms. The teacher called the child protective services office. Ms. Dawn investigated and talked to the family. A medical examination performed by Dr. Anttien found many more severe bruises on his buttocks and lower back. One bruise seemed consistent with the outline of a belt buckle. Ms. Dawn talked to Ms. Balinger who said she used a belt to discipline Jimmy and his younger sister Katie, age 3. She said, "My folks never believed in sparing the rod and that's the way I was brought up." Ms. Balinger seemed reluctant to accept that this kind of discipline method was no longer allowed if it led to physical injury, such as bruising. Ms. Dawn suddenly remembered a story told to her by the rancher's wife, and she retold the story to Ms. Balinger:

In a Great Plains family, there were generations of women who always cut the end of their Easter ham off before they baked it. One year it was time for the youngest of the family to bake the ham. She asked her mother why they practiced this tradition. The mother told the girl to ask her grandmother. The grandmother answered that she did not know why they cut the end of the ham off now. She said she had to do so because her small oven was not large enough to hold a full ham.

Ms. Dawn explained to Ms. Balinger that there was a lesson that could be gleaned from this story, which she put this way: "Do you continue to use the traditional discipline methods or do you change them to avoid having CPS come into your family? This is your decision." Ms. Balinger held her chin in her hand for a moment, gave a sigh, and then said "Yes, I would like to change the way I'm disciplining Jimmy. It's not working very well anyway." In this vignette, the worker was simply using the cultural values of the local people in communicating with a mother who had physically abused her child. She had learned the regional tradition-versus-change values by spending a few minutes listening to a local woman tell a story and engaging in a bit of self-reflection about the possible cultural messages therein.

## Practice Application

Learning to use aspects of local culture can help social workers communicate more fully and deeply with their clients. Understanding as many aspects of a community as possible allows the social worker to use the community assets to help clients. As the author demonstrates in this chapter, familiarity with and integration into the community happen when the social worker takes the time and energy to fully understand the culture, language, and issues surrounding the lives of people within that community. Learning to live in a rural community and taking the time to develop relationships enables the social worker to build social capital and to develop survival skills for professional practice.

## DISCUSSION QUESTIONS

1. What supplies do people need in a rural survival kit in your rural area?
2. How is food used to convey friendship?
3. Identify some personal characteristics that would prepare a child welfare worker for rural social work practice on the Great Plains. To what extent may these apply to your rural area?
4. Give an example of how a professional could use a "local story" or local data in an individual, family, group, community, or policy-advocacy activity.
5. In the case vignette, Ms. Dawn told a story to help the mother learn a new behavior. What are some other ways of attaining behavior change? What would have happened if the mother continued to beat her child with the belt? What are Ms. Dawn's obligations as a child welfare worker no matter where she works?

## LEARNING ACTIVITIES

1. Formal Community Assessment Techniques
   a. Have participants break into small groups to research how to find data about a specific rural community or area. Have them list at least 10 specific sources of information.
2. Informal Community Assessment Techniques
   a. Complete a community windshield and/or walk about assessment as a course assignment and have the participants present their communities to the class.

## SUGGESTED READING

### FAMILY-CENTERED SERVICES

https://www.childwelfare.gov/famcentered/overview/approaches/family_group.cfm
National Rural Social Work Caucus
www.ruralsocialworkers.org

## COMMUNITY ASSESSMENT

University of Kansas. (2016). *Community toolbox*. Workgroup for Community Health and Development. http://ctb.ku.edu/en/table-of-contents/assessment/assessing-community-needs-and-resources

## HISTORY OF THE GREAT PLAINS

Frazier, I. (1988). *The Great Plains*. New York, NY: Picador Press.

## REFERENCES

Carr, P., & Kefalas, M. (2009). *Hollowing out the middle: The rural brain drain and what it means to America*. Boston, MA: Beacon Press

Data Masher. (2008). *Population density 2008 census*. Retrieved from http://www.data-masher.org/mash-ups/people-square-mile#map

National Indian Child Welfare Association. (n.d.). *The Child Welfare Act of 1978*. Retrieved from http://www.nicwa.org/indian_child_welfare_act/

Rölvaag, O. E. (1927). *Giants in the earth*. New York, NY: Harper & Row.

University of Kansas. (2016). *Community toolbox*. Workgroup for Community Health and Development. Retrieved from http://ctb.ku.edu/en/table-of-contents/assessment/assessing-community-needs-and-resources

Vallandares, S., & Moore, K. A. (2009). The strengths of poor families. *Child Trends Research Brief*, 26, 1–8.

## CHAPTER 4

໖

# Matchmaker, Matchmaker, Make Me a Match

## *Rural Resource Family and Child Matching*

HEATHER CRAIG-OLDSEN

Two Paths. Rural land provides regular recreation for rural people. This path is used by hikers and those riding off road vehicles.

Barbara J. Pierce

## LEARNING OBJECTIVES

- Describe the historical foundation of resource (foster and/or adoptive) family home-finding and support in rural communities
- Describe important policy practice considerations in a typical rural statewide system for matching children with resource families
- Identify barriers to effective matching of children with resource families in rural settings
- Determine ways to develop working relationships with children and resource families in rural statewide child welfare systems
- List three or more unique matching considerations for children who are eligible for tribal enrollment

## HISTORICAL BACKGROUND OF RESOURCE FAMILY AND CHILD MATCHING IN THE RURAL MIDWEST

Finding, approving, licensing, and supporting rural resource (foster and/or adoptive) families has historically faced significant challenges. With rural child welfare programs beginning in the mid 1850s, Midwestern and other rural states faced significant challenges when trying to find and support resource families. Child welfare agencies, largely located in urban settings, likewise faced challenges meeting the needs of children at risk of poor outcomes because of neglect, abuse, or abandonment. Many of those challenges centered significantly on clashes of cultures. The challenges of the 1800s and early 1900s changed somewhat during the 20th century as it became easier for social workers to interact more regularly with resource families in rural communities and to begin to address the systemic cultural clashes inherent in the early child welfare history. Resource family home-finding and support changed dramatically at the turn of the 21st century as technology dramatically opened the options for systemic changes designed to support resource families; yet challenges remain.

### Resource Family Home-Finding and Support in the 19th Century

The history of rural resource family home-finding and support in the 19th century emerges from a fascinating history of forced transportation of children across the plains. Two parallel and intertwining transporting histories produced a child welfare system that impacts support of resource families today.

Midwestern rural states were the focus of home-finding for children who from 1854 until the early 1930s came on trains from the city of New York to live with farming families in the rural United States who were in need of labor. An estimated 150,000 poor urban children (largely children of recent immigrants) were sent to farm families in the effort that they be saved from "vice, beggary, and filth" (Cook, 1995, p. 181). Most were not orphans but children of poor and largely unskilled workers (many immigrants) trapped in what Nelson (1995) describes as a "vortex" of poverty that resulted from low wages, high unemployment, inflated prices, and housing shortages (p. 61). Charles Loring Brace, an Evangelical minister, led the "placing out" movement. He and his agency staff members from the Children's Aid Society believed that the only way to save these children (many of whom were Jewish or Roman Catholic) from lives of hereditary sin, poverty, sloth, and other bad habits was to remove them from their families and place them, ideally, with good, Protestant farm families; the placement families were approved by the Children's Aid Society through very limited contact (Cook, 1995; Nelson, 1995; Schene, 1998).

According to interviews with adults who were involved with the orphan trains as children, decisions were made by the prospective parents about the suitability of a child to live with the family, rather than through a systematic approval processes (Hearn & Petzall, 1991). Matching a child with a family was a matter of a cursory approval process and a conversation with the parents about what sort of child they needed to live with their family, usually in exchange for labor. The challenges of meeting the wants and needs of the rural families continued to be a challenge well into the early 20th century. Birk (2012) suggests that by using labor in exchange for care, institutions placed the burden on children to behave in a way that proved their worthiness and to live up to the expectations of their placement parents.

The process of matching American Indian and Alaskan Native (AI/AN) children with rural families was nearly nonexistent in the 19th century. Their story was very different. While children from the East coast were being moved to rural America, AI/AN children were being transported from tribal lands all over the country to boarding schools, often far away from their homes. From 1789 through 1871, federal policy was aimed at exterminating American Indians. From 1871 until 1928, policy goals switched to assimilation and dependency (Halverson, Puig, & Byers, 2002) in the 1880s and running through the 1950s, boarding schools were used to speed assimilation of Indians into dominant White culture. Captain Richard Henry Pratt, the architect of the Indian boarding school movement, said, "We accept the watch-word. There is no good Indian but a dead Indian. Let us by education and patient effort kill the Indian in him, and save the man!" (US Congress, 1886, p. 25). Forcibly separating Indian children from their families and harshly forbidding their involvement in Indigenous culture, language, and religion were key to assimilation. Like the street children of New York City, American Indian children were considered "salvageable," though their parents were not. Boarding schools were to teach children a trade, help them adopt an "appropriate" belief system (Catholic or Protestant Christian), and cut their ties with family and community (Burger, 1995). However, many more AI/AN children were affected by boarding schools. From 1879 to the present day, it is estimated that hundreds of thousands of AI/AN children attended boarding schools (Brown Foundatiion, 2001; Magagnini, 1997). Many children never left their boarding school, especially in the early era. The 1928 Meriam Report found that the death rate among AI/AN children was 6.6 times higher than any other ethnic group, largely due to malnutrition and the spread of influenza, trachoma, tuberculosis, and other diseases at boarding school. Enrollment in boarding schools peaked in 1973, with 60,000 children estimated to have been enrolled. In 2007, enrollment was 9,500, including 45 reservation boarding schools, 7 off-reservation boarding schools, and 14 other dormitories (Bear, 2008).

## Rural Resource Family Home-Finding and Support in the 20th Century

Both the orphan train and boarding school stories involve children being separated from family and culture to be placed with families or in institutions with little or no thought of matching specific children with specific families. In both situations the goal was to acculturate the children in an effort to improve their lives and their futures, largely by cutting them off from their families and communities of origin and arranging for them to be raised up in the dominant Anglo-Saxon culture. This policy of moving children to very different environments created a child welfare history based on stories of loss of family connections, loss of culture, and loss of respect. Both histories created the foundation for child welfare practice in much of rural America in the 20th century.

The beginning of the 20th century brought rapid and significant changes to child welfare programs and systems all over the United States. Opened on April 9, 1912, the US Children's Bureau became the first national government agency in the world to focus solely on the needs of children. During the 20th century the Children's Bureau played a critical role in addressing vital issues affecting families, with an important focus on preventing child maltreatment and promoting permanency for children and youth.

During the late 20th century the focus on child welfare was sharpened in the United States. According to the Children's Bureau the number of children in out of home care skyrocketed from 177,000 in 1961 to 503,000 by 1978 (Children's Bureau, 2012a). During that same time the general population of children was decreasing (Calhoun, 1980). This was a wake-up call in the United States. In subsequent years, significant changes occurred through the passage of federal child welfare laws and policies such as the Child Abuse Prevention and Treatment Act of 1974, the Adoption Assistance and Child Welfare Act of 1980, the Multiethnic Placement Act of 1994, and the Adoption and Safe Families Act of 1997 (Children's Bureau, 2014a). Each of these acts significantly strengthened the potential for support of resource families in America and provided child welfare professionals the legal basis to begin selecting resource families to meet the needs of children and matching specific children with those families. For example, during the late 20th century statewide resource parent training programs grew dramatically in both urban and rural communities. According to the Children's Bureau (2014b), approximately 44 states and the District of Columbia require in law or policy that prospective resource parents complete a course of orientation and training prior to licensure, which provides an avenue for agency staff to begin to understand the strengths and needs of each family.

One important law passed in the 20th century was designed to direct practice decisions about matching AI/AN children with resource families. The Indian Child Welfare Act of 1978 (ICWA), a legal agreement between the US government and multiple Native American nations, assures tribal courts have legal jurisdiction for all children eligible for enrollment in a recognized tribe. According to Cross (2006), ICWA was established to stop the child welfare practices that contributed to the break-up of AI/AN families, and several legal decisions have weakened the act's strength. Regrettably, the ICWA is also the most ignored federal law ever established (Eveleth, 2005). Child welfare social workers must educate other social workers, legal professionals, and resource parents to always inquire about the possibility of a child being AI/AN, even when the child does not appear to be AI/AN.

Even into the end of the 20th century, rural child welfare programs faced logistical constraints in the process of approving, licensing, and supporting resource families (Children's Bureau, 2012a). Rural public child welfare agency offices were generally located in county seats. Without the benefit of technology improvements, child welfare workers frequently found it necessary to travel over hundreds and sometimes thousands of square miles to recruit, approve, and support resource families in rural settings. For example, a resource family social worker in Montana was responsible for working with families in a 30,000 square mile area (J. Clark, personal communication, 1999).

## Rural Resource Family Home-Finding and Support in the 21st Century

The advent of the 21st century brought with it a rapidly changing utilization of technology, the increase in transient populations in rural areas, and significant changes in organizational structures for delivery of child welfare services. In rural child welfare practice, professionals, used to developing and maintaining personal relationships in their communities, saw changes in practice because of increases in transient workers such as farm workers or oil field workers. The use of technology in centralized locations took some child placements out of their hands (and out of the realm of relationships) and into the hands of a centralized call center. Privatization was a notable structural change in rural child welfare service provision in the late 1900s and the advent of the 21st century. Privatization is the transfer of public agency functions to a private for-profit or not-for-profit organization. Privatization of child welfare has had mixed results in the United States. Barillas (2011) points out:

> Government must have the capacity to carry out the activities associated with private sector contracting including the establishment of measurable results, cost efficient reimbursement rates, performance incentives, and competitive bidding and accountability systems. If privatization is instead a response to low state capacity, then already strained public resources are wasted. (p. 115)

It is not surprising that the Children's Bureau funded a National Quality Improvement Center on the Privatization of Child Welfare Services beginning in 2001 to assess the status of privatization and analyze other aspects of the new phenomenon of privatization of child welfare in the United States.

Whether in public or privatized child welfare programs, rural social workers began expanding their use of technology in the 21st century to support the challenges of rural geography. The Fostering Connections to Success and Increasing Adoptions Act of 2008 placed greater emphasis on connecting and supporting relative caregivers, improving outcomes for children in foster care, providing for tribal foster care and adoption access, and improving incentives for adoption (Children's Bureau, 2014a). All of these connecting outcomes became more possible with the rapid advance of technology usage in child welfare agencies. The previous logistical constraints of the 20th century led to new systemic responses to finding, approving, licensing, and supporting resource families. The new technology opportunities additionally created challenges to traditional rural resource home-finding and matching approaches.

Technology is used by both resource parents and child welfare agencies. Prospective resource parents in rural America can today find resources to meet training requirements online. Organizations like Foster Club (www.fosterclub.com) and Foster Parent College (www.fosterparentcollege.com) offer a variety of online courses for resources parents, as do several private and public child welfare agencies around the United States. Private and public child welfare agencies rely on technology to help them track resource family recruitment, training, support, and matching activities. With all these technology advances come new challenges, some of which are addressed in the case vignette.

## CASE VIGNETTE

Thomas Olson is a BSW child welfare social worker in a rural regional office of a state public child welfare agency. The statewide system in this predominantly rural Midwestern state has privatized the child welfare functions previously managed by Thomas. In the past, Thomas was responsible for recruiting and training resource (foster and/or adoptive) families, recommending families for specific children needing a resource family, and providing support to the resource families during a child's placement. These functions had been performed for years by public child welfare social workers and other staff who were placed in regional and county child welfare offices. As a result of his physical proximity to the resource families, Thomas and other social workers were able to get to know the resource families well. Thomas and his colleagues understood the importance of social capital and worked consistently and over time to build trusting relationships with the resource families. One negative consequence of this system was that some families who were well known and trusted by the social workers were overutilized and families not known as well were underutilized. Thomas acknowledged that the resource families he knew and trusted were often the first to be called when he was asked to locate a resource family for a child.

Because of privatization all home-finding, training, support, and matching positions were eliminated in the public child welfare agency and were transferred from the public child welfare agency to a statewide private agency, here called PCW Org. State administrators selected PCW Org, a private, not-for-profit child welfare organization, because of its impressive plan for creating more efficiencies in home-finding, approving resource families, supporting them, and matching children with families in primarily rural communities. PCW Org offices were elsewhere in the state and were not located in the community housing the regional public agency offices.

Thomas was not in a position to move to another community, so when his position was eliminated in the regional office, he applied for another position in the agency, working with children in foster care and their families. As a result of his new position he was able to continue working with resource families he had known and supported in his past position, as well as new resource parents now supported by PCW Org.

"Matching" refers to the process where PCW Org locates resource families who would be the best possible "match" for a child in need of foster care. In an effort to maximize resources, PWC Org consolidated all matching functions (locating a specific resource family for a specific child) to a single call center in one of the larger urban centers in a more populated part of the state with a large workforce. Privatization was expected to address the problems associated with the public agency staff overutilizing some resource families and underutilizing others. As a result of the changed system, rural child welfare workers looking for a resource family for a child would call the center and give the staff a child's information. From there, the call center would use the database to locate an appropriate match for the child and call resource families in the service area.

Thomas understands that when a resource family is approved and licensed, PCW Org puts the family's information into its database so they can "match" the family to a child who needs foster care. The PCW Org matching staff reviews the age range and gender of children the resource family is willing to foster, the location of the resource home relative to the child's birth home, and the resource family's ability to accommodate a child's special needs or behaviors.

At the point in time when the public child welfare agency refers a child in need of a resource family, PCW Org uses a referral form to ask the public child welfare agency staff questions about the referred child and enters this data into a database. PCW Org uses this database, and also communicates with local public agency staff, to match the resource family's strengths to a child's needs with the goal of creating stable placements for children while they are away from their birth parents.

The child's situation dictates how quickly the call center staff must locate a resource family. Most children require emergency placements, within two hours of the call (urgent). Some children need a family within two to three days (specified dates). A smaller number of children require placements within five days. Children moving from residential settings often require a match within 30 days. Technically, the call center staff assigned to a specific service area in the state is expected to consider the age of the child, the location of the family (near the birth family), and the special needs of the child. In actuality, the call center staff focuses on the age of the child and location of the family, placing the special needs of the child at a lower level of priority.

At 4:00 on a Friday afternoon Thomas receives a call from the supervisor in the Child Protective Services Unit informing him that a nine-month old child, Hank Parker, has entered foster care in an emergency situation and has been placed in the John and Susan Jensen resource home. Thomas will be the ongoing worker assigned to Hank's case.

On Monday morning Thomas receives a call from resource parent Susan Jensen, who lives in a rural part of the county, bordering another state where there is a Native American reservation. Thomas has known the Jensen family for most of his life, having recruited them as resource parents four years earlier and gone to high school with their youngest daughter. Mrs. Jensen is clearly upset. Susan reminds Thomas that they are licensed to parent school-age children to age 18. They accepted nine-month-old Hank into their home under duress on Friday afternoon. According to Susan:

> We took Hank because that call center on the other side of the state told us that they had called ten other resource families in our community Friday afternoon and could not reach anyone. They told us that they were desperate to find a place for this poor baby to stay, so we broke down and said we would take him. We just couldn't say no. You know us, Thomas. We will stretch. But we are not set up for a baby and this doesn't seem the right way to do things. We didn't get much information about Hank, but to top it off, I know the Parker family from across the river and I'm sure that this baby is eligible to be enrolled in his tribe, if he isn't already. This is a mess, and I want to know what you are going to do about it.

Thomas reflects upon his challenge. Given changes in the use of technology to match children with resource parents, rural social workers are still today required to use their social capital to strengthen relationships between resource parents, birth families, and representatives of sometimes numerous local and statewide agencies. Equally important, he knows he has a role to play in educating the local community about how technology impacts child welfare work and in modeling ethical problem-solving with multiple players.

Thomas feels that he is faced with multiple problems that he must address as quickly and as judiciously as possible. His challenges include

- Using his social capital and exercising ethical professional boundaries to convey empathy to Susan Jensen. It is not unusual for resource parents to overextend themselves in an effort to help children and families. In this case, the Jensen family members know they have overextended themselves and are feeling bad that they did so. It is likewise not unusual for organizations like PWC Org to face difficulties reaching prospective resource families by phone on a Friday afternoon, miles across the state. He knows that this is a tough situation and people need to hear that social workers understand where they are emotionally.
- Thomas knows that he must immediately determine if Hank Parker is an enrolled member of a Native American tribe or eligible for enrollment. If so, he will contact the tribe immediately as they have legal jurisdiction per the ICWA. Because many legal and social service professionals are not aware of the requirements of ICWA, Thomas knows that he may find it necessary to educate others throughout the process.
- As in all difficult situations, it is best to engage others. Social workers seldom, if ever, solve problems on their own. Thomas understands that he has an opportunity to bring together all the people who will be involved with Hank Parker to determine the next best steps. These people will include Hank's family and tribal members, the Jensens, the PWC Org support worker who will be working with the Jensens, the child protective services investigator, supervisors, and others.
- Feedback is essential for program improvement, so Thomas will strengthen child welfare practice by remembering to document strengths and problems with the remote matching process and provide feedback to PWC Org.

## Practice Application

In this vignette, Thomas the social worker confronts learning to cope with the challenges of a new job in the private sector in a rural community that is connected to a centralized call center, which makes assignments for rural workers but is located in an urban community. He must cope with the mandates of his new agency but translate those mandates into rural practice, as he understands the needs of the community and the resource parents in that community. Further, Thomas understands that in his area of the state he must be ever vigilant for children who might be tribal members as there is a federal law (ICWA) protecting and guiding the placement of those children who might come into state care. Thomas integrates the needs of his agency with the needs of the child, the resource family, and the tribe to whom the child might belong. His experience, use of his relational capital with the resource family, and cultural acumen are essential to a successful outcome for this child.

## DISCUSSION QUESTIONS

1. Why is Thomas worried about the tribal connection? What is ICWA? How does it relate to Thomas's worries?
2. What are other examples of potential problems for rural child welfare social workers needing to place a child with a resource family? What are ideas for ways to address those problems?
3. To what extent does the history of placements seem similar and different than the centralized placement assignment system encountered by Thomas?
4. What are other examples of potential problems for the urban call center staff? What are ideas for ways to address those problems?
5. What are potential problems for the rural resource development and support staff? What are ideas for ways to address those problems?
6. What are possible policy changes and strategies that might promote best practice in the rural areas of the state?

## LEARNING ACTIVITIES

1. Paychecks Activity
   a. To explore the importance of relationship building with resource parents, brainstorm all of the types of "paychecks" or positives they anticipate receiving when or if they become child welfare social workers in their communities. List all of the ideas so that they are visible to all members of the class and challenge the learners to list as many paychecks as possible.
   b. When the participants have created a sufficiently long list, ask them to identify which of the "paychecks" on the list are also rewards of resource parenting. Circle each "paycheck" that is also a reward or paycheck for resource parents. Cross off "paychecks"

that are clearly not rewards for resource parenting. For example, few resource parents are salaried or paid to foster. Unless they are a professional therapeutic resource parent, they are most likely to receive a partial reimbursement for the cost of caring for children in their home, not a salary or gainful wage. Likewise, they generally do not receive health care or retirement benefits as resource parents. Referencing the case vignette, ask the participants to consider the list of "paychecks" that are likely important to resource parents like the Jensens and to consider ways a rural social worker might assure that the listed nontangible rewards are provided through the social worker's practice and interactions with rural resource parents. Ask the participants to consider ways the state call center staff might offer nontangible rewards in the ways they interact with the resource parents on the phone.

2. Group or Individual Interviews with Resource Parents

   a. If you are in a rural community, provide participants with names and contact information for resource parents who are willing to be interviewed. Direct the participants to interview the resource parents about their experiences being "matched" with children and to compare and contrast that information with information in this chapter, as well as with information they can locate on the public child welfare agency website or through an interview with a child welfare social worker in the community. An example of a rural resource on a website can be found at http://www.iowakidsnet.com/sites/default/files/Quick%20reference%20guide.pdf. Participants may present their findings through oral reports or papers.

## SUGGESTED READING

American Bar Association. *Model family foster home: Licensing standards:* http://www.grandfamilies.org/Portals/0/Model%20Licensing%20Standards%20FINAL.pdf

Foster Parent Bill of Rights: http://nfpaonline.org/page-1494336 (10 states with legislated bills)

Indian Child Welfare Act Online Training: http://www.nicwa.org/icwa_course/

McGuinness, T. M. (2009). Almost invisible: Rural youth in foster care. *Journal of Child and Adolescent Psychiatric Nursing, 22*(2), 55–56.

National Foster Parent Association: www.nfpainc.org

National Indian Child Welfare Association: www.nicwa.org

National Resource Center on Diligent Recruitment. *Support matters: Lessons from the field on services for adoptive, foster, and kinship care families:* http://www.nrcdr.org/_assets/files/AUSK/support-matters/support-matters-resource-guide.pdf

# REFERENCES

Barillas, K. H. (2011). State capacity: The missing piece in child welfare privatization. *Child Welfare, 90*(3), 111–127. Retrieved from http://search.proquest.com/docview/918652398?accountid=9720

Bear, C. (2008, May 12). *American Indian boarding schools haunt many.* National Public Radio, Morning Edition. Retrieved from http://www.npr.org/templates/story/story.php?storyId=16516865

Birk, M. (2012). Supply and demand: The mutual dependency of children's institutions and the American farmer. *Agricultural History, 86*(1), 78–103. Retrieved from http://search.proquest.com/docview/929021828?accountid=9720

Burger, R. (1995). *Effects of the boarding school experience on American Indian families: Practice guidelines.* St. Paul, MN: Augsburg College.

Brown Foundation. (2001). The challenges and limitations of assimilation: Indian boarding schools. *The Brown Quarterly: Quarterly Newsletter for Classroom Teachers, 4*(3).

Calhoun, J. (1980). The 1980 Child Welfare Act: A turning point for children and troubled families. *Children Today, 9*(5), 3.

Children's Bureau. (2012a). *The Children's Bureau legacy: Ensuring the right to childhood.* Retrieved from https://cb100.acf.hhs.gov/sites/default/files/cb_ebook/cb_ebook.pdf

Children's Bureau. (2012b). *Rural child welfare practice.* Child Welfare Information Gateway. Retrieved from https://www.childwelfare.gov/pubs/issue-briefs/rural/

Children's Bureau. (2014a). *Fostering Connections to Success and Increasing Adoptions Act of 2008 (P.L. 110-351).* Child Welfare Information Gateway. Retreived from https://www.childwelfare.gov/topics/systemwide/laws-policies/federal/fosteringconnections/

Children's Bureau. (2014b). *Home study requirements for foster parents.* Child Wellfare Information Gateway. Retrieved from https://www.childwelfare.gov/pubPDFs/homestudyreqs.pdf#page=2&view=Training requirements

Cook, J. F. (1995). A history of placing-out: The orphan trains. *Child Welfare, 74,* 181–193.

Cross, S. L. (2006). Indian family exception doctrine: Still losing children despite the Indian Child Welfare Act. *Child Welfare, 85*(4), 671–690. Retrieved from http://search.proquest.com/docview/213808448?accountid=9720

Eveleth, S. (2005). *Overview of ICWA: The most ignored federal law ever.* Retrieved from www.throughtheeyes.org/resources/nejournal_articles.php

Halverson, K., Puig, M. E., & Byers, S. R. (2002). Culture loss: American Indian family disruption, ubanization, and the Indian Child Welfare Act. *Child Welfare, 8*(1), 320–335.

Hearn, W., & Petzall, J. (Producers). (1991). *The end of the line: Orphan trains* [DVD]. New York, NY: Heritage Account Inc.

Magagnini, S. (1997, June 30). California's lost tribes: Long-suffering urban Indians find roots in ancient rituals. *Sacramento Bee.*

Meriam, L. (1928). *The problem of Indian administration: Report of a survey made at the request of Honorable Hubert Work, Secretary of the Interior, and submitted to him, February 21, 1928.* Baltimore, MD: Johns Hopkins University Press.

Nelson, K. (1995). The child welfare response to youth violence and homelessness in the nineteenth centruy. *Child Welfare, 74,* 56–68.

Schene, P. A. (1998). Past, present, and future roles of child protective services. *The Future of Children, 8*(1), 23–38.

US Congress. (1886). First Session of the 49th Congress. *Congressional Record, 2398,* 25.

# CHAPTER 5

∿

# Cultural Humility within Rural Practice Wisdom

## DEBRA NORRIS

Rural downtown. This small town has a classic downtown area where rural residents connect at a locally run "Mom and Pop" restaurant, the hardware store, and several churches.

David G. Riebschleger

## LEARNING OBJECTIVES

- Provide a definition of practice wisdom
- State the importance of cultural humility

- Identify how the concept of cultural humility can assist workers in dealing with the complexities and relationships in rural communities
- Specify how interagency cooperation can help build culturally responsive and ethical practice

## CULTURAL HUMILITY

Practice wisdom is the process of developing skill and lasting understanding by acquiring and applying knowledge to guide good judgment. Practice wisdom for rural areas must include professionals' use of *self-reflective cultural humility* awareness. Rural professionals who practice cultural humility embrace the *diversity* between and among rural areas. They recognize that one community or region can be different than another, and they work to understand these cultural contexts that affect the socialization of the people served. Professionals who understand diversity within and among rural areas can better know with whom and how to connect with in a particular community in order to increase their social capital so they can better serve children, families, organizations, and communities.

The concept of cultural humility could strengthen the "purposeful *use of self*" noted by Riebschleger (2007, p. 208). When workers employ self-reflection, that includes a recognition of the *power imbalances* that influence clients, workers, and the services they share (Ortega & Faller, 2011). Further, professionals practicing in rural areas need to develop a sense of self that goes beyond their professional identity and allows for the acceptance and recognition of the many *dual relationships* in which they find themselves. Riebschleger conducted focus groups with rural social workers; they said rural practitioners "need to understand that nearly everything is *connected*" (p. 207). Families are connected. Clients and their families are connected to differential power positions such as teachers, coaches, law enforcement officers, as well as community elders and leaders. All these individuals and families are connected to the families that rural workers serve. In rural social work, practice wisdom must include self-reflection and acceptance of dual relationships in order to sustain longevity within child welfare practice.

Another critical point made by the concept of cultural humility is *openness*. Being open to the complexities of themselves, their clients, and the systems of communities allows workers to accept that they cannot understand many of the complexities of a client's life. Ortega and Faller (2011) propose that *accepting complexity* with its limitations frees a worker to engage in client care were workers *continually learn from the client* and *assesses organizational structures that may not be responsive* to the needs of clients, particularly the families and children served.

Early attempts to prepare social work professionals for work with diverse groups may have reinforced stereotypes and power imbalances by the superficial application of case studies (Stevenson, Cheung, & Leung, 1992). Studies and struggles in the area of cultural competence echo what Davis noted in her 2009 article "communication and *relational competence* [emphasis added] are integral to any successful intercultural exchange or relationship" (p. 47). Cultural humility may help practitioners appreciate the complexities of relational competence by allowing practitioners to engage in solution-focused conversations where they do not have all the answers.

The history of *negative experiences with service providers* was found to be a powerful contributor to the mistrust of professionals in rural communities (Chipp, Dewane, Brems, Johnson, Warner, & Roberts, 2011). Recognizing mistrust as part of the complexities of rural work will help professionals acknowledge the need for approaches incorporating cultural humility. Stereotypes of rural people and the tendency of policymakers to leave small communities to struggle add to the cultural complexities for why many rural residents *mistrust* professionals. In contrast, professionals' relational competence with rural people, demonstrated over time, can enhance their abilities to connect with clientele, colleagues, and other community professionals. Relational competence builds connections and information about a particular rural area. Professionals can learn how to *adapt service delivery* using an "accurate understanding of a community's culture, diversity, and strengths . . . [this can be done by] "building on existing resources and strengths in creative and meaningful ways" (Chipp et al., 2011, p. 28).

In summary, a self-reflective culturally humble stance helps rural practitioners to engage in use of self and to build relationship competence. They can use these skills to (a) learn more from clients and other residents, (b) embrace rural community/region cultural differences, (c) recognize dual relationship challenges, (d) consider complex and connected community linkages, (e) consider the impact of regional culture on client and family development, (f) reduce client-worker power differences, and (g) collaborate with other professionals to promote more ethical and culturally responsive service organizations and systems of care. These *practice wisdom* actions would be likely increase openness and trust, a critical element for change among workers and those receiving child welfare services. The case vignette that follows helps illustrate some of these constructs within a particular area of Appalachia and a specific extended family.

## CASE VIGNETTE

Tucked deep in a little hill town in the Appalachian Mountains is an area where most of the tourist industry service workers live. Many of the residents in this area of the town work two to three-part-time jobs and struggle to maintain incomes above the poverty threshold. To protect the tourists who are drawn to the flourishing business district, the impoverished housing section is found down a gravel road off one of the town's secondary throughways. In this complex of trailers and rundown houses, it is common to find two or three generations of a family living together. How family members are related does not seem matter to many of the residents. They may describe someone without a "blood" relationship as family and welcome him or her to bed down on a cot, couch, or recliner. Many families are a blend of cousins, stepsiblings, adult children, children, grandchildren, and, sometimes, warring in-laws and outlaws (a term many families use for past partners and relatives with active warrants out on them). It is not unusual for some children to have six sets of grandparents and three or four different combinations of parents. With large intergenerational combination families where adults are working two to three part-time jobs, the care of children is sometimes assumed by whoever is available. Impoverished multiproblem intergenerational families where the care and custody of children have been a source of dispute become familiar to child protection professionals. It is not unusual for family members to "call social services" on other family members. This practice leads to long histories, large files, and preset perceptions of the families by workers. In this story, other complexities ensue. There is a family member illness, kinship quarrels over the children, additional burdensome family expenses, and worry over protecting pain prescriptions. Each family stressor builds accumulating tension in the family system.

As a social worker with a small home health agency, Debora Bennett was ordered to open a care plan for the family described here. The nurses in charge of Mary Johnson's care were from the area and familiar with the family. She identified as Caucasian and said she was 28 years old. Ms. Johnson was the mother of three children—Mary Beth, age 10; Jeremiah, age 8; and Daniel, age 5. Each of the children had a different father. Mary Johnson was very ill with Stage IV pancreatic cancer. She and the children were living with her biological mother, Grace Samuels, along with her stepfather, John Samuels, a half-brother, Larry Samuels, and various cousins who moved in and out as work became available. The 10-year-old was a feisty girl who was often left to chase after her brothers while the adults busied themselves with work, sleep, and an occasional cold beer out on the town. Disputes over custody involved the many grandparents, fathers, and the fathers' latest live-in partners. All of the extended family members were reportedly from the area, and their relational histories were long, complicated, and often contentious. It was not unusual for arguments and squabbles to end with a call to social services with allegations of child abuse allegedly perpetrated by another family member.

Ms. Bennett adopted the practice of visiting with families she worked with and openly sharing that she was a mandated reporter and that she often was included in Child Protective Services (CPS) case reviews. She had some knowledge about the history of the family as a matriarchal-led system so she obtained permission to visit with CPS from the mother and grandmother. They said they were accustomed to CPS visits and shared their distrust of the agency and workers. The two women summed up the contacts that ended badly as the result of not being listened to and being treated disrespectfully. Both said that there were grateful to have someone "in their corner," and they asked that Ms. Bennett work had to work with "that office" (CPS). Further, they asked Ms. Bennett to talk with CPS worker "Cindy," whom they said was the "only worker we can trust."

The latest call following an argument raised the level of concern for the family because the call alleged that the grandfather was sexually abusing the youngest boy. With the day-to-day supervision of the boys reportedly usually left to the sister, CPS was compelled to investigate. Meanwhile, Ms. Bennett was scheduled for a healthcare home visit with Ms. Johnson. Debora Bennett knew there was something terribly wrong as soon as she pulled up to the house. The grandfather was walking down the drive and hollered that "The ole girl cleared the house." Mary was in the bedroom napping and the house was empty except for the grandmother and the youngest boy. The home was always before teeming with activity, noise, and the three children running in and out. The grandmother informed the social worker of the impending investigation she caught wind of from overhearing a "social services" person in the local tavern talk about "the old drunk down the street who has a kid in the office." Needless to say, overhearing about the alleged sexual abuse of her grandson by her spouse in the local bar reinforced family members' mistrust and animosity toward CPS.

Ms. Mary Johnson's health condition was worsening, and the grandmother did not want her to have to go through "this mess and worry." The grandmother and her husband had been the "go to" place of safety for Mary and her children for years. Mary did have the care of the children settled. Once she learned her condition was terminal, Mary made provisions for her children to be cared for by another set of grandparents who lived out of the region. The grandmother agreed the children needed to get out of this "hornets' nest." The latest allegation seemed more than the grandmother could bear.

> What were those assholes thinking . . . Mary is so sick, the kids are scared enough and they pull this? I can't stop working, Mary can't get well, and they are going to rip those kids right out of here on a lie and farm them out to strangers.

Ms. Bennett met with the child welfare family conference team and shared the breach of confidentiality and that the grandmother's report of hearing of the abuse allegation. The CPS office was organized with an intake/investigation team that was distinct from the intervention team. Cindy Allen had been promoted to the intervention team and according to agency policies would not be available to work with the family unless the investigation merited intervention. Debora Bennett could not be sure but she wondered if the breach of confidentiality and the anger of the grandmother helped convince the supervisors they could allow Cindy to lead the CPS investigation.

Cindy Allen was from the area and versed in the culture of the impoverished hill folks who were the seasonal workforce for the tourist industry. Ms. Allen was well acquainted with the family and the many different people within it. She had worked with them a number of times during the tourist season when Mary Johnson came home to live with her mother. Cindy Allen said she was sure the family's poverty, Mary's previous "transient lifestyle" and the strained relations of the extended family had a lot to do with the number of allegations the office received. She also knew none of the previous investigations ever warranted action and she knew how ill Mary was.

Like the grandmother, Debora Bennett expected that news of the allegation would be very hard on Mary Johnson, who was in a late terminal stage of cancer. She was concerned the children would not be present for Ms. Johnson's death. She visited with Cindy Allen as she reflected on how the possible separation of the children so close to the end of Mary's life would add trauma to the grief the children would be facing. It was not clear if state involvement would interfere with the plans Mary Johnson had made for the children. It seemed they needed to plan how to complete the investigation quickly. Ms. Bennett said she hoped to investigate in such a way that Mary Johnson was spared dealing with the matter. The professionals were also aware that community members had learned of the allegation and that it was just a matter of time before an allegation would be turned into "a nasty bit of gossip." They were also aware that CPS would be sure to be getting some heat when it did. They agreed that they needed the help of the grandmother, the good judgment of the family, and their multiagency teamwork.

## Practice Application

In this vignette, the health agency social worker becomes involved in a CPS case as a member of a "system of care" for children at risk. Even without a system of care approach, it is quite common for non-child welfare social workers to have contact and work within a case that becomes a child welfare matter. All social workers must understand that their duty to report abuse is only part of how they might have to work with CPS with any given family. In this case, working with the CPS worker and advocating for the family enabled the social worker to mitigate more harm to her own client, the dying mother of the children. Being able to navigate multiple professional systems, using principles of cultural humility, and understanding family cultural dynamics helps social workers to provide for good outcomes for all members of the family. This is true ecological social work.

## DISCUSSION QUESTIONS

1. Identify the cultural considerations of this case for the family, community, the CPS worker, and the medical social worker.
2. What are the strengths of the family?
3. Identify the issues involved in minimizing harm to this family.
4. Identify the components of practice wisdom needed to resolve the situation.
5. What are the principles of cultural humility in the case?
6. How comfortable would you feel in working with this family?
7. To what extent were the professionals attending to the "do no harm" aspect of professional practice?
8. To what extent may growing up in a rural area help, or not help, the professionals to work with this family effectively?
9. What do you think about the intergenerational family approach considered by the CPS, medical worker, and the family?
10. What might the worker be thinking about in her self-reflections? How would the background of the worker influence some differences in self-reflective content?

11. What else would you like to know in order to understand the situation and the need for a response decision? How could this information be gleaned?

## LEARNING ACTIVITIES

1. Role Play with Some Family Members
   a. Role play how Cindy Allen and the Debora Bennett might elicit the grandmother's (Mrs. Samuel's) assistance.
2. Role Plays with All Family Members
   a. Break up the class into small groups by family members' roles. Be sure to include the children. Ask each group to report on how the particular family member may be feeling and thinking about the situation.

## SUGGESTED READING

Child Welfare Information Gateway: http://www.childwelfare.gov
FRIENDS National Resource Center for Community-Based Child Abuse Prevention: http://www.friendsnrc.org
National Center for Children in Poverty: http://www.nccp.org
Responding to child abuse and neglect: http://www.childwelfare.gov/responding
Risk and protective factors for child abuse: http://www.childwelfare.gov/can/factors

## REFERENCES

Chipp, C., Dewane, S., Brems, C., Johnson, M. E., Warner, T. D., & Roberts, L. W. (2011). "If only someone had told me . . ." Lessons from rural providers. *The Journal of Rural Health, 27,* 122–130. doi:10.1111/j.1748-0361.2010.00314.x

Davis, T. (2009). Diversity practice in social work: Examining theory in practice. *Journal of Ethnic & Cultural Diversity in Social Work, 18,* 40–69.

Ortega, R. M., & Faller, K. C. (2011). Training child welfare workers from an intersectional cultural humility perspective: A paradigm shift. *Child Welfare, 90*(5), 27–49.

Riebschleger, J. (2007). Social workers' suggestions for effective rural practice. *Families in Society, 88*(2), 203–213.

Stevenson, K., Cheung, K., & Leung, P. (1992). A new approach to training child protective services workers for ethnically sensitive practice. *Child Welfare, 71,* 291–305.

## CHAPTER 6

cɣɔ

# Adoption Social Work
# in Rural New England

## BARBARA J. PIERCE

Rural School. This rural school was the main educational setting for early regional settlers.
David G. Riebschleger

## LEARNING OBJECTIVES

- Highlight differences between agency and private adoption
- Discuss the role of adoption social workers in child welfare

- Discuss the role of the support system in helping the case birth mother
- Identify the ethical concerns of the social worker in the vignette
- Provide specific rationales for the necessity of home and community visiting in rural communities

## INFANT ADOPTION AS AN OPTION
## FOR UNINTENDED PREGNANCY

The child welfare continuum includes public child welfare and a vast array of private, not-for-profit agencies serving children and families. While adoption from the public child welfare system does occur, infant adoption most often occurs within not-for-profit agencies or private law firms that provide assistance to birth parents who wish to place a child for adoption with families identified by the agency as appropriate adoptive families. Adoption is a permanent, legal process by which a family is formed when one parent(s) transfers parental rights to another parent(s) who, in turn, assumes those rights. The adoptive parent or parents become the legal and permanent parents for the child. Infant adoption occurs when a birth mother and father decide that they cannot, for whatever reason, parent the infant that they have conceived and birthed. About 2% of US families are formed through adoption (Vandivere & Malm, 2009). Adoptions can occur through private adoption or social service agencies, private attorneys, or public child welfare agencies via foster care.

While adoption has been practiced in the United States since colonial times, it began legally in the mid-19th century when Massachusetts enacted the first adoption statute (Spaulding for Children, 2005). Adoption has evolved from a time when a pregnant young woman who had an unintended pregnancy would leave her home to go live in a maternity home, deliver her baby, which was placed for adoption, and then return home from "visiting her aunt" in another state. This practice allowed the young woman to avoid the stigma of having given birth out of wedlock. Since then, societal norms around unintended pregnancy have changed dramatically, and unmarried women give birth to children every day.

Some women or unmarried couples choose to have an early abortion when they find out they are pregnant, but others either parent their children or place them for adoption. Adoption practices have evolved from a closed legal process in which no information was shared between birth and adoptive parents to varying degrees of openness in which the parents share information and even have contact with each other. At the very least, medical information, in as complete a form as is possible, is given to the adoptive parents. US adoptive parents have also pursued overseas adoptions; however, many countries are now restricting these adoptions. In public child welfare, children become legally eligible for adoption when their parents, voluntarily or involuntarily, relinquish their parental rights.

The vast majority of children adopted as infants have high levels of well-being. They tend to be better educated than the general population, have good health, and have good relationships with their adoptive parents. While children adopted from the foster care system tend to have a rougher time in life, children adopted as infants and placed from birth develop their primary attachments to their adoptive parents, so they are more apt to flourish (Pierce, 2006). In general, in the United States today, children grow up with the knowledge of adoption and the alternative ways that families can be formed. The many books available to and written for adopted children help with this life event.

While infant adoption from the hospital is not as common as it once was, it is a choice that birth parents can make. Social workers who work with these couples or birth mothers learn to navigate the complex needs of these clients: options counseling, attachment, healthcare needs, and, sometimes, the limits that poverty imposes. Many times birth mothers make an adoption plan because they want to be able to give their baby a life that they know they cannot provide. In some instances, they are high school or college students who have other aspirations, and in others they are women who may have a child and know that they cannot provide for another. Adoption social workers counsel birth parents during the pregnancy and up to a year postadoption. Within the counseling process, the social worker assesses the readiness to place the baby and the attachment level. In addition, the social worker may provide maternity clothes and/or food, assist with affordable healthcare, provide transportation, and work with extended family members. Ultimately the decision to place a baby for adoption in voluntary infant adoption lies with the birth parents as long as they are of legal age. Younger birth parents, depending on the obtaining statute, may need permission from their parents.

Part of the counseling process involves helping the birth parents to devise an adoption plan for themselves and their child. They must decide how much information to share or have shared with them postadoption. They also may work on a "life" or "baby" book for their child in which they might include pictures, their adoption story, a letter from themselves to the child and/or adoptive parents, and any other meaningful material they want to share with the child. In addition, they provide complete medical histories in case this information becomes necessary as the child grows up. Birth parents may also choose the adoptive parents for their baby. This process can involve reading biographies of couples and then interviewing them. While no one thinks that making an adoption plan is an easy task, it can be an empowering part of the life of the birth parents because, from the act of creating one, they often sense they have made the best and most loving plan for their child. The case vignette presents Jennifer Garvey, a resident in a rural New England state. She chooses to place her newborn infant in an adoptive family home.

## CASE VIGNETTE

Jennifer Garvey was a 25-year-old woman who called the not-for-profit local adoption agency after finding out that she was 13 weeks pregnant. Her phone call to set up services was sent directly to the desk of the infant-adoption social worker. When the social worker called to set up an appointment, Jennifer said she did not drive and lived an hour away from the agency in a small and very rural New England town. This set of circumstances was typical of most of the adoption social worker's caseload. She did not want the social worker to make a home visit, so she proposed, instead, that they meet at her workplace: a small sandwich shop located in a strip mall in her rural town. Jennifer was a part-time worker there. The social worker immediately discussed privacy and confidentiality issues with Jennifer who stated that the shop owner, her boss, knew about her situation and even offered to provide assistance. They met a couple of days later in a break room in the back of the sandwich shop.

The social worker was known in many communities within a hundred miles of the agency as she was the only adoption worker in that half of the state. It was incumbent upon the social worker that her client knew those facts about her professional role. Before they met, then, she offered Jennifer the option of talking at a private location to ensure confidentiality. Jennifer reassured the social worker that she was fine meeting at the restaurant. When they met, Jennifer was neatly dressed and did not appear obviously pregnant. After initial pleasantries, she disclosed that she went to the local family-planning clinic after doing a home-pregnancy test. The nurse practitioner indicated that she was about 13 weeks pregnant. Jennifer had been having many of the presumptive pregnancy symptoms, including morning sickness, but was beginning to feel better. She indicated that she called the agency because she knew she would not have an abortion and wished to place the baby for adoption. The principal role of the infant-adoption social worker is to make sure the pregnant woman understands all of her options. To that end, the social worker asked about the third option of parenting the child. Jennifer stated that would be impossible since she had no "real" job, no education or training, and she did not know who the father of the baby was. She stated that she did not want to live on "welfare" forever and thought the best thing she could do for the child was to make sure it had a good home. As the worker gathered more information, she learned that Jennifer had also worked at the local truck stop as a sex worker in order to supplement her meager income. Since her clients tended to be long-haul drivers, she really had no idea who the father was, nor did she know their names. But she was emphatic that she would not parent a child alone. She also said that her family lived in another state and that she had no intention of revealing her pregnancy to them. She described her mother as a devout Catholic who "would not deal well" with this situation. Jennifer did, however, have a couple of friends in town and used them for emotional support. After hearing about Jennifer's "other" work and knowing the dangers attached to it, the social worker worried for Jennifer's safety. Jennifer added, however, that she no longer worked "the streets" and that the sandwich shop was now her only form of employment.

Jennifer indicated that she would like to continue with adoption planning and stated that she would like to meet every month to continue the planning process. The social worker indicated that she would call every couple of weeks to check on her and that she was always available by phone at any time between those monthly meetings. Jennifer indicated that she would continue with her clinic appointments and would follow up with WIC (the government-sponsored nutrition program for pregnant women, nursing mothers, and infants). The social worker made referrals to Medicaid and the local food bank and was able to provide maternity clothes for Jennifer.

The two met monthly at the restaurant. On one occasion, Jennifer revealed that the baby had been kicking her and she was developing an attachment to the baby. She knew that the adoption would be best but also was realistic enough to recognize that, when the time came, relinquishment would be emotionally difficult. Jennifer was involved in every aspect of the adoption planning. She provided a detailed medical record, wrote a pregnancy diary for the baby, and chose the adoptive parents whom she declined to meet. She was compliant with all of her medical appointments, ate well, and did not drink, smoke, or take drugs during her pregnancy. As indicated, she also did not engage in sex work, largely because she feared a sexually transmitted disease might harm her baby. To the knowledge of the social worker and the local midwife who provided her maternity care, she stayed true to her word. All of her check-ups indicated that she was healthy, clean and sober, and infection-free.

Each time the social worker met Jennifer at the restaurant she indicated that she could make a home visit if the client would be more comfortable. The social worker knew this town well from driving around it to find other clients she had worked with. The worker even went to festivals with her family and friends in this town. So, from the address provided, the worker knew that the client lived in a camper trailer in a trailer park and suspected that living arrangement was perhaps a source of embarrassment to Jennifer. To put Jennifer's mind at ease about this possibility, the worker talked about her experiences throughout the different parts of the state and the types of domestic settings in which she met and worked with clients. Although the other waitresses at the restaurant were quite discrete and kind when the social worker and Jennifer met, the social worker remained concerned about confidentiality. Picking up those signals, Jennifer insisted that her coworkers at the restaurant were always kind to her and that she considered them a support system. In fact, she already had told all of them about the adoption plan. At the last visit the two had at the restaurant before the birth, the other waitresses gave Jennifer a present. Inside the box were a hand-crocheted blanket, sweater, hat, and booties, along with a note indicating support and care for Jennifer.

Because she used Medicaid as her health insurance, Jennifer had to travel about two hours away to deliver her baby in a hospital that accepted her insurance. She had no transportation so the social worker and her supervisor were on call for the delivery to provide transportation and support. One snowy afternoon in late March, Jennifer called the agency to say that she needed to go to the hospital. The social worker and her supervisor both hurried to pick Jennifer up and take her to the hospital. Jennifer appeared to be in active labor and delivered a healthy baby girl about two hours after arriving at the hospital. She elected to care for the baby while she was in the hospital. On the day after delivery, the social worker and supervisor drove separate cars so one could take Jennifer home and the other could take the baby to the agency foster home overnight in preparation for the placement of the baby the next day. Jennifer indicated that she would like to take the baby to the agency-sponsored foster home.

After a quick phone call to the foster mother, who agreed to the arrangement, they drove to the foster home where Jennifer handed the baby, dressed in her new sweater, hat, and booties, to the foster mother. Jennifer left the lifebook containing a letter and a picture for the baby, the pregnancy diary, a few outfits, and toys for the baby. The baby's hospital picture would be added from the online website. Jennifer was allowed private time with the baby to say goodbye before leaving to go home. Jennifer was sad to say goodbye but also stated that she felt that she was doing the right thing for her baby. She told the worker that this was the first time in her life that she felt that she had made a good decision and said she felt proud of herself for making a good plan.

The next morning the foster parents drove to the agency with the baby and handed her to her new adoptive parents who cried when she was put in their arms. The social worker called Jennifer to see how she was and asked if she could come to check on her. She agreed. The social worker made her first home visit to the camper trailer on a small piece of trailer-park land on a country road. Jennifer finally indicated that she was embarrassed to be living in a camper but was tired and did not feel physically up to walking to the restaurant a few blocks away. Her camper had food and heat and was quite cozy. The social worker spent time letting the client know how the placement earlier in the day went and then gave her a letter from the adoptive parents. The letter was heartfelt and kind. They thanked Jennifer for the opportunity to become parents and wished her well. They also indicated that they would keep in touch with the agency in the event that she wanted pictures or updates about how the baby was doing.

A few weeks later, the social worker picked Jennifer up and they went to the County Judge's chambers where Jennifer signed formal relinquishment documents. The judge, a kind older woman, indicated that she thought Jennifer had made a good decision. Choking back a few tears, Jennifer agreed. She told the judge that it was a difficult decision but was also, as she believed, the best way she could love her child. The judge asked Jennifer to continue to work with the agency for a while to make sure she was doing well. Jennifer responded that she and the social worker had already begun the follow-up counseling.

The social worker continued to have contact via phone and visits for the next year for postadoption counseling. Jennifer actually did well. She returned to her job at the sandwich shop part-time, had visited her mother, and was beginning to think about options for her future. She did not return to working as a sex worker. She asked for and received updates on the baby for the first few months, but after six months she did not ask again.

## Practice Application

Infant adoption social work is a highly specialized field in which social workers must learn to help women to sort out all of their options for a usually unintended pregnancy. These social workers help women and couples to best identify which option fits their situation best and then provide support for the duration of and after the pregnancy. It is important to understand that this practice requires integration of the biopsychosocial and spiritual needs of their clients as well as community resources for all of the options. In rural communities these resources are usually lacking, and the worker must learn to use informal systems of resources and support. In the case of Jennifer, her supports came from her job, which provided a space to meet, emotional support from her coworkers, and an income. Social workers must learn to identify both formal and informal resources while maintaining good ethical boundaries and confidentiality. Working in a rural community affords little confidentiality, because everyone knows everyone else and generally everyone knows the social worker. Rural social workers must remain vigilant about their ethical obligation to confidential provision of services while using their social capital and the resources of the community.

## DISCUSSION QUESTIONS

1. Why was the social worker sensitive about confidentiality and privacy? To what extent could it involve (a) a rural area (she was well known in the town); (b) a restaurant as a public place; (c) pregnancy and adoption plans, which are very personal and private; (d) HIPPA protections?
2. What are the legal protections for birth fathers in your state?
3. If your client wanted to place her baby for adoption, where would she go? Research the infant-adoption process in your town.
4. What are the long-term psychological consequences of making an adoption plan for the birth mother and for the child? Do some research.

## LEARNING ACTIVITIES

1. Personal and Professional Values Clarification
   a. Ask learners to write a short essay about their feelings about infant adoption. Ask them to consider the pros and cons of making an adoption plan for a newborn. Discuss their reactions to infant adoption in class.
2. Adoption Thoughts
   a. Watch the film *Juno* (available free online) in class and discuss the role adoption plays in the lives of both Juno and Paulie.

b. Role play ways to discuss options for couples who experience unintended pregnancies. Pay particular attention to the role exact and correct language plays in emotional responses. How does using the term "making an adoption plan" differ from "giving the baby up for adoption"?

c. Ask the class to research the role of lifebooks in adoptions and how they can help any child for whom an adoption plan is made.

## SUGGESTED READING

Adopt US Kids: http://www.adoptuskids.org

Dave Thomas Foundation for Adoption: https://davethomasfoundation.org/adopt/
    general-adoption-resources/

Infant adoption resources: https://www.childwelfare.gov/search/?q=infant+adoption

Lifebooks: https://www.childwelfare.gov/search/?q=lifebooks

National Council for Adoption: https://www.adoptioncouncil.org

## REFERENCES

Pierce, B. J. (2006). Adult adopted person's psychosocial adjustment. In K. S. Stolley
    & V. L. Bullough (Eds.), *The Praeger handbook of adoption* (pp. 59–62). Westport,
    CT: Praeger.

Spaulding for Children. (2005). *Infant Adoption Training Initiative: Understanding infant
    adoption.* Southfield, MI: Author.

Vandivere, S., & Malm, K. (2009). *Adoption USA. A chartbook based on the 2007 National
    Survey of Adoptive Parents.* US Department of Health and Human Services, Office
    of the Assistant Secretary for Planning and Evaluation. Retrieved from https://
    aspe.hhs.gov/report/adoption-usa-chartbook-based-2007-national-survey-
    adoptive-parents?id=1

# CHAPTER 7

cho

# Working with Aboriginal Families in Canada

KHADIJA KHAJA

## LEARNING OBJECTIVES

- Describe five or more aspects of Aboriginal and First Nations culture
- Identify the advantages of having social capital in a cultural community
- Identify the merits and challenges of having Aboriginal or First Nations workers in the agency to work with these families

## CHILD WELFARE IN CANADA WITH ABORIGINAL FAMILIES

The Constitution Act (1982) designates the Aboriginal population as consisting of three main groups, which include the First Nations, Metis, and Inuit peoples. Approximately 65% of Aboriginal children are First Nations (Sinha & Kozlowski, 2013). First Nation children in Canada make up approximately 6% of the child population, estimated to comprise 26% of children who are eventually placed in out-of-home care in child abuse investigations. Many Aboriginals still hold painful historical memories of the systematic removal of Aboriginal children from their homes. The children were placed in poorly funded residential school facilities or non-Aboriginal homes as a result of settlement by Europeans who wanted to "assimilate them into colonial culture" (Sinha & Kozlowski, 2013, p. 3).

This led to separation from families, the destruction of cultural practices, and increased needs for family interdependence. Some reserves lost almost a whole generation of children. The residential schools spread disease due to poor hygiene and living conditions with speculation that 50% of children died. There were also allegations of physical and sexual abuse (Sinha & Kozlowski, 2013). In some Canadian provinces and territories at least 60% to 78% of Aboriginal children are in child welfare systems. In the 1960s and 1970s many Aboriginal children were apprehended by provincial child welfare agencies; social workers were known to have put children in residential homes or to adopt them out to non-Aboriginal homes (National Collaboration Centre for Aboriginal Health, 2009–2010).

During the 1970s, Aboriginals started to develop their own child welfare agencies, which were generally managed by their communities. One goal was to try to lessen the overrepresentation of Aboriginal children in out-of-home care. Underfunding of Aboriginal child welfare agencies on reserves has been reported frequently. Approximately half of the Aboriginal population now lives in urban areas; this was followed by the development of Aboriginal-led private child welfare agencies in big cities such as Vancouver, Toronto, and Winnipeg (Statistics Canada, 2009). There appears to be a significant variation of Aboriginal delivery of child welfare services based on "child welfare statutes, assessment tools, competency based training programs" and diversity in services offered to Aboriginal children and families based on different structures of "governance, and law making authority, service providers and funding control" (Sinha & Kozlowski, 2013, p. 5).

Then there is also the critical component that a band has the right to be involved in some areas in development of care plans for Aboriginal children being placed out-of-home or adopted. Band leaders appointed representatives to deal with child welfare protection services, including legislation. For example, in Alberta the law states that there needs to be consultation with Aboriginal representatives when child welfare services workers are involved with Aboriginal children and families. The First Nations Aboriginal Child Welfare agencies, for instance, can intervene in numerous ways. First, this can be done under provincial/territorial child welfare laws to provide child welfare services including investigations of child abuse and neglect. Second, band-designated agency workers can provide family support services. Third, guardianship and voluntary care agreements can be used, but workers must have legal permission to investigate child abuse reports. There are other self-governing models in which child welfare agency staff provide a diverse range of child welfare services due to specific self-governance agreements and/or treaties; those same agencies may have "voluntary mandates" to provide some services to the

Aboriginal population (Canadian Child Welfare Research Portal, n.d.). It is also important to note that many former Aboriginal children still work as adults within mainstream public child welfare agencies. Federally, the Canadian government often pays for child welfare services on reserves with provinces paying for child welfare services outside of reserves.

Any type of child welfare service that assists Aboriginal children should work in consultation or collaboration with elders, band members, and extended family members. In 2016, a landmark decision from the Canadian Human Rights Tribunal ruled that the federal government had "discriminated against First Nations by persistently underfunding and providing inferior on-reserve child protection services" (Come, 2016, para. 3). For example, one out of two Aboriginal children lives in poverty whether from a reserve or off-reserve setting. Aboriginal families are four times more likely to experience hunger than non-Aboriginal populations. Some unemployment rates on reserves are has high as 90%. Rates of substance abuse and suicides are significantly higher than those found in non-Aboriginal communities (Jones & Finlay, 2010). These issues have often been attributed to the trauma that Canadian Aboriginal families have faced historically and across multiple generations of families.

## CASE VIGNETTE

This case takes place on a remote Aboriginal First Nation reserve community on Grande Island in eastern Canada. The first settlement on the island was founded between 1897 and 1903. It has a population of approximately 1,500 people, and the majority of the population is registered to the band that oversees the community. It is rather geographically isolated in the sense that the only way to get there is either by plane or ferry. All food and most supplies are shipped in by ferry. The main livelihood is the fishing industry. The island has a general store, a community school, several small restaurants, a small medical clinic, and a hospital. A police detachment is open only during the daytime on weekdays. There is an outreach office for a private child and family service agency. Child protection and guardianship services are provided to the reserve by an office located approximately two hours from the community by plane.

The child and family services agency has an executive director, family preservation worker, and other program and support staff. There is also a child protection and guardianship worker who resides in the community and is virtually attached to the remote, outreach office. The child protection and guardianship worker has an office in the child and family service agency on reserve. The majority of the staff members are First Nation people. The agency has a mission to provide child welfare services such as community-based foster homes, family support services, and other intervention and prevention services.

An anonymous person called the island's child and family services agency to express concerns about a family living on the island. The family was described as a couple named John and Tina Cross and their 14-year-old son, Tom. The caller stated that John has "a severe drinking problem" and that he was worried about the welfare of the child, Tom. The caller said he had never seen Tom abused physically but that he was worried about the home environment due to Tom's father's "drinking binges."

The worker recorded some general information. Reportedly, the father, John, was 40 years old and the mother, Tina, was 35. Both of them worked seasonally in fishing, which was the main sustenance for people living on the reserve. During the season of fishing John did not drink. However, once the fishing season ended in winter, he would "binge drink for weeks on end, then take a break for a couple of days and start again." The caller reported that there had also been increased "arguing" in the home between John and Tina, perhaps due to his drinking. As is required by law, the child and family services agency provided the information to the in-house child protection worker for evaluation and response. The child protection worker consulted with her supervisor and the child and family services agency regarding the response to the information. It was decided that it would be best to make an unannounced visit to the family home the next day.

The public child protection worker, Nate Walker, went to the home unannounced the following day. A worker from child and family services, Susan Dey, accompanied him. John and Tina answered the door, and they seemed quite very upset that a child protection worker and a worker from the child and family service agency had been sent. They reported that they "provide well" for their child. Tina shared up front that she only trusted First Nations people, upset that the workers "are not Aboriginal." She reported that historically many non-Aboriginal social workers had systematically removed their children from Aboriginal homes, and it was very hard to trust anyone not from the community. John also shared that he had the same fears and was "terrified" that their son, Tom, would be sent away and put in a non-Aboriginal home somewhere on the mainland of Canada.

Nate and Susan empathized with John and Tina and reassured them compassionately that they could understand why they were afraid given the past history of how Aboriginal children and families had been separated and put in residential schools. Nate clarified that they were required by law to investigate any allegations of neglect and that Susan was there to act as the band representative, to ensure that children stay in the community with their families or extended families and to offer other family support services to assist the family to address the child/youth safety concerns.

John and Tina both said that they were frustrated and they would only speak with Nate and Susan if a family elder were present. They indicated that they would not permit Nate to talk with their son Tom. Nate could see Tom from a distance. He was playing video games. Nate could not smell any alcohol on John, and he appeared lucid. However, Nate also knew from the anonymous callers' information that it was possible that John was a binge drinker, drinking for a few days and stopping. He also knew that there had been allegations of increased arguing happening in the home when John was allegedly drinking, and he was worried about the potential for domestic violence.

Nate informed John and Tina that he would be agreeable to the family having an elder band member present. John then made a call on his cell phone to the family elder, Argon Duquette. The family elder said he would be over in a few minutes. Once the family elder was there, John and Tina seemed much more relaxed. Argon said it would make sense to first talk to the parents and then to bring the son in for a conversation.

Family elder, Argon along with Nate, and Susan sat with John and Tina around the dining room table. Nate shared the concerns about Tom's alleged binge drinking and concerns about the growing arguing in the home between him and Tina. Initially, John looked defensive, but once Argon asked him to respond truthfully, the dynamic changed. John shared that over the last few years his drinking had "gotten out of control "and that when he started to drink he "could not stop." Nate thanked John for being honest and trusting him enough to share. Tina broke into tears and said that when John drank he would "get mean and start yelling." She did not report any physical abuse.

Nate then said that he wanted to speak with Tom privately to get his perspective as well. John and Tina got very upset, speaking loudly "This is stupid" and pointing at the workers with a shaking first finger. However, Argon said he would stay in the room and that way the parents might feel more comfortable. John and Tina agreed to this plan and left the room with a few worried back glances.

Tom came into the room and shared very honestly that he was worried that Nate was going to take him away and put him on the mainland. Nate assured Tom that would not happen and that he would not be removed from the reserve. Tom then started to slowly share that his father's drinking had been getting "worse and worse" and that both his parents "argued constantly" when his father drank. Tom said that he felt his father needed serious help and treatment. Tom said he had not seen any domestic violence but was worried it could happen. Tom denied any physical abuse toward him by either of his parents. Further, he appeared to be well nourished. The home was clean and well-kept, and there was plenty of food to eat. Tom did say that he was having increasing arguments with both his parents over "regular stuff," meaning teen issues like going out with his friends, staying out too late, and playing his music too loud. He wanted some help "to get along better with my parents."

Nate then called the whole family back in the room with Argon. John said that he felt that he needed treatment, but there was no place to do this on Grande Island. Nate agreed and advised that he could set up counseling for John at the local health center. Nate said John would need to attend some counseling sessions with his drug and alcohol counselor and that the counselor should be able to assist him in making arrangements to attend treatment on the mainland in Canada. Given this was the off-season of work, John was agreeable. Argon also advised that it would be helpful for some members of Tina's family to support her and assist her through John's recovery. He offered to help Tina talk to her family members.

In addition, Argon, John, Tina, Tom, Nate, and Susan worked on a plan to try to ensure a safe environment for Tom and Tina should John drink again before going to treatment. The plan identified resources, supports, and actions to access and activate should Tom and/or Tina feel unsafe.

Nate suggested that the parents enter a group parenting program or have a visiting family support worker come to the home. A family support worker would visit once weekly to assist the family to meet their outlined goals and to address the child safety concerns given Tom was worried about the potential for domestic violence.

Tom could obtain support through the Aboriginal Supported Childhood Development Program, or he could attend a child and youth mental health weekly program for boys grounded in traditional practices and culture (singing, drumming, camping, fishing, etc.). Family meetings and family-directed plans in response to regular parent/adolescent conflicts was suggested. The hereditary chief or elder spokesperson for the family could be involved. The family was receptive to the plan, which included clear and measurable goals and a plan to evaluate those goals. Once everyone agreed to the plan, it was signed and copies were provided to each participant.

## Practice Application

This vignette highlights the importance of using a cultural guide and advocate (in this case, the family elder from the band) and to provide the option of culturally sensitive and nearby treatment for the family. The social workers both knew the job they had to do (ensure the child's safety), and they were able to use their cultural knowledge to ensure safety by working with the band elder to help the family. This vignette points out the importance of working *with, rather than at* a family and including community resources necessary to try to ensure that the family gets the help they need. Further, this vignette points out the importance of a thorough assessment and the necessity for a broad knowledge of health, mental health, and substance abuse, including how these disorders affect the child and family. These social workers used ecosystems theory to assess the family, access the community and band resources, and provide for culturally sensitive treatment for the family within their own tiny rural community.

## DISCUSSION QUESTIONS

1. What kind of impact do you think the John's binge drinking has had on his wife, Tina, and their adolescent son, Tom?
2. Why do you think that having someone involved from the Aboriginal band is important in future family meetings?
3. John is going into a treatment center on the mainland to deal with his alcohol addiction for several weeks. Is there a potential for future relapse? Why or why not?
4. If in the future you learn that Tina has experienced domestic violence, what might you do?
5. Canada has a prior history of assimilative practices of the Aboriginal peoples. What impact do you think it has had on Aboriginal families as a whole?
6. Explain how the intervention plan included formal and informal rural community resources.
7. Explain how the intervention plan addressed individual, family, and community levels of care.

## LEARNING ACTIVITIES

1. Family Group Conference
   a. Plan and run a family group conference with various participants taking the parts of the people in this family. If your state uses the family group conference model, invite a caseworker graduate of your program to facilitate the group.

2. Substance Abuse
   a. Discuss options for addiction treatment for rural families. Use your own or a neighboring community as an example. How would you secure treatment for your clients?
3. Cultural Group Discovery Project
   a. Research Aboriginal and First Nations customs and present various customs to the class. Be clear about the methods you used to discover the information.

## SUGGESTED READING

Canadian Child Welfare Research Portal: http://cwrp.ca/aboriginal-child-welfare
Indigenous and Northern Affairs Canada-First Nations Child Welfare: https://www.aadnc-aandc.gc.ca/eng/1100100035204/1100100035205
Rae, L. (2011). Inuit Child Welfare and Family Support—Aboriginal-Related Documents. Ottawa: National Aboriginal Health Organization. Retrieved from http://www.naho.ca/documents/it/2011_Inuit_Child_Welfare_Aboriginal_Documents.pdf

## REFERENCES

Canadian Child Welfare Research Portal. (n.d.). *How do Canadian child welfare systems work for Aboriginal children?* Retrieved from http://cwrp.ca/faqs
Come, M. C. (2016). *We must end gross underfunding of reserve communities.* Retrieved from http://ottawacitizen.com/opinion/columnists/matthew-coon-come-we-must-end-gross-underfunding-of-reserve-communiti
Jones, M., & Finlay, J. (2010). Systemic social issues: Aboriginal child welfare. *Relational Child and Youth Care Practice, 23*(4), 17–30. Retrieved from http://www.cyc-net.org/journals/rcycp/index.html
National Collaboration Centre for Aboriginal Health. (2009–2010). *Child welfare services in Canada: Aboriginal and mainstream.* Retrieved from http://nccah-ccnsa.ca/docs/fact%20sheets/child%20and%20youth/NCCAH-fs-ChildWelServCDA-2EN.pdf
Sinah, V., & Kozlowski, A. (2013). The structure of Aboriginal child welfare in Canada. *The International Indigenous Policy Journal, 4*(2), 1–21. doi:18584/iipj.2013.4.4.4
Statistics Canada. (2009). *Aboriginal peoples in Canada in 2006: Inuit, Métis and First Nations, 2006 Census.* Retrieved from http://www12.statcan.ca/census-recensement/2006/assa/97-558/p1-eng.cfm

# CHAPTER 8

∾

# A New Social Ill in Ishpeming

## JOANNE RIEBSCHLEGER

Washed Out Road. Distance and road conditions are a rural challenge especially for child welfare home visits.
Laura Harvey

## LEARNING OBJECTIVES

- Provide three or more reasons that ongoing community assessment is a critical practice activity for a rural practitioner
- Describe and give an example of the concept of rural community "pastoral myths"

- Identify the impact of substance abuse on a rural family
- Define micro, meso, and macro systems for social work or other professional practice

## INTRODUCTION

Rural practitioners need to pay attention to the community/region environment. It is important to consider and engage in micro, meso, and macro areas of practice within the work at-hand (Mackie, Zammit, & Alvarez, 2016), even if one's job description seems entirely clinically focused. Micro means working with individuals. Meso means working with families and small groups. Macro means working with/for large groups of people, such as those who live and work in organizations, institutions, agencies, neighborhoods, communities, and social policy arenas. Professionals who work across these levels use an ecological approach (Brofenbrenner, 1979). This means they regularly think about child welfare agency clientele as a person or persons in a multilayered and interactive social environment (Riebschleger, Norris, Pierce, Pond, & Cummings, 2015). This multisystem assessment and intervention process is one of the core concepts found in generalist practice, which is recommended for effective rural practice (Daley & Pierce, 2011).

Rural practitioners especially need to examine community interactions within the framework of larger social and economic systems. They need to continually observe and reflect upon community assets, stabilities, strengths, as well as community challenges (Scales & Streeter, 2004). They also need to stay attentive to those regional, state, national, and international factors that influence and change the social and economic realities of their practice-communities.

The case vignette in this chapter illustrates how rural practitioners must be prepared to address the ways in which new social ills can tear at the fabric of the rural communities they serve. Even though the case this vignette sets forth took place 17-plus years ago, it still teaches lessons of ongoing relevance. Simply put, one must keep abreast and be prepared for changes that impact people in their local rural environments. One should never equate rural communities solely with some idealized "pastoral myths." A rural pastoral myth means that someone envisions rural areas as all wonderful, clean, healing, and beautiful, with no problems whatsoever. At the same time, rural practitioners should never view rural communities through with a solely negative, stigmatizing sociocultural lens. One must always avoid labeling clients as "lesser" people because of the location of their residence.

"Homegrown" providers are those who grew up in a rural area. Homegrown providers have to consider, but not remain locked into, whatever past experiences they have had that may color their perception of a particular rural area. They also need to work toward objective assessments. The main lesson is that rural practitioners need to mindful about current events; put their ongoing, objective community observations to good use; regularly reflect upon the possible varied meanings of their observations; and consider how the elements within multiple rural ecosystems figure in the world of child welfare clients and consumers.

## CASE VIGNETTE

Juanita Elliot, a social work professional, grew up in the town of Ishpeming, Michigan, and had deep ties to it. When she married Bo Elliot, a state park ranger, in the 1990s, she was determined to stay in Ishpeming. Bo reportedly found no reason to disagree. By the turn of the 21st century, they had two young children and lived on a 10-acre piece of property with a pond located about 9 miles outside of Ishpeming "in the sticks," as local residents called the surrounding thin-trunked trees of the pine and deciduous forests.

The many acres of remote forests that surrounded Ishpeming made that area of Michigan seem almost untouched by human hands. Its beauty and resources were sufficient to support a population of about 7,000 late into the 20th century. Logging and government were major sources of revenue, as was tourism. Tourists came to camp, hunt, fish, swim, hike, cross-country ski, and snowmobile in the tranquil forests that surrounded the many spring-fed lakes. A number of the locals could be counted on to promote Ishpeming as being a "good place to raise kids" due to its clean, safe environment, low cost of living, many natural resources, and "connectedness" among many local residents. Volunteer mayor Wylie Jung echoed that sentiment when he remarked, "We care about our kids here. We want there to be good jobs for them so they can stay here when they grow up." But by 2000, the population was down 13% from its peak during the previous decade because of rising employment and "more businesses going bust."

In many respects, child welfare worker Juanita Elliot serves as an example of a "homegrown" rural social work professional. She commuted to Northern Michigan University where she earned her degree in social work and then earned an MSW through the Michigan State University School of Social Work distance education outreach program. Early in 2000, she took a job as a protective services worker with the Michigan Department of Human Services public child welfare agency.

In late October of that year, the Ishpeming, Michigan Department of Human Services child protective services (CPS) supervisor, John Hennessey, received a suspected child abuse and neglect call from Ms. Susan Cape, the principal at the Ishpeming Middle School. She reported that 11-year-old Tiffany Hollingbeck had missed the last two weeks of school; Tiffany was a 6th-grade student. The principal said she was also concerned because Tiffany sometimes came to school in "dirty, oversized clothing that smell like cat urine." She also disclosed that Tiffany's home-room teacher Mr. Kane said Tiffany sometimes appeared hungry and tired. According to Ms. Cape, Mr. Kane said that he sometimes gave Tiffany food to take home if he had any available. Ms. Cape said Tiffany was a quiet, well-behaved child who did okay in school when she was there. Tiffany had reportedly lived in the area for about two years. Ms. Cape noted that there had been "some problems with attendance but nothing like a two-week lag." She also reported repeated attempts to make contact with the parents, though they "never called back."

John Hennessey asked Juanita Elliot to go with him on a home visit. Tiffany Hollingbeck lived with her mother Sally Winter and her stepfather Justin Winter. They had no information about the location of her birth father. School records indicated that Tiffany had two younger siblings, Jake and Justin Winter, who were ages 4 and 2, respectively. There were no former CPS complaints on file for the local county, but a neglect complaint had been filed two-years prior by a "downstate" (lower peninsula) public health nurse who had formalized her concern about the low weight gain of Justin Winter at four months, as well as his severe diaper rashes. Department of Health Services (DHS) case records indicated that Dr. Ahmed, a pediatrician from the federally designated rural health clinic, was overseeing the case at that time. The neglect allegation was not substantiated by DHS.

Early in the afternoon, Mr. Hennessey and Ms. Elliot traveled some 8 miles out of town and then another half-mile down a "two-track" driveway through the forests to arrive at the Hollingbeck/Winter residence. The driveway and roadside entrance featured a number of "No Trespassing" signs. That fact was not unusual in the area as many people "posted" their property to keep hunters from trespassing. The home was a small log cabin with a large external wood stove located about 50 feet from the property. The cabin itself was painted white, though the paint had peeled, especially on the west side of the building. Stacks of cord wood were near the outdoor stove. A German shepherd was tethered to its dog house by a long chain; its water bowl had overturned. The dog growled and appeared menacing, but the chain seemed secure. Ms. Elliot noted that the main picture window on the front of the house was covered in plywood with the words "Keep out" spray-painted in black, sprawling letters.

When they knocked on the door, a small blonde woman opened it an inch or two. She looked through the opening. Mr. Hennessey said he and Ms. Elliot were there to see whether things were okay with Tiffany because "some folks are worried about her missed schooling." After an awkwardly long hesitation, Ms. Winter let them into the home. She was still in her bathrobe, despite the hour, and looked as if she had just awakened. The workers entered a closed-in porch with stacks of garbage about 4 feet high against the north wall. Next to the garbage on the linoleum floor were several empty bottles of bleach and a bottle of brake-repair fluid. The south side of the entry was littered with an array of shoes and coats, some hanging up on hooks, some on the floor. There was a lockable door between the covered porch and entry to the main living area. They entered a single room that took up most of the home: a combination kitchen, dining room, and living room. A very large flat-screen television was on, and its volume was painfully loud. There were three mounted deer heads above the television. Despite possible "red flags," the house was comfortably warm.

The workers could hear children in an adjacent room behind a closed door. Ms. Elliot noted the presence of a large bag of cat litter near the dining-room table. A glass sliding-door looked out into a wooded area. Altogether, the house smelled of cat urine and wood smoke. Dishes were piled high in the kitchen; a kitchen garbage bin occupied the center of the room. Several plastic water bottles with long drinking tubes were on the kitchen counters and the floor. The garbage bin was overflowing with diapers and plastic bottles. The flooring in the kitchen was tile, and the living room seemed to have newer carpeting and matched traditional furniture. There was a black spot about 9 inches wide on the tile floor in the kitchen. A baby bottle, which appeared to contain curdled milk, was on the floor in the living room as were several pieces of scattered clothing. A couple of unused diapers were on the coffee table, in addition to several children's books. A dozen or so children's toys were piled in a corner of the dining room.

Mr. Winter was not present. Ms. Winter said he had gone to the store to get some medicine for Tiffany who, she said, had a cold. "I think she may be allergic to the cat too," Ms. Winter volunteered. About that time, Tiffany came into the room carrying the two-year-old. Tiffany stared briefly at the visitors before she poured a bottle of apple juice for the baby, who appeared irritable and cried intermittently until he was given the bottle. Tiffany held him while he sucked vigorously on the bottle. Both children were dressed in t-shirts and pants that seemed appropriate; they appeared to be reasonably clean. Tiffany sat at the dining room table and seemed reluctant to talk to the workers, shrugging her shoulders when asked questions and looking to her mother. Ms. Winter explained that Tiffany had been kept home with a cold and their cell phone only worked when they went to town as there was "bad coverage" near their home. She reported that Mr. Winter said he was going to call the school and let them know Tiffany would be back tomorrow as she seemed to be feeling better since getting on cold medicine. Mr. Hennessey and Ms. Elliot noted, however, that an already opened bottle of cold medicine was on the kitchen floor and another near the top of the garbage bin. Ms. Winters said that Mr. Winter worked in the logging industry and also added, "He just got paid so he's going to the store for groceries too." It was agreed that Tiffany would be returning to school the next day.

As Mr. Hennessey was driving away from the Hollingbeck/Winter residence, he looked over at Juanita Elliot and said, "We're going to have to call the police on that meth lab." Ms. Elliot looked startled and replied, "What are you talking about? We don't have meth labs in Ishpeming!"

## Practice Application

This vignette focuses on a family whose child has been absent from school. CPS workers frequently investigate children under these circumstances as school officials report absences. In the course of the visit, the workers view signs what *may* be the signs of a methamphetamine lab (e.g., cold pills, cat smell, cleaning supplies, break repair fluid, and a burned floor). While today almost no one would be surprised to hear about methamphetamine production in rural areas, it was a *new phenomenon* during the late 1990s and early 2000s (Anderson, 2011). Sadly, methamphetamine production has become a major source of revenue for many rural people. Systemic poverty is certainly a factor in accounting for that explosion (Potter, 2004; Rural Health Information, 2015). Additionally, people may be attracted to the remoteness of rural areas because "cooking meth" has a distinctive, strong odor. Furthermore, they may believe that rural areas offer opportunities for increased privacy; there may be less chance of being observed when they manufacture methamphetamine in their kitchens, outbuildings, RVs, and neighbor-less backyards. Rural practitioners must be sharp in how they observe rural communities and reflect critically upon the changes they spot. Child protection workers frequently happen upon illegal drug activity and must understand the biological and social-emotional-cognitive impact of that activity on children. While in this case there is suspicion that would need to be investigated by law enforcement, if this was a known methamphetamine lab, the children would very likely be removed for their safety as most child welfare jurisdictions have policies about removal in these instances. It would be important for the workers in this case to work together with law enforcement and other agencies as soon as possible to ensure the safety of the children.

## DISCUSSION QUESTIONS

1. What are some of the positives and negatives we tend to associate with rural communities? What might these perspectives have something to do with Ms. Elliot's lack of awareness (in 2000) of the potential for a meth lab?
2. What are some of the signs in this vignette that could be indicative of a meth lab?
3. What are the risks for children, families, and communities who live in close proximity to meth labs?
4. What does this case vignette tell about the need for social workers in rural areas to stay in touch with emerging social ills? How can workers do this? Be specific.
5. What will likely happen next in the case vignette?
6. If there is an arrest for a meth lab, how likely is it that the local media will report it? What factors might weigh in the media's decision to publish or not publish the story?
7. To what extent may Ishpeming parents think their children may move away as adults? What is known about the "brain drain" in rural areas?
8. What are possible child welfare, health, and mental health workforce recruitment and retention issues in rural areas? What is a "homegrown" professional? What makes a person want to stay working in child welfare in a rural area?
9. What are your recommendations for increasing recruitment and, especially, retention of child welfare workers in rural areas? Be sure to think about things that can be done by individual workers, supervisors, agencies, communities, and others.

## LEARNING ACTIVITIES

1. Educational Video on Methamphetamines
   a. Participants can listen to the Front Line video about methamphetamine and discuss the impact this substance has reportedly had on a rural community.

2. Interview Child Welfare Workers
   a. Participants can interview a child welfare worker about substance abuse in rural communities and ask specifically about how alcohol, marijuana, methamphetamines, and opioid abuse have affected rural children and families.

3. Paper on Risk Factors for Children and Families
   a. Write a short paper about co-occurring risk factors for children and families: polysubstance abuse; child abuse/neglect; mental health disorders, physical health problems; unemployment; and incarceration. Create a case scenario involving substance abuse and other co-occurring risk factors in child maltreatment and then role play or create a system sculpture (in the manner of an in-class theatre scene).

4. Emerging Abused Substances: An Online Exercise
   a. Complete online research and investigate newly emerging substances abused by people today. Report on the incidence, prevalence, and signs of the substance use/abuse. Identify sources of information about local, regional, and statewide incidence of the abuse of particular substances. Be sure to include treatment recommendations and resources for dealing with the problem in a community taskforce or planning group.

5. Community Observations Journal
   a. Keep a journal of reflective comments and ideas derived from observations about a particular community. Themes of the journal can be shared during class discussion and/or via a community-assessment paper.

6. Child Welfare Workforce Recruitment Analysis and Discussion
   a. Participants can be asked to use small-group presentations to analyze difficulties with recruitment and retention of child welfare workers, especially in rural areas. They should offer recommendations for improving recruitment and retention.

## SUGGESTED READING

Anderson, S. T. (2011). *How meth-driven crime is eating at the heart of rural America.* Folsom, CA: Coalition for Investigative Journalism.

Frontline. (2006, February 14). *The meth epidemic.* Portland, OR: National Public Broadcasting System. http://www.pbs.org/wgbh/pages/frontline/meth/

Hohman, M., Oliver, R., & Wright, W. (2004). Methamphetamine manufacture: The social work response. *Social Work, 49,* 373–381. doi:10.1093/sw/49.3.373

Rural Health Information Hub. (2015). *Substance abuse in rural areas.* https://www.ruralhealthinfo.org/topics/substance-abuse

# REFERENCES

Anderson, S. T. (2011). *How meth-driven crime is eating at the heart of rural America*. Folsom, CA: Coalition for Investigative Journalism.

Brofenbrenner, U. (1979). *The ecology of human development: Experiments by nature and design*. Cambridge, MA: Harvard University Press.

Daley, M., & Pierce, B. (2011). Educating for rural competence: Curriculum concepts, models, and course content. In L. Ginsberg (Ed.), *Social work in rural communities* (5th ed., pp. 125–140). Alexandria, VA: NASW Press.

Mackie, P. F., Zammitt, K., & Alvarez, M. (2016). *Practicing rural social work*. Chicago, IL: Lyceum.

Potter, M. (2004). *Meth labs, a toxic threat to rural American—One small town grapples with the scourge of addiction*. NBC News—Crime and Courts. Retrieved from http://www.nbcnews.com/id/4489307/ns/us_news-crime_and_courts/t/meth-labs-toxic-threat-rural-america/#.V3exjaJvl-8

Riebschleger, J., Norris, D., Pierce, B., Pond, D., & Cummins, C. (2015). Preparing social work students for rural child welfare practice: Emerging curriculum competencies. *Journal of Social Work Education, 51*(Suppl. 2), S209–S224. doi:10.1080/10437797.2015.1072422

Rural Health Information Hub. (2015). *Substance abuse in rural areas*. Retrieved from https://www.ruralhealthinfo.org/topics/substance-abuse

Scales, T. L., & Streeter, C. L. (Eds.). (2004). *Rural social work: Building and sustaining community assets*. Belmont, CA: Brooks Cole/Thomson.

## CHAPTER 9

✧

# On Your Country

### Living and Working Respectfully with
### Aboriginal Families in Rural Australia

ROCHELLE HINE

Australian Forest. Australia has a plethora of climates. Rural people are usually familiar with the flora and fauna of the area.
Rochelle Hine

## LEARNING OBJECTIVES

- Describe the importance of collaboration and partnership to enhance outcomes for Aboriginal children and families
- Identify the potential complexity and multiplicity of relationships in small rural communities
- Explain the development of Aboriginal cultural awareness and cultural sensitivity for rural social work and welfare practitioners
- Explore critical reflection as a tool to conceptualize gender, diversity, culture, and context

Took the Children Away
The welfare and the policeman
Said you've got to understand
We'll give them what you can't give
Teach them how to really live.
Teach them how to live they said
Humiliated them instead
Taught them that and taught them this
And others taught them prejudice
You took the children away
The children away
Breaking their mother's heart
Tearing us all apart
Took them away
© Archie Roach, 1990

## INTRODUCTION

This chapter is founded on my experiences of working with Aboriginal people in South Western Victoria over the past 16 years. The traditions, practices, social and cultural structures, histories, and issues of Aboriginal people and communities in other parts of Australia will differ; therefore, local protocols and processes need to be followed and Traditional Owner groups and Elders consulted.

The relatively high living standards and wealth enjoyed by many in contemporary Australia exist under the shadow of a brutal and racist history that continues to permeate society today. Colonial residue is evident in the paternalism of many current social and welfare policies. Social workers have multiple roles in working to rectify the effects of past social injustice for at least two reasons. First, redressing social justice issues and engaging in social and political advocacy to promote equity are core components of the social work profession. Beyond the provision of individual counselling and support, we need to be capable of conceptualizing and working toward improving the equality of the social and economic contexts in which people live, which influence their access to the resources needed to lead a healthy life. Second, social workers need to take responsibility for the roles welfare and social work practitioners have had in implementing destructive and inhumane policies.

This chapter begins with a brief history of Aboriginal Australia and outlines the social welfare, health, and community services that are available today. Numerous issues confronting Aboriginal families are both presented and explored through a practice vignette. The role of the rural social worker is outlined, including an examination of values, principles, actions, and processes that may be useful in engaging families, demonstrating respect, building capacity, and cultivating hope.

The aim of this chapter is to underscore the importance of cultural awareness and the development of respectful, sensitive, and supportive practice. The social and economic disadvantage faced by many Aboriginal people in Australia is duplicated among other Indigenous populations. It is though improving our awareness, our self-reflection, our knowledge and skills and through forming genuine partnerships with Aboriginal people and communities that we can commence redressing past injustices and atrocities.

If you are reading this as a non-Indigenous person, begin by reflecting on your own assumptions, experiences, values, and perspectives as they relate to Indigenous people. Where do these come from? Who or what has influenced you? How representative are your views? How has *your* culture and personal history shaped your perspectives? What personal and professional challenges might you face? How will you manage these matters, and who or what might support you?

If you are reading this as an Indigenous social work or welfare practitioner, how does your personal and cultural history influence the way you approach and conceptualize your role? What additional strengths and skills will you bring to work with rural Aboriginal families and communities? What personal and professional challenges might you face? How will you manage these matters, and who or what might support you?

# HISTORICAL CONTEXT OF "WELFARE" POLICY AND PRACTICE IN AUSTRALIA

## Aboriginal History

Aboriginal people have lived in Australia for at least 60,000 years (Morrissey, 2001; Pascoe, 2012), with recent geological evidence suggesting occupation in a location in southern Australia that dates back to at least 80,000 years ago (Warrnambool City Council, 2015). These data account for the usual response from Aboriginal Australians when asked where they come from: "We have always been here" (Pascoe, 2012, p. 5) and substantiates the assertion that Aboriginal Australian society has the longest continuous culture on the planet (Morrissey, 2001). Prior to invasion, Indigenous inhabitants resided in approximately 700 discreet language groups (Australian Museum, 2015), with each such group having its distinct set of sophisticated land management, legal, economic, social, and spiritual cultural practices that evolved over tens of thousands of years. There are no accurate estimates of the population of Australia before European settlement. Estimates were based on post-1788 observations of a population already reduced by introduced diseases and other factors and range from a minimum pre-1788 population of "315,000 to over one million people" (Australian Bureau of Statistics [ABS], 2010).

Beginning in 1788, Aboriginal populations were decimated as Australia was established as an English penal colony, with large scale migration to follow. The brutal practices of early settlers included the widespread killing of Aboriginal people who defended their homes against invasion (Clark, 1990; Pascoe, 2007; Reynolds, 1987). That carnage, conducted through localized wars, lasted over a period of 150 years. Cumulative effects of discriminatory government policies and practices along with the introduction of new diseases also contributed to the loss of Aboriginal life (Campbell, 2002). The Indigenous population had limited resistance to the diseases that the Europeans brought with them, and the instances of large-scale murder were so many that some have characterized them as attempted genocide (Bottoms, 2013). While Aboriginal people fought valiantly against the invaders, their traditional weapons and strategic attacks were ultimately unsuccessful against the guns and treachery of the English.

Other impacts upon Aboriginal communities continue to have resounding implications today. This is especially true for the loss of traditional lands and, with that, access to food sources, cultural lore, practice and sites, language, and spiritual connections (Dudgeon, Milroy, & Walker, 2014). Subsequent government policies of protectionism and assimilation resulted in layers of systemic discrimination that led to ongoing generational poverty, stolen wages, stolen children, and transgenerational trauma (Gunstone & Heckenberg, 2009). As agents of those policies, social workers have participated in the removal of Aboriginal children from their families, which country and culture now recognize as the Stolen Generations (Stolen Generations Victoria, 2009). National "Sorry Day" arose as one of the recommendations from the 1997 "Bringing them Home Report," in recognition of the devastation caused by the forced removal of Aboriginal children, who were often subjected to horrendous physical, emotional, and sexual abuse in institutional or foster care (National Sorry Day Committee, 2015; Stolen Generations Victoria, 2009). Aboriginal people were subjected to a suite of discriminatory legislative frameworks, and it was not until the 1967 national referendum that they were finally recognized as citizens.

Current Aboriginal population figures are also contested. It is commonly estimated that Indigenous people make up around 2% of the total Australian population; however, underrepresentation in census data collection activities means that reliable data are still not available (ABS, 2010). The resilience, ingenuity, dignity, and tenacity of Aboriginal people have been repeatedly demonstrated and celebrated over the past two centuries, resulting in increased understanding of the depth and breadth of knowledge, innovation, and skill that have remained deeply embedded in Aboriginal culture. Many Aboriginal communities have maintained and continued to practice and teach cultural traditions. In fertile farming areas, Aboriginal people were removed and dispossessed of their traditional homelands and forced into government "missions" where speaking one's language and practicing one's culture were forbidden. The painstaking work of reviving or restoring cultural practices has been initiated by descendants and continues today (Gunditjmara People with Wettenhall, 2010).

Aboriginal people now take part and often excel in all aspects of society, including academe, business, arts and culture, sports, politics, science, and healthcare. However, there remains significant disparity across the spectrum of social and economic determinants of health, which require an urgent and dedicated response from mainstream and Aboriginal-specific services (Dudgeon, et al., 2014). Inequities that exist between Aboriginal and non-Indigenous Australians can be found in areas including mortality and morbidity rates, educational outcomes, economic opportunities, housing, experience of violence, incarceration rates, and living standards (Al-Yaman, Van Doeland, & Wallis, 2006; National Aboriginal Community Controlled Health Organization [NACCHO], 2013). An Aboriginal woman is 35 times more likely to be hospitalized as a result of family violence than a non-Indigenous woman (Australian Institute of Health and Welfare [AIHW],

2014). The numbers of Indigenous people imprisoned in Australia have increased by 6% over the past decade; in the state of Victoria, for instance, people identifying as Aboriginal or Torres Strait Islander make up 8% of the prison population; in the Northern Territory, they make up 86% (ABS, 2014).

The expected lifespan of Indigenous Australians is 10 years shorter than for the general population; Indigenous Australians are twice as likely to report having asthma and more than three times more likely to be diagnosed with diabetes compared to the general population (AIHW, 2014). Compounding these issues for rural families is lack of specialist services close to home, which necessitates long three- to four-hour trips to metropolitan centers. With limited transport and financial resources, many Aboriginal people decide to forego their medical needs rather than make the journey. Some experts also view current state and federal funding levels wholly inadequate to address the cumulative disadvantage Aboriginal Australians continue to endure. Health and community organizations and service providers have a responsibility to know about and accept the brutal collective history that defines Australia, as well as to appreciate the need for mechanisms and collaborative efforts that will improve the health outcomes and advance the socioeconomic interests of Aboriginal communities and families. Resources to assist this endeavor have been developed by Aboriginal organizations (NACCHO, 2013; Victorian Aboriginal Community Controlled Health Organization, 2014).

## CONTEMPORARY SETTINGS AND SERVICES

Australian children and families are supported through a range of systems and services from the universal to the highly targeted. Within the framework of its tiered governmental structure, Australia delivers a complex range of health services funding by national, state, and local governments, often in partnership (Willis, Reynolds, & Keleher, 2009). While a mix of prevention, early intervention, and treatment services exists, health promotion advocates argue that the funding allocations perpetuate an imbalance toward direct-service delivery or "downstream" interventions (Keleher, 2009).

### National

The national government funds and coordinates a universal health system with access to general practitioners as the central pillar. The Commonwealth records childhood immunizations and funds selected programs in mental health, Aboriginal health services, and child care. Homelessness services are also administered federally.

The Australian Association of Social Workers (2015) has developed practice guidelines to inform culturally responsive social work practice with Aboriginal and Torres Strait Islander people. This guidelines document recognizes the historical role social workers played in the removal of Aboriginal children from their families. The nature of the experience of oppression, disadvantage, and discrimination that has resulted in the health conditions described earlier means that Aboriginal and Torres Strait Islander populations are frequently in need of services that social workers provide. The role of social workers in implementation of racist government policies, such as the ongoing removal of Aboriginal children and the recent Northern Territory "intervention" (Calma, 2011), has meant that the social work profession has had a conflicted relationship with Aboriginal people that still occasions significant mistrust today.

In 2006, the "Close the Gap" campaign was established. This rose from a collaboration of bipartisan political support from national and state governments. The campaign is currently led by Aboriginal and Torres Strait Islands people. The aim of the campaign is to achieve health equality by the year 2030 through a human rights–based approach (Holland, 2016). The latest progress report, 10 years after the campaign's inception, demonstrates a modest gain: "improvements in infant and child health outcomes that bode well for the health of the future adult population"; however, the report also cautions that "there is still tremendous effort and resources needed if Aboriginal and Torres Strait Islander life expectancy equality is to be achieved by 2013" (Holland, 2016, p. 5). Racism in public hospitals was found to be a significant barrier to health services for Indigenous people, with overt as well as systemic discrimination resulting in people failing to receive the treatment they require when attending hospitals.

In order to reverse the compounding impacts of loss, racism, ill health, and cumulative trauma, all mainstream health, education, and community sectors need to be guided by culturally sound strategies, actions, and programs that have been found to be safe and effective with Aboriginal communities. To help advance these endeavors, evidence-based Closing the Gap resource sheets have been produced to summarize various health issues Dudgeon, Walker, Scrine, Shepherd, Calma, and Ring (2014). For example, Atkinson's (2013) trauma-informed care sheet contains pertinent information for service providers about the experience of trauma among Indigenous Australians.

## In the State of Victoria

State governments directly manage the bulk of health and education programs and services that operate through a combination of state and federal funds. The legislative, policy, and practice frameworks vary over time and from state to state; in the state of Victoria, for instance, the state government funds and administers services delivery in hospitals and health services, primary health, public health, mental health, alcohol and drugs, as well as ageing and aged care. Under these broad domains falls public housing, child protection, disability, family services, family violence, and sexual assault sectors (Victorian State Government Department of Health and Human Services, 2015). The State Government Department of Education and Early Childhood Development also manage kindergarten and public schools.

## Local Government

Local government's role in health and welfare service delivery is fundamentally implementation of programs funded by state or federal governments within their municipality. Examples of services include aged care, child care, maternal and child health, home and community care, youth development, as well as some health promotion and public health programs.

## CULTURAL AUTHORITY

Organizational leaders considering the delivery of services to Aboriginal populations must seek the approval of the Aboriginal community on whose land the activities will take place. This must be done in the initial design and throughout the implementation and evaluation process. Protocols need to be developed to facilitate Aboriginal authority and ensure that projects address Aboriginal-identified priorities. The project's scope, methodology, evidence of need, evaluation mechanisms, and, most importantly, the monitoring and management of programs all need to be determined within the context of Aboriginal decision-making authority. Demonstration of the cultural appropriateness and Aboriginal outcomes of the undertaking will be assessed, and special amendments or requirements may be needed to ensure that no misappropriation or misrepresentations occur, especially in research activities.

Depending on the type of endeavor undertaken, it may be appropriate to consult and collaborate with multiple stakeholders. This could mean working with Traditional Owner groups, individual recognized community Elders, the board or reference group associated with an Aboriginal Community Controlled Health Organization, or, in some instances, all of these.

## In Small Communities

In small rural communities, it is common for individuals to have multiple roles and relationships as the pool of people to undertake the range of professional and volunteer tasks pales in comparison to existing practice in metropolitan settings. Having such a small pool to draw from may in fact impact colleagues and clients alike in the kinds of relationships they have with one another.

As an example, consider the intersections in the lives of Susan Markita and Donna Janith. Susan is an Early Years educator now working in Family Services; she provides intensive support to vulnerable families. Donna is a social worker practicing as a senior mental health clinician. As a day-care educator in a child-care facility, Susan cared for Donna's son when he was an infant. Ten years later, Susan participated in professional-development training facilitated by Donna on supporting parents with mental illness. As a result of Susan's continued interest in this area and her previous Early Years' experience, Susan and Donna subsequently cofacilitated a workshop. Later that year, Susan led a parenting program that Donna participated in as the parent of her youngest child. In this scenario Susan was to Donna a service provider, training-program participant, colleague, and educator. It also happened that they were friends outside of professional life and often saw one another at social functions as well as at their children's sporting events.

For Aboriginal health and community workers, this phenomenon is often compounded as the community network is always smaller and interrelated and its number of culturally safe employment opportunities diminished. Rather than clients being acquaintances from the same township, they may indeed be family members of the people they are providing services to. This can make setting personal and professional boundaries an impossibility and can lead to carer burden and expedite professional burn-out. Other workplace issues have been identified by Aboriginal health practitioners that often emanate from inequitable power dynamics with non-Indigenous counterparts. Issues stem from a lack of empowerment, trust, respect, and recognition within health teams where clinical qualifications are more highly valued than cultural and community knowledge and skills. Low remuneration and lack of supportive workplace conditions can lead to retention issues. Cultural security in workplaces is often lacking; in addition, difficulties with leadership and management abound when service goals and practice methods differ, and Aboriginal workers are constantly under the kind of scrutiny to which other professionals are not subject to (Health Workforce Australia, 2011).

The proximity of family networks in Aboriginal communities underscores the critical importance of maintaining positive relationships and avoiding "burning bridges." News travels fast in Indigenous communities, and while it can take years for a non-Indigenous health practitioner to develop trust and cultivate a positive reputation, this can be destroyed in an instant if the practice is not consistently high-quality, reliable, and authentic.

## CASE VIGNETTE

Prior to being employed as a primary welfare officer at the school, Shannon Lovenjoy had often seen Carol Winters at the school gate in the afternoons as they had both been picking their children up. Living in a small town with a population of just 1,500, one could nott help running into people at the supermarket, at the children's weekend sports, or around the one-and-only school. A polite smile and greeting had been the extent of their relationship until each became pregnant with her third child within two months of the other. With this fundamental mothering experience in common, they gradually began to share some of the challenges and joys of pregnancy, but, still, their communication remained superficial, and an unspoken cultural divide persisted.

Shannon applied for the new social worker position at the school 12 months later, with the benefits of working part-time and close to home very enticing in this particular life phase. Her two older children were teens now and traveled by bus to a nearby secondary school, with her 15-month-old baby beginning to attend a child-care facility on work days.

Soon thereafter, Carol's two children's teachers referred them to Shannon for individual support around emotional and behavioral issues. At six years of age, Cassie was the youngest and had been found crying in the playground. After some comforting, she revealed that she was feeling sad and worried about a baby cousin who was very ill and had been admitted to hospital on the previous day. Knowing that Aboriginal mortality rates for babies was high, Shannon took Cassie's fears seriously and was conscious of the need to be both reassuring and realistic, focusing on the emotional impact for Cassie.

Shannon and Cassie talked about families and emotions and especially worries. Emphasizing the importance of sharing fears, they drew a "worry tree," listing in the leaves all the worries Cassie could think of. Together, they divided them into big and small, Cassie's own worries and those that belonged to others. Cassie colored the tree, once complete, in red, yellow, and black, stating "I'm using my Aboriginal colors." She talked about the storytelling and dance workshop that she and the other Aboriginal students had participated in with Harry Mondoolgan, the Koori Education Support Officer (KESO), who made regular visits to the school.

The following week, Cassie's brother Jeremy, age 8, arrived to see Shannon in a very angry state because of an altercation he had had with another student. As the conversation progressed, Jeremy described frequent verbal fights between his stepfather and mother, including racial abuse by his non-Indigenous stepfather toward his Aboriginal mother. Shannon and Jeremy spoke about the characteristics of healthy and unhealthy relationships. Afterward, Shannon phoned Carol to invite her to meet and discuss the work she was doing with the children. She also encouraged Carol to bring her infant along to a supported playgroup Shannon had established for parents of preschool children. Her aim was to build attachment, increase social connection among parents, and develop preliteracy skills for the young children. This would be achieved through simple facilitated activities, including singing nursery rhymes, reading stories, and providing play opportunities.

Carol attended the following Wednesday, but Shannon observed her to appear reserved and uncomfortable, particularly with the singing. It was not until the other parents departed that Carol began to open up and a fruitful discussion ensued. Shannon listened as Carol shared her difficult upbringing, removal from her own birth family, teen pregnancy, financial difficulties, parenting challenges (especially managing the children's behavior), and acute social isolation. Carol's husband and the father of her two eldest children had died suddenly at the age of just 42 of a heart condition, and her grief was still raw. Carol's next-door neighbor, Kathy Awatōtō, was described as her "savior," and they forged a strong bond through assisting each other in times of adversity over the past seven years. Kathy, a Maori woman indigenous to New Zealand, was a single mother with four children of her own. Hardly a day would go by that the two neighbors, after dropping their kids to school, would not share a coffee and discuss their plans for the day.

Carol informed Shannon that she did not know much of her family or cultural history, except that the traditional country of her ancestors was interstate in northern Queensland, thousands of miles away. As such, she was on the periphery of the local Aboriginal community and stated that she derived no spiritual or cultural strength from her Indigenous origins, which brought her only hardship and discrimination. Shannon shared with Carol her hope and observation that things may be different for her children, as they had demonstrated pride in their culture on a number of occasions. Carol and Shannon agreed to meet again in a week to continue the conversation and explore how the school and other services in the community might be able to offer additional support.

Shannon's next working day was Friday, and on arrival she was immediately ushered into the principal's office. There had been an incident of family violence witnessed by all of Carol's children. The screaming was said to be so loud that neighbors phoned Child Protection Services. A preliminary court hearing took place that day and the three children were removed from Carol's care while an investigation took place. In addition to the escalating family violence, concerns were raised regarding possible neglect. Over the ensuing six weeks, child protection practitioners assessed the level of risk posed to the well-being of all three children because of their stepfather's alleged violence and both parents' reported alcohol use. In the course of the investigation, Carol revealed that she had experienced significant symptoms of anxiety, which she hoped the alcohol would alleviate or, failing that, mask.

While the investigation was being conducted, baby Leila was cared for by a relative of her father's, and a foster care family was identified that could take Jeremy and Cassie. However, that family lived in a town an hour's drive south, so a change of school was necessary. Shannon did not see the kids at school for the rest of the term. She phoned Carol a number of times with an offer of support; during those exchanges Carol was abrupt and noncommunicative. Other staff at the school had seen Carol when she had come to collect some of her children's belongings; they described her as distraught. She was acutely aware of numerous other Aboriginal families who had had children removed and how rare it was for those children to be returned home. Historical narratives about the stolen generations and her own troubled childhood spun in her head.

Her drinking increased, as did her reliance on her next-door neighbor. Kathy was staunch in her support of Carol. She visited daily to get Carol out of bed and to brew strong cups of coffee. Kathy would then turn the stereo up while she tidied and cleaned; she attempted to motivate Carol to get organized so that she could show those child protection workers how dedicated she was to getting her children back. Kathy drove Carol to an appointment with a family violence service, where she was able to get support from a worker who advocated around the injustice of the removal of her children, given that her partner's violence had caused the harm that, in the process, had also victimized her.

After completing a detailed investigation, child protection staff identified a number of strengths in Carol's parenting capacity. The children's
school attendance had been consistent, and, when interviewed, Jeremy
and Cassie spoke about the things they enjoyed doing with their mother.
They both mentioned fishing in the river. In the throes of this traumatizing experience, Carol separated from her partner and evicted him from the
house. She had applied for an intervention order from the court, preventing him from legally entering her home. Kathy continued to be a supportive
friend, and Carol engaged with a health program through one of the local
Aboriginal health services. Child protection stipulated conditions under
which the children could be returned to her care, and Carol readily agreed
to terms. This included ceasing alcohol use, maintaining contact with the
health program support worker, commencing counseling to develop strategies to manage her anxiety, and ensuring that her ex-partner did not enter
her home.

After being in care for six weeks, Jeremy, Cassie, and their baby sister
were reunited and returned home. The two eldest went back to school, and
Shannon saw each of them individually in the initial week. It was apparent
from their retelling of the incident and their separation from parents, sister, and home that they had been traumatized. A family meeting was con-
vened, in accordance with the "Wannik" or Koori Education Strategy for
Koorie children in the state of Victoria, called KESO. ("Koorie" or "Koori"
is the name that Indigenous people originating from the states of New
South Wales and Victoria use for themselves). For this meeting, attend-
ees included the school principal, several class teachers, a KESO staff person, the Aboriginal family support worker, Carol, and Shannon. Individual
learning plans were developed for each child, focusing on their culture,
strengths, and interests. The aims were to maintain and strengthen the
children's engagement to school and community.

Subsequently, Jeremy and Cassie continued to work with the KESO
staff. They were also referred to a specialized visiting counseling service
that could be accessed at school. Carol and her baby Leila started to attend
a Koori playgroup where the local Aboriginal language was being revived
and taught to children and parents through stories and songs. Leila, who
had been delayed in speech, started to put together three- to four-word
sentences. She also displayed her enjoyment of the songs and learning
activities with enthusiastic participation, laughing, and clapping.

Shannon continued to support the children individually around promoting positive strategies to manage their emotions and relationships,
especially around the separation from their mother and the ending of their
relationship with their stepfather, whom they no longer saw. Shannon

decided to draw on her relationships with the local Aboriginal community, which she had developed many years by attending and supporting Aboriginal community events, participating in cultural awareness training, and initiating collaborative projects around health issues identified by the community members.

She telephoned an Aboriginal visual artist she has worked with previously to discuss a proposal to employ the artist to work with Carol's two children and another five Koorie students in order to create a "meeting place" on the school grounds. After refining the project plan with a steering group made up of an Aboriginal Elder, a KES staff member, the artist, the school principal, and an Aboriginal health promotion worker, Shannon got the project underway. The students worked with the artist and the KESO staff member to design and build a circle of seats around a fire pit. They used locally sourced logs and rocks. The process and completion of this project supported the students in building build social and communication skills as well as personal and cultural pride. Through their efforts, they hoped to be recognized and even celebrated by their peers and the school leadership. This project also enabled local Aboriginal and mainstream families to have a welcoming meeting place where they could work on reducing the anxiety and fear of attending school, which remained enduring problems for Aboriginal parents who experienced the bitterness of discrimination and racism when they were in school.

Four years later, Shannon no longer works at the school. However, she continues to see the children most weeks in the local supermarket, at the playground, or at Aboriginal community events. The youngest child attends swimming lessons with Shannon's youngest son. The local kinder that Leila attends has many Aboriginal books and toys; a Koorie educator attends regularly to teach all the children, Indigenous and non-Indigenous, about Aboriginal history and culture. This change represents a positive social development that demonstrates how education settings can be used to foster cultural pride and belonging and to reduce discrimination and prejudice.

Jeremy now often approaches Shannon for a chat in the street or the park and speaks to her in a friendly and enthusiastic manner. Currently in sixth grade, he has been identified as the "buddy" or mentor for Shannon's four-year-old son when he commences school next year. Last week he was positively glowing as he shared that his mum is taking them to her own country for the first time, where they will be introduced to aunts, uncles, and cousins they have never met before. On that trip, they will also visit the places Carol used to frequent when she was growing up.

Shannon reflects on the blurring of professional and personal relationships and boundaries by virtue of working close to home. Of concern to her, especially, is in how best to negotiate the confidentiality of the families she works with and the privacy of her own family. Different practitioners will have varying levels of comfort about these "grey areas," but ultimately Shannon feels that sometimes in rural communities the boundaries are either artificial or irrelevant. She decides that everyone brings with them diverse perspectives according to their own experiences, backgrounds, financial resources, cultures, and personal histories; we are all community members, confronting challenges in life, sharing resources, and supporting one another. At the same time, she respects the need to pay attention to power differences in relationships, boundary issues, and self-awareness reflections.

That Shannon is well known to all the children in the town through her work at the school and outside of it as a member of the community has not meant that others judge Carol's children as "welfare clients." Engaging in casual conversations within the community increases social connectedness and a sense belonging for everyone.

## Practice Application

There are no shortcuts to building one's cultural awareness or to developing respectful reciprocal relationships with Aboriginal · organizations, Aboriginal Elders, and Aboriginal families and communities. Demonstrating a preparedness to listen, learn, share, and contribute over an extended period is the only sure way to build meaningful practice frameworks and activities that will lead to sustained improvements in health and well-being. Creating "Aboriginal-inclusive" programs and services leads to better outcomes for all, as the foundations of Aboriginal understandings of holistic well-being include spiritual and ecological components that are often overlooked in mainstream settings.

Seeking out Aboriginal accounts of history and contemporary issues and challenges will help to counter the lack of Indigenous content in Australian educational institutions. Thankfully, this exclusion is now being remedied as Aboriginal history and culture are fast becoming embedded in early-year to tertiary-level curricula. However, caution is required when applying knowledge to social work practice. Be alert to your own assumptions regarding the experiences an Aboriginal person may have had as diversity is immense and every life circumstance unique.

For many Aboriginal people, reviving cultural practice and participating in traditional customs and ceremonies may be healing and empowering, as these forces strengthen identity and facilitate renewed connection to country, family, and heritage. But as one woman recently stated, "I want to *know* my culture, but I don't want to *do* my culture . . . and I don't want to perform." Her words allude to the perception that Aboriginal culture is sometimes experienced as an art form put on display for the gratification of a non-Indigenous audience. While Aboriginal culture is imbued with a rich aesthetic conveyed through painting, sculpture, story, music, dance, and every other artistic endeavor, it is a privilege to be invited to witness and participate.

This vignette allows the reader to see the value of having a social worker in schools. This social worker was able to provide a safe person with whom the children and their mother could trust and work with. This worker demonstrated cultural humility and not only worked to provide help for this family but broadened the care to all of the Aboriginal families in her school by beginning programming for these children and families. For rural social workers in any setting, the core professional values surrounding authenticity, transparency, mutual respect, active listening, and genuine partnership will go a long way to establishing solid relationships with Aboriginal communities. The benefits of having a positive reputation within the community is amplified in the rural context where word of mouth and the practice of "vouching" for individuals who demonstrate culturally sound practice move at lightning speed. Focusing on our many commonalities and valuing the diverse skills, knowledge, perspectives, and experiences of others assist in overcoming barriers and enable us to advance a health and social justice agenda together.

## DISCUSSION QUESTIONS

1. When the dichotomy between professional and personal life erodes, how do you manage living in the same community with families you work with?
2. What circumstances might threaten your clients' or your own privacy? How can this be prevented, minimized, or managed?
3. How might you use innovative approaches to engagement and relationship-building (e.g., group work, community art projects)?
4. Who are the key stakeholders in your service system and community? How can you build strong, respectful, and enduring relationships with Aboriginal services and communities?
5. What historical or transgenerational events might influence your work with individuals and families of Aboriginal descent?
6. How might individuals or families express their needs and preferences around welfare interventions?

7. How do we make overt our values and assumptions so that we are transparent yet also reflective in our social work practice?
8. What strategies might be employed to build cultural awareness? What are the issues and tensions between being culturally aware but also individually focussed? How do we avoid making assumptions about people's experiences, needs, or preferences just because of a cultural or background characteristic?

## LEARNING ACTIVITIES

1. Finding Cultural Guides
   a. Learners are instructed to identify where they could begin to look for a cultural guide in a new community. This can be assigned to work on in one class and bring the information back the following week.
   b. Cultural Intersectionality
      Use the cultural intersectional "pie" chart in Ortega and Faller (2011) to have participants identify how many facets of their cultural identities and backgrounds intersect toward developing their own unique person in environment. This works best if the learner has to talk to at least two rural community professionals about their experiences with cultural guides and ways to find cultural guides. Learners should write up a two-page summary of their learning and share the lessons learned with the class.

## SUGGESTED READING

Department of Child Protection and Family Support. (n.d.) *Home page*. Western Australia. https://www.dcp.wa.gov.au/Pages/Home.aspx
North Coast Area Health Service. (2009). *Cultural respect and communication guide*. NSW Health. http://www.healthinfonet.ecu.edu.au/uploads/resources/19163_19163.pdf
Ortega, R., & Faller, K. C. (2011). Training child welfare workers from an intersectional cultural humility perspective: A paradigm shift. *Child Welfare, 90*(5), 27–49. Retrieved from http://www.cwla.org/child-welfare-journal/

## REFERENCES

Al-Yaman, F., Van Doeland, M., & Wallis, M. (2006). *Family violence among Aboriginal and Torres Strait Islander peoples*. Cat. No. IHW 17. Canberra: AIHW.

Atkinson, J. (2013). *Trauma-informed services and trauma-specific care for Indigenous Australian children*. Resource Sheet No. 21. Close the Gap Clearinghouse. Institute for Family Studies. Retrieved from www.aihw.gov.au/closingthegap

Australian Association of Social Workers. (2015). *Preparing for culturally responsive and inclusive social work practice in Australia: Working with Aboriginal and Torres Strait Islander peoples*. Retrieved from http://www.aasw.asn.au/document/item/7006

Australian Bureau of Statistics. (2010). *Year book Australia*. Retrieved from http://www.abs.gov.au/ausstats/abs@.nsf/0/68AE74ED632E17A6CA2573D200110075?opendocument

Australian Institute of Aboriginal and Torres Strait Islander Studies. (2015). Home page. Retrieved from http://aiatsis.gov.au/

Australian Institute of Health and Welfare. (2014). *Australia's Health 2014:Indigenous health*. Retrieved from http://www.aihw.gov.au/australias-health/2014/indigenous-health/#t2

Australian Museum. (2015). *An introduction to Indigenous Australia*. Retrieved from http://australianmuseum.net.au/indigenous-australia-introduction

Bottoms, T. (2013). *Conspiracy of silence: Queensland's frontier killing times*. Sydney, Australia: Allen & Unwin.

Calma, T. (2011). Challenges for the social work profession and Aboriginal people in working together. Speech delivered at 70th Anniversary Colloquium, February 14. Melbourne, Australia: University of Melbourne.

Campbell, J. (2002). *Invisible invaders: Smallpox and other diseases in Aboriginal Australia 1780–1880*. Melbourne, Australia: Melbourne University Press.

Clark, I. (1990). *Aboriginal languages and clans: An historical atlas of Western and Central Victoria, 1800–1900*. Monash Publications in Geography 37. Melbourne, Australia: Monash University.

Dudgeon, P., Milroy, H., & Walker, R. (Eds.). (2014). *Working together: Aboriginal and Torres Strait Islander mental health and well-being – Principles and practice* (2nd ed.). Canberra: Commonwealth of Australia.

Dudgeon, P., Walker, R., Scrine, C., Shepherd, C., Calma, T., & Ring, I. (2014). *Effective strategies to strengthen the mental health and wellbeing of Aboriginal and Torres Strait Islander people*. Issues Paper 12. Close the Gap Clearinghouse. Canberra, Australia: Institute of Health and Welfare & Melbourne, Australian Institute of Family Studies. Retrieved from www.aihw.gov.au/closingthegap

Gunditjmara People with Wettenhall, G. (2010). *The People of Budj Bim:Engineers of aquaculture, builders of stone house settlements and warriors defending country*. Victoria, Australia: Em PRESS.

Gunstone, A., & Heckenberg, S. (2009). *The government owes a lot of money to our people: A history of Indigenous stolen wages in Victoria*. Melbourne, Australia: Australian Scholarly Publishing.

Health Workforce Australia. (2011). *Aboriginal and Torres Strait Islander health worker project: Interim report*. Retrieved from https://www.hwa.gov.au/sites/uploads/atsihw-project-interim-report-20111017.pdf/

Holland, C. (2016). *Progress and priorities report 2016*. The Close the Gap Campaign Steering Committee for Indigenous Health Equality. Retrieved from http://www.oxfam.org.au/closethe gap

Keleher, H. (2009). Public health in Australia. In E. Willis, L. Reynolds, & H. Keleher (Eds.), *Understanding the Australian health care system* (pp. 61–74). Sydney, Australia: Elsevier Churchill Livingstone.

Morrissey, P. (2001). *Aboriginal Australia and the Torres Strait Islands: Guide to Indigenous Australia*. Melbourne, Australia: Lonely Planet Publications.

National Aboriginal Community Controlled Health Organisation. (2013). *Investing in healthy futures for generational change: NACCHO 10 Point Plan 2013–2013*. Canberra, Australia: Author.

National Sorry Day Committee. (2015). *Welcome to the National Sorry Day committee*. Retrieved from http://www.nsdc.org.au/

Pascoe, B. (2007). *Convincing ground: Learning to fall in love with your country*. Canberra, Australia: Aboriginal Studies Press.

Pascoe, B. (2012). *The little red, yellow, black book: An introduction to indigenous Australia*. Canberra, Australia: AIATSIS, Aboriginal Studies Press.

Reynolds, H. (1987). *Frontier*. Sydney, Australia: Allen & Unwin.

Roach, A. (1990). Took the children away. On *Charcoal Lane* [CD]. Melbourne, Australia: Author/Hightone.

Stolen Generations Victoria. (2009). *Between two worlds: Understanding the stolen generations. A guide for health and human service professionals*. Melbourne, Australia: Deadly Design.

Victorian Aboriginal Community Controlled Health Organisation, & La Trobe University (2014). *Koorified: Aboriginal communication and wellbeing*. Melbourne, Australia: Author.

Victorian State Government Department of Health and Human Services. (2015). Home page. Retrieved from https://www2.health.vic.gov.au/

Warrnambool City Council. (2015). *Moyjil*. Retrieved from http://www.moyjil.com.au/

Willis, E., Reynolds, L., & Keleher, H. (2009). *Understanding the Australian health care system*. Sydney, Australia: Elsevier Churchill Livingstone.

# CHAPTER 10

ᴄᴠᴏ

# Rural Social Work in
a Native American Community

## TONI HAIL

Memorial to Lost Children. Native American tribal members walk to remember the children that were taken from their families and sent to government- or church-run Boarding Schools.
Heather Craig-Oldsen

## LEARNING OUTCOMES

- Describe social capital in a cultural context
- Identify ways that social capital may be useful in resource development
- Explain the significance of trust in Native American communities

- Identify potential barriers in working with Native American families
- List two or more strategies for building rapport with Native American families

## SOCIAL WORK WITH NATIVE AMERICAN PEOPLE IN CHILD WELFARE PRACTICE

### Social Capital

Working with children and families can be rewarding as well as challenging. Generalist social workers learn a range of skills that prepare them to deliver the services that best promote the well-being of children and families. No matter how solid that preparation, however, social workers often deal with challenges that require social capital, which stresses the importance of relationships as well as specific knowledge about information and social networks. Social capital is the crux of working with historically oppressed populations; Kahn, Rifaqat, and Kazmi (2007) call social capital "the glue that holds society together" (p. 3). What this means is that when people come to trust each other they are more likely to be part of community networks that reciprocate, cooperate, and engage in collective, shared actions toward a common goal. There is a "helping out" exchange process that goes back and forth between individuals, groups, families, and sometimes, communities. There are many examples of the use of social capital as a primary influence toward rural community project building projects. These include building new community employment resources (Crofts & Begg, 2007) and setting up community resident groups to manage natural resources (Kilpatrick & Abbott-Chapman, 2007).

For social workers in rural communities, that lack of sufficient formal resources commonly has a direct impact upon child welfare practice (Belanger & Stone, 2008).

Rural social workers must often use social capital to build rapport, as well as to access, allocate, and generate informal resources when formal resources are not readily available. For example, a small, rural hospital unit member may keep a little known cache of medication for patients from the area who had no way to pay for their medications. The availability of this secret hospital "stash" was shared with the community social worker after she helped the emergency room staff deal with a series of child and family health emergencies in the hospital. In the years that followed, these interactive helping exchanges facilitated further trust and sharing between the workers and their respective agency and institutions toward helping people living in the rural community.

The literature of social capital theory mentions the concepts of bonding and bridging as part of the building up and drawing upon social capital (Giorgas, 2007). In social work practice, this means that the professionals, residents, business community members, and other members of the community may have interactions that may lead to them considering themselves connected or attached to each other; they often view themselves as parts of a bigger picture, such as connected contributors toward a healthier rural community. They may think of children of the area as "our children" and not just limit their view of children as merely part of a nuclear family. Further they may link, or bridge, their resources, including helping each other access people in their networks who can provide additional resources in a time of need (Giorgas, 2007). In this sense, they may even serve as organizational and cultural guides to the "secret stashes" of helping resources that can be accessed or created with some creative thinking and a network of trusted relationships.

## Use of Social Capital with American Indians/Native Americans

Situating social capital in a *cultural* context is a concept that is not easily defined. Cultural contexts are often complex and require close attention to various nuances in order to achieve optimal outcomes in working with diverse populations. The focal point of this chapter is utilizing social capital to access child welfare resources in a rural setting with a specific population, namely Native Americans.

According to the National Congress of American Indians (n.d.), there are 566 federally recognized nations, or tribes, in the United States; it is imperative to understand, given that number, that "tribes are ethnically, culturally and linguistically diverse" (para 3). Relationships between tribal child welfare and state child welfare entities are critical for the purpose of restoring families and maintaining compliance with the federal mandate of the Indian Child Welfare Act (ICWA) of 1978. The primary goal of the ICWA is to preserve cultural connections and address the issues of Native American children who are placed in non-Native homes by involving tribes in the placement decision-making process. Consideration of placement of Native American children is prioritized by kinship within the same tribe as the child or within another tribe respectively.

Despite ICWA implementation, Native American children and families are still disproportionately represented in child welfare. Native American people make up 1% of the total population, but they represent 2% of children in the foster care system (Children's Bureau, 2013). This fact offers a glimpse into how Native American children and families have been and continue to be adversely affected under the history of colonization in the United States. The photograph at the front of this chapter shows a tribal march to "remember the children" that were forcibly removed from their family homes to enter boarding homes to be "civilized" according to the dominant White culture. There are places in this country where one can take a walk near the former boarding homes to find many graves of children who died there.

The continued overrepresentation of Native Americans involved in the child welfare systems may be influenced the lack of knowledge the generalist social worker may have in terms of Native American culture and self-awareness. A study examining culturally competent services for social work with Indigenous people conducted by Weaver (1999) highlights the significance of understanding that tribal communities are quite diverse and recommends exercising caution when assessing "Native American culture." In addition to the generalist skills of social work, practicing social workers should also "be aware of his or her own biases and need for wellness" as well as "value social justice [in order to] decolonize his or her own thought processes" (p. 223). However, there is evidence from intersecting rural and cultural literature that using social capital to get things done has been used with success even during difficult times in history. An Aboriginal Elders group in the rural Australian community of Wagga Wagga were able to accomplish numerous new social capital building ventures including hosting oral history events and developing more self-governance (Krivoikapic-Skoka, 2007). Even government led social-capital-fueled initiatives can be useful if time is taken to build trust (Brooks, 2007).

Still, working with such children and families may prove difficult to navigate, particularly when social workers have to adapt to unfamiliar cultural practices and function with limited resources. These ideas are illustrated in the case study of generalist practice social worker Christine Cornell in her work with the Hancock family.

## CASE VIGNETTE

Christine Cornell, a Native American, grew up in a small, rural town in the lush and mountainous region of the northeastern area of Oklahoma. Although the town is relatively small, with a population of slightly over one thousand, it is surrounded by many smaller communities and is situated approximately 25 miles from the county seat.

Elementary and middle schools are located within her community; however, she had to attend high school outside of her community. She graduated from high school and attended the local university, from which she received a bachelor of social work degree approximately three years ago. While Christine was in college, she worked as a case aid for her tribal child welfare agency and transported children and parents to visits, court hearings, and appointments. Her work as a case aid helped her to decide to pursue a career in child welfare. Upon completion of college, she acquired a position as a caseworker specializing in permanency placement for the same tribal child welfare agency. Her primary role is to secure a permanent placement for tribal children in custody when reunification with the biological parents is an unlikely outcome. Christine is a member of the tribe she works for and has developed both personal and professional relationships with other departments in her tribe throughout her years as a tribal member, an aid, and a caseworker. Christine has become familiar with her role and feels fairly confident in her abilities to assist her clients and meet their needs.

Christine acquires a case involving a family that lives in the same community in which she was raised. The county child welfare agency conducted the initial investigation and then notified the tribe that the client in question belonged to their tribe, at which point the tribe took over the case. Upon reviewing the information and allegations provided by the county child welfare agency, along with the case files of her tribal agency, Christine realizes the case involves Ms. Lucy Hancock, whom she recalls when Ms. Hancock was a young girl in her community; through the grapevine, she has also heard that Ms. Hancock had some struggles as a teen stemming from her tumultuous relationship with her boyfriend and father of her three children, Mr. Joe Ross. Ms. Hancock is a full-blood Native American and belongs to the same tribe as Christine. Mr. Ross has no tribal affiliation. Christine staffs the case with her supervisor; they determine that Christine's work with the family would not constitute a dual relationship because even though she knows of the family, she does not have a personal connection to any of its members. As she proceeds, she learns the details of Ms. Lucy Hancock and Mr. Joe Ross' three children. The case file states that the eldest, Kimberly, who is eight years old, alleges she has taken on a parental role in caring for her younger siblings. She is very protective of them and has attended to their needs (bathing, cooking, helping with homework) and demonstrates anxiety over potentially being separated from them. She seems extremely intelligent but has fallen behind in school due to excessive absences from class.

Her younger brother, Junior, is six years old. His teacher describes him as "extremely shy. He does not engage with his teachers or his peers." He demonstrates some degree of cognitive delay perhaps influenced by his mother's substance abuse while she was pregnant with him. In addition, he is below average in terms of height and weight for his age but has no apparent physical disabilities. The youngest child, Susan, is two years old and appears to have normal cognitive and physical development. Susan also seems rather shy; both she and Junior appear rely on Kimberly for nurture and support.

Christine learns the children were removed from their biological mother, Ms. Lucy Hancock, approximately 18 months ago due to a referral from the local probation office. The investigation by the state and tribal child welfare agencies disclosed that the children were exposed to severe neglect. Ms. Lucy Hancock admitted she left the children unattended for several days at a time in a trailer-home she rented on the outskirts of town. Ms. Hancock also acknowledged she had a history of substance abuse and would "use from time to time to deal with stress"; however, the primary reason she would leave for days at a time was due to her gambling addiction. Ms. Hancock was unemployed and had been on probation for petty theft and writing "hot" checks for the past two years. Her probation officer was conducting an unannounced visit to the home and discovered the children alone. The food available to them was rotted; they had neither electricity nor water as the utilities had been disconnected.

The three children were immediately placed in a tribal shelter while the probation officer, state, and tribal child welfare worked in collaboration to locate Ms. Hancock. The probation officer was able to locate her several days later via social media activity in which a friend "tagged" her at a casino approximately 30 minutes away. Ms. Hancock admitted that she was under the influence of alcohol and bath salts at the time she was initially interviewed. She stated she felt that Kimberly was capable of caring for the younger children and had "left them with food." However, she had forgotten to apply for assistance for her utilities and did not realize they had been disconnected. As events unfolded, her probation officer determined she had violated her probation, and therefore she was arrested. As a result, she was jailed where she awaits a court hearing and adjudication of her violation.

Christine learns that the biological father of Ms. Hancock's children, Mr. Joe Ross, passed away approximately six months prior to the removal of the children. Mr. Ross had a history of addiction to alcohol and prescription painkillers since his early teenage years and overdosed in the trailer home they shared with their three children. In addition, the case report indicates several incidents of suspected domestic violence that had been reported to authorities. However, Ms. Hancock and the children denied the accusation, nor did any evidence surface to support it. Ms. Hancock reports that Mr. Ross had minimal involvement with the children due to his alcohol and substance abuse issues and had no contact with his family primarily because of his involvement with her. Mr. Ross's problems with addiction also strained relations with his family or origin. Among other things, his family never approved of his relationship with Ms. Hancock as they contended that "mixing White people with Native people" was wrong. According to Ms. Hancock, the Ross family expressed no desire to be involved with the Hancock-Ross children; moreover, they were not entirely convinced the children actually belonged to their son, even in the face of DNA evidence obtained by the local Department of Human Services when Ms. Hancock was applying for TANF benefits after the birth of Junior.

After several days in the shelter, the children were temporarily placed with an extended family member of Ms. Hancock. The agreement reached stipulated that no placement would be permanent until after Ms. Hancock had completed a treatment program for addiction and was reassessed in terms of suitability as a mother. The relative, a distant cousin, stated that she would be willing to care for the children for "no more than six months" as she had small children of her own and was emotionally and financially unable to maintain a household increased by three on a long-term basis. The probation officer and judge agreed that Ms. Hancock be given the option of treatment over prison for her violations; however, an unsuccessful treatment would mean a two-year sentence at a women's correctional facility. The judge indicated that this approach was her "last chance to get it together." After her court hearing and the temporary placement for the children, Ms. Hancock was sent to a treatment facility approximately six hours away. She abandoned the required program after her third day in the facility. She has not been seen or heard from since. Despite the combined efforts of the probation officer, tribal child welfare, and families to locate her, they have not been successful. The tribal child welfare agency made the decision to secure a permanent placement for the children, as Ms. Hancock will likely be incarcerated once found.

Due to the unlikelihood that the children will be returned to Ms. Hancock in the near future and the pressure from the current caregiver of the children, the case is given to Christine and she begins working toward establishing a safe, permanent environment for the three children. Because of tribal involvement in this case, the agency has been in regular contact with the maternal grandparents, Mr. Bill and Mrs. Lisa Hancock. Mr. and Mrs. Hancock have been married for 25 years. Mr. Hancock works for a local construction company on an "as needed" basis, and Mrs. Hancock cleans a few homes in town for cash. Mr. and Mrs. Hancock say they are devastated about their missing daughter and very concerned about what will happen to their grandchildren. They maintain contact with the children regularly and have expressed a strong desire to take permanent custody of the children. Christine considers this alternative an ideal fit and wonders why it was not the initial placement for the children. She consults with the worker who, instead, made the decision to place the children with a distant relative and learns that the conditions of the elder Hancock home were not suitable for the children. Christine contacts Mr. and Mrs. Hancock and arranges a home visit to assess what resources might help them to bring the home up to the standard necessary for placement of the grandchildren with their maternal grandparents. Christine is fairly confident that she will be able to access resources and feels that the previous assessment may have been exaggerated due to the urgent need for a placement. Although Christine is familiar with the very rural areas of the tribal community, she must drive around for some time, searching in vain for the home of the elder Hancocks. Along the way, she even stops at a home in an attempt to secure directions. The residents of that home offer her helpful instructions. Eventually she is able to locate the correct vicinity and drives to a very remote area where she finds what appears to be a shed. She is apprehensive but notices an old car and decides to ask for further direction in locating the family. She approaches a makeshift shed made of what appears to be plywood with a tarp overlapping the top layer of plywood.

As she walks up to the shed, Mr. Hancock emerges and thanks her for coming. Christine is a little confused as she has been in many marginal, make-shift homes, but the dilapidated structure before her did not even appear to qualify as a "shed," much less a home. She enters through the front and quickly realizes that this is indeed their home. Inside the very small area, there is a large rug covering the plywood floor, a couch and a small dining table for two. She notices a sheet that is hanging from the ceiling that divides the home into two parts. Mrs. Hancock greets her and asks her if she would like something to drink. Christine is cautious and tries to mask her surprise at the living conditions. She accepts the offer, and Mrs. Hancock brings her a glass of water she got from a large Igloo water container. Mrs. Hancock explains that they get their drinking water from a neighbor since they do not have running water. Christine is relying on her foundational skills she learned during her Interviewing Skills class and can actually hear the voice of her instructor, Dr. Green, explaining how to handle situations like this and how to maintain nonverbal communication.

Mr. and Mrs. Hancock appear somewhat anxious about the visit and initially only respond to her open-ended questions with very brief responses. Christine begins to realize that English is the second language for the Hancock's and that she, unfortunately, is not well-versed in their native tongue. She also realizes she will need to take another approach with this family if she hopes to gain their trust in her efforts to help them gain custody of their grandchildren. She refocuses her efforts and places more emphasis on building rapport. She decides to do this by mentioning that she stopped at the tire shop to get gas on the way. She recalls how she used to stop by there on Saturdays with her grandfather when she was a little girl and how it still looks about the same as it did then. Mr. Hancock asks who her grandfather is. Christine understands the fine line of disclosure and knows that in order to develop a working relationship and establish rapport with the Hancock family, a little self-disclosure will be beneficial in this situation. Christine is not what would be considered "identifiably" Native American. She has some of the features but is one-quarter Native American and three-quarters Caucasian. The Hancocks—Bill, Lisa, and Lucy—are full-blood Native American. She explains that her grandfather lives on the other side of the creek and her family name is Beaver. Mrs. Hancock asks if she is the daughter of Johnna? "Yes," she replies. Mrs. Hancock states that she knew of Johnna and knew that she had lived nearby until she passed away. Christine is curious to hear memories of her mother but remains focused on her immediate responsibility of assisting the family.

Mr. and Mrs. Hancock tell Christine they know their home is not sufficient but feel strongly that having their grandchildren with them is what they believe is best for them. Their home is situated on five acres of land that they purchased, after many years of saving money, with the intention of utilizing tribal resources to have a home built. The grandparents have no desire or means to relocate as they own the property and need to maintain possession of it in order to be eligible for assistance for home ownership through their tribe. The waiting list, however, is rather long. During the course of several meetings with the Hancocks, Christine presents several options in terms of relocating. They are adamant, however, that they do not want to live in Section 8 housing and do not want to give up the only thing they own and the opportunity to eventually have their own "real" home. Mr. Hancock states, "I have worked my whole life for that land and I want to have something to show for it, but I need to know my grandkids are taken care of. We raised our kids in what you call an unfit home and, aside from Lucy, everyone is just fine, this is how we live."

Mrs. Hancock tells Christine that they sought assistance "some time ago" at the county Department of Human Services to help with clothing and food for their own children when they were younger; however, they did not fully understand the process because English is not their first language. They report feeling "humiliated" at having to ask for assistance in the first place and that it was just worsened when they inquired as to what some of the words on the form meant. They were told that no one in the agency spoke their language so the Hancock family would have to find someone to bring with them to help them translate the documents. Mrs. Hancock recalls Mr. Hancock saying there was no way he was going to ask the only bilingual elder they knew to come to the welfare office as they already felt ashamed of their situation and having to ask for assistance. "So that was the end of that—and we managed. We either did without or made do with what we had," Mrs. Hancock says. Christine knows that she must comply with the ICWA; she also knows that the safety of placement is vital to helping the family. The children desperately want to be with their grandparents. Their current placement meets the housing standards, but the relative is not able to keep the children any longer. Christine has a list of ICWA compliant foster homes; however, none has the availability to take all three children together.

In considering the ICWA and what would be in the best interest of the children in custody, Christine has determined that placement with the maternal grandparents is the best permanency plan for the children. She consults with her supervisor and everyone agrees that this would be the best placement; however, they are also in agreement that the home is not in livable condition for the children. Christine has several obligations. The first is to comply with the mandates of the ICWA, and the second is to act in the best interest of the children in custody. Lastly, she must adhere to the clients' right to self-determination.

Christine's determination and use of formal and informal resources were significant in her work with the Hancock family. She had no doubt that keeping the children together and with their maternal grandparents was in the best interest of the children. Not only was this option in accord with the ICWA, it was also a permanent plan that kept the siblings and family together. She had attempted on several occasions to reach out to the paternal grandparents to determine whether they had changed their minds about involving themselves in the lives of their grandchildren, but those attempts proved unsuccessful. Adequate housing remained her primary obstacle. Thus, she reached out to the tribal housing department. Representatives from the tribal housing agency again indicated that the waiting list was very long and that it would take "a couple of years" before Mr. and Mrs. Hancock qualified for tribal construction. Because of their lack of steady income, they would not qualify for any tribal home loans.

Christine did, fortunately, have a strong working relationship with the other departments in her tribe, which drew upon her earlier employment as well as from personal connections she had made through tribal gatherings and events outside of work. That relationship enabled her to connect with another resource that offered small loans to tribal members with very low incomes. In addition, she was fully aware of the informal practices that obtain in her tribal community; that knowledge allowed her to present Mr. and Mrs. Hancock with an idea that might improve their conditions and help them to gain custody of their grandchildren.

With the approval of Mr. and Mrs. Hancock, Christine set her plan into motion. She located a bilingual worker in the tribe to assist Mrs. Hancock in beginning the process of applying for Social Security benefits for her grandchildren. Mrs. Hancock agreed that she would be willing to go back to the Department of Human Services if she had someone that would help explain what she did not understand.

This would provide a more stable income; however, housing was the main barrier. Christine explained to Mr. and Mrs. Hancock that they could work with the tribal loan agency and use the land they currently own as collateral to purchase materials. She assured them that the loan was low-risk and worked on a budgeting plan that both Mr. and Mrs. Hancock felt was feasible for them. The Hancocks seemed apprehensive but said they trusted Christine because they believed she would not mislead them into signing up for something that would cause them to lose the land they had worked so hard for.

Altogether, the Hancocks seemed to be empowered by the intervention plan: it offered them a good chance of keeping their land and taking care of their grandchildren. Mr. Hancock reached out to his construction coworkers and shared his situation. He explained to them that he would qualify for a loan to construct a small home on their land; however, such a loan would only cover the basic costs for materials. His coworkers and tribal community responded to his plea; over the course of four weekends, they worked nonstop and were able to build a very small but suitable structure that met the criteria for placement of the grandchildren. The tribal housing director approached the local lumberyard and some of the building contractors in town he knew from their professional relationships. He was able to get windows, leftover carpet and tile, and other basic materials donated to assist this family. In addition, many members of their small community came together to donate bunk beds, bedding, and other items to help the Hancock family provide a safe and permanent placement for Kimberly, Junior, and Susan.

Christine was able to utilize her culturally-informed social capital, based upon her knowledge of the tribal community and, by extension, the local community, to assist the Hancock family. Due to her access to resources, her relationships, and determination, she was able to reunite the children with their maternal grandparents without compromising Mr. and Mrs. Hancock's lifetime of hard work.

### Practice Application

Christine, the social worker with this family, uses many micro and macro skills to help the family to care for their grandchildren and mitigate further trauma for the children in the family. First, she checks her ethics with her supervisor making sure not to have a dual relationship or cross boundaries with this family. Second, she conducts an assessment of the needs of the children and the capability and desire of not only the grandparents but the tribe. She determines what seems to be the best interest of everyone involved. Next, she uses her social capital in the community to advocate for her clients by helping them to get a loan and then empowers the family to use their informal resources to help them to build and furnish a small but sound structure in which to raise the grandchildren. Many grandparents are raising their grandchildren because their own children are involved with the judicial or mental health systems. By using her own strengths and those of her clients, Christine was able to help this family to be reunited and to continue their filial and tribal bonds.

## DISCUSSION QUESTIONS

1. Consider the significance of social capital and established cultural connections between the worker and her tribe. Within that frame, what do you think may have been the most beneficial actions for helping the family reach their goals of establishing permanency and addressing the issue of substandard housing?
2. What other formal resources might have been beneficial in this situation?
3. How did informal resources of the tribal and local community assist Christine in providing permanency for the children?
4. The probation officer in the vignette utilized social media to "track down" Ms. Lucy Hancock. What social work ethical considerations can you identify in using social media during investigations?
5. How might you build a "strong, working relationship" in a rural context?
6. How might your approach in building a strong, working relationship differ when working with Native American communities?
7. To what extent is personal disclosure appropriate in a rural context? What are some of the costs/benefits associated with self-disclosure?

## LEARNING ACTIVITIES

1. Exploring Social Networks and Social Capital in Tribal Contexts
   a. Initiate a discussion of social networks and social capital in tribes. How might you utilize established connections within the tribe to help form a network to accomplish permanency goals for this family? What avenues, within the tribe, would be advantageous in assisting you in brokering for the family?

2. Community Resources
   a. Ask participants to identify resources in their own communities that might assist the grandparents. What are some of the barriers you may face in allocating resources for the maternal grandparents in this tribe?
3. Building Partnerships
   a. Discuss the ways that state DCS units can form coalitions or partnerships with tribes. How might you approach tribal stakeholders in the quest for placing the children with the maternal grandparents? Would non-Native allies in the community be useful in this situation? If so, who and how?

## SUGGESTED READINGS

National Congress of American Indians. (n.d.). *Tribal nations and the United States: An introduction*. Retrieved from http://www.ncai.org/about-tribes
National Indian Child Welfare Association. (n.d.). *Foster care and adoption*. Available at https://www.nicwa.org/foster-care-adoption
Weaver, H. N. (1999). Indigenous people and the social work profession: Defining culturally competent services. *Social Work, 44*, 217–225. doi:10.1093/sw/44.3.217

## REFERENCES

Belanger, K., & Stone, W. (2008). The social service divide: Service availability and accessibility in rural versus urban counties and impact on child welfare outcomes. *Child Welfare, 87*, 1–124.
Brooks, K. (2007). Social capital: Analysing the effect of a political perspective on the perceived role of government in community prosperity. *Rural Society, 17*, 231–247. doi:10.5172/rsj.351.17.3.231
Children's Bureau. (2013, September). *A roadmap for collaborative evaluation in tribal communities*. Retrieved from www.nicwa.org
Crofts, P., & Begg, P. (2007). Defying the odds: Enterprising social work practice in a rural employment project. *Rural Society, 17*, 331–347. doi:10.5172/rsj.351.17.3.331
Giorgas, D. (2007). The significance of social capital for rural and regional communities. *Rural Society, 17*, 206–214. doi:10.5172/rsj.351.17.3.206
Kahn, S. R., Rifaqat, Z., & Kazmi, S. (2007). *Harnessing and guiding social capital for rural development*. New York, NY: Palgrave Macmillan.
Kilpatrick, S., & Abbott-Chapman, J. (2007). Modelling how communities deliver outcomes for members. In M. Osborn, K. Sankey, & B. Wilson (Eds.), *Social Capital, Lifelong Learning and the Managment of Place: An International Perspective*. New York, N.Y.: Routledge.
Krivoikapic-Skoka, B. (2007). Negative social capital and conflicts: Asian entrepreneurs in New Zealand agriculture (1870s to 1920s). *Rural Society, 17*, 286–298. doi:10.5172/rsj.351.17.3.286
National Congress of American Indians, (n.d.). *Tribal nations and the United States: An introduction*. Retrieved from http://www.ncai.org/about-tribes
Weaver, H. N. (1999). Indigenous people and the social work profession: Defining culturally competent services. *Social Work, 44*, 217–225. doi:10.1093/sw/44.3.217

# CHAPTER 11

∽

# Providing Services to Children
# of Recent Military Veterans

## ANDREA KEPHART

## LEARNING OBJECTIVES

- Explore the effect of war on the veteran and that person's family
- Discuss the trauma response of the child and the parent in the chapter vignette
- Describe the role of each social worker (agency and child protection services) in helping families to successfully negotiate a case plan

As the wars in Iraq and Afghanistan come to a close, the returning veterans will surely face many challenges integrating back into a civilian population. In order to prepare for the influx of service members requiring mental health services as well as social services, social workers should prepare themselves for the challenges that this population may face by learning about the major issues faced by veterans during war and as part of the reintegration process.

Traumatic brain injury (TBI) and posttraumatic stress disorder (PTSD) are considered the "signature wounds" of these wars. In the context, the widespread use of improvised explosive devices (IEDs) as agents of warfare has occasioned many concussive injuries. As there is a spectrum of brain injuries spanning from minor to major, the impact of these injuries may also vary. Understanding the symptoms and repercussions of these injuries will prepare social workers for the varied reactions and situations they may encounter when working with this population. Veterans with TBI may experience headaches, mood instability, memory lapses, impulsive behaviors, difficulty concentrating, and difficulties with their speech. Some veterans have such severe TBI that they will require care-assistance for the rest of their lives. Some veterans also experience PTSD as a result of the trauma of war. PTSD also affects mood, creates trust issues, results in hypervigilance and the re-experiencing of traumatic events, and blocks the experience of positive emotions that can potentially create a pattern of self-destructive behaviors.

There is a disproportionate representation of minorities and rural service members in the military (Heady 2007, 2011). Service members from rural areas are more likely to preserve their family and communal ties, which may mean they will return to the rural areas for support and familiarity after the completion of their service (Heady, 2011). Social workers who encounter veterans will need a working knowledge of the military culture. For example, they need to understand that veterans may be facing many real contemporary challenges as a result of their previous service experiences.

Military children often have unique life experiences that include dealing with long and frequent deployments (Park, 2011). While military children appear to be resilient, the challenges they face can impact their mental and physical health (Chandra, Burns, Tanielian, Jaycox & Scott 2008; Flake, Davis, Johnson, & Middleton, 2009; Park, 2011). The effects on the mental health of military children are evidenced by the doubling in the number of military children seeking mental health services since the beginning of the war in Iraq (Hefling, 2009). Some factors that may elevate the need for psychological intervention may include a family history of mental issues, younger families, longer deployments, more frequent deployments, and fewer coping mechanisms utilized by the nondeployed spouse or partner (Park, 2011). A protective factor for some of the stress is close military unit affiliation, but this phenomenon can be negated for some families whose service member has served in the National Guard or Reserve Units (Shepard, Maltras, & Israel, 2010). Reserve unit families are at a higher risk for stress than their active duty counterparts. Military resources for these units are less than for active duty soldiers.

Shepard, Maltras, and Israel (2010) found that child maltreatment and neglect increases significantly during a deployment. During parental deployment, a child in a military family is often expected to take on additional responsibilities in order to help the family (Park, 2011). In light of these additional stressors and the increased possibility of maltreatment of military children at such times, social workers who work with these children may require additional insight into the challenges this population faces.

## CASE VIGNETTE

Arthur Brown first met his social worker when he applied for financial and housing help through an agency that assists veteran in a rural southern state. In trying to assess the nature and extent of his need, the social worker discovered that Arthur, a 35-year-old African American male, is a medically retired Army veteran and single father of three young children: Ali, age eight; Anisha, age six; and Anna, age four. While deployed to Iraq, he sustained a TBI when he was involved in an IED explosion; two of his fellow soldiers were killed when this incident occurred. While Arthur was recovering at an Army hospital, his wife confessed to him that she had been having an affair during his deployment and that she intended to leave him when he came home. She also stated that she felt she had spent "enough time as a single parent" while he was in the Army and did not want to pursue custody of the children.

Arthur spent some time in the Warrior Transition Unit (WTU). This unit provides teamwork and chain of command that is familiar to soldiers, while holding a primary mission of recovery. The WTU operates as a regular military unit with exceptions, as it includes a civilian case manager, primary-care physicians, and nurses. One objective of the unit staff is to ensure that soldiers attend their health and recovery appointments. Arthur was going through the Medical Evaluation Board to find out if he would be designated as fit for duty, medically retired, or medically discharged. The difference between a medical discharge and retirement is that the latter allows service members to keep all of their benefits, including health insurance for the service member and family.

Arthur soon found himself separated from the military and his wife. He decided that his best chance of successfully raising his children was to move back to his rural hometown where he believed he would have the support of his family. With some help from his mother, he registered the children for school and tried to begin a normal life. Arthur, however, described beginning to feel overwhelmed even in his small town, finding that he often felt isolated with no one to discuss the things he had been through. He had nightmares every night, lacked trust in others, felt that he had to know an exit strategy for every situation, and often had trouble maintaining the speed limit because he believed that driving at indicated speeds would subject him to IEDs hidden along his rural routes. He struggled to manage the children's schedule, as well as deal with his injuries. He said that he tried to explain his struggles to his family, but they did not seem to understand his mood swings, memory issues, and the financial stress of having three children and little opportunity for employment. Arthur said that he loved his children and was committed to being a good father. However, Arthur began to isolate himself and the children in order to avoid having to explain himself to others. He said this was also to avoid the rejection and lack of understanding from his relatives.

One day Anisha's kindergarten teacher called Arthur to discuss his middle daughter's behavior in class. The teacher stated that she had been acting out in a sexual manner in class. Specifically, she was drawing explicit pictures of body parts and writing inappropriate words on the walls in the bathroom. The teacher also stated that Anisha was showing the other children how she was "touched" by someone. The school social worker notified child protective services (CPS). The investigators began by scrutinizing Arthur. As a single father, Arthur needed to be excluded as the perpetrator before CPS could move forward. He was cleared after a thorough investigation. Despite his TBI, Arthur acted appropriately and in a fully supportive manner toward his daughter. He told her that he believed her, worked with her on safety and trust issues, and fully complied with the CPS case plan.

As part of the case plan, Arthur took his daughter to a counselor and discovered that while he was deployed, the babysitter had molested two of his three children: Anisha and Anna. Arthur discovered that the babysitter had not only touched the children but also took pictures of them in various sexual positions with each other. The children described that the events happened when Arthur was deployed, a fact that CPS verified with the Army. Arthur did, however, have to live with the fact that he felt he had not protected his children while he was away serving his nation, that his children had been victimized. Arthur understandably felt betrayed and mistrustful of people and systems. At times, Arthur did not have the mental capacity to negotiate the issues he needed to address. He often forgot appointment times and was clearly overwhelmed when dealing with the caseworkers, legal system, and school administrators.

The veteran agency social worker, Rasheeda Brooks, helped Arthur in many ways. The major impact was that she helped him to access numerous assistance systems necessary for him and his children. She introduced him to systematized ways of keeping track of appointments and offered continued support as Arthur negotiated his way through legal, CPS, and school systems.

The challenges he faced were vast. In a rural area without a military base close by, and with little support, the social worker assisted Arthur with finding adequate evidence-based trauma counseling for the children that would also take his military insurance. He also needed to access counseling himself, as he felt betrayed by his wife and the babysitter. At the same time, he lived with survivor's guilt (his fellow soldiers had died while he lived) and also exhibited some symptoms of PTSD. While the CPS social worker was able to locate counseling for the children, the co-pay for services was $25 dollars per child. This may not seem like an enormous amount, but Arthur was on a fixed income. Working together with the CPS worker, the agency social worker assisted with the primary objective of helping this family secure adequate financial resources for the costs associated with counseling and getting Arthur into a counseling setting he could relate to and would attend. Military veterans often have the sense that those who are not associated with the military cannot truly understand the struggles that veterans face once they return from combat. That belief does not imply a critique of civilians or civilian services, but it does underscore the importance veterans attach to those who have lived and shared the military culture. Military services would have provided the most immediate relief, but Arthur and his family lived too far away from the services they needed. The agency was able to locate financial assistance through several nonprofits set up to assist wounded veterans. The agency also offered counseling services for Arthur at a mobile vet center that travels to rural areas to engage veterans who may not have access to the veteran center.

Arthur was able to engage in counseling services, which enabled him to cope with the symptoms of PTSD. The social worker continued to work with him to learn to use checklists and a daily schedule to make sure he and the children made it to their counseling and medical appointments. Arthur was able to receive job retraining through the Department of Vocational Rehabilitation, which took his TBI disability into account. He now works at a local chicken processing plant and is described by his supervisor as a "good worker." Arthur continues to do well with his children who are learning to cope with the aftermath of the abandonment of their mother and their molestation. The therapist for the children stated that she believes that Arthur's support of the children helped to ameliorate some of the trauma effects of their molestation. The children are doing better in school. Arthur and his family still require the support they receive from Arthur's mother as he continues to suffer from some cognitive impairment as a result of the TBI. She assists with some parenting and after-school care and helps Arthur to manage his finances.

## Practice Application

In the case of Arthur and his children, the social worker used brokering, coordination, and advocacy skills to make sure that Arthur got what he needed in order to be able to care for his children. Knowing that members of this family were not only physically and psychologically traumatized by war but also by child maltreatment, the worker had to use her trauma lens to elucidate the strengths of this father, teach him new skills, and assist him to be able to parent his traumatized children. Living in a very rural southern town meant the worker also had to find veterans resources as close as possible to them since her client had a TBI and had transportation concerns. Every member of this family endured some sort of trauma. The social worker helped Arthur and his children stay together.

## DISCUSSION QUESTIONS

1. What was the impact of the veteran assistance agency on the outcomes for this family?
2. Discuss the possibility of using formal and informal resources with this family. What are your suggestions for engaging the community on behalf of this family?
3. How can having military health insurance help and hinder the care received by a military family?
4. If you were working with the daughter, what sorts of information might you need to elicit? What are some evidence-based treatments available for her?
5. How might you intervene with the family unit with regard to the abandonment by the wife/mother in the family?
6. What is the impact of trauma on all members of the family? What forms of trauma exist?
7. How might trauma experiences affect the trajectory of this family's functioning?

## LEARNING ACTIVITIES

1. Research Child Abuse and Parent Attitude
   a. Provide an opportunity for participants to research the effects of parental attitude toward the molestation and the child's veracity on the mediation of the effects of molestation.

2. Discuss Developmental Expectations and Sexual Behaviors
   a. Facilitate a discussion of the typical development of preschool and young school-age children. What is to be expected with regard to sexual knowledge, and why was the teacher right to be worried?
3. Active Military and Veteran Resources
   a. Explore the differences between services for active military personnel and their families and those of veterans.

## SUGGESTED READING

National Institute of Neurological Disorders and Stroke (TBI): http://www.ninds.nih.gov/disorders/tbi/tbi.htm

Veteran and military family resources: http://www.samhsa.gov/veterans-military-families

Working with military families: https://www.childwelfare.gov/search/?q=military+families

## REFERENCES

Chandra, A., Burns, R. M., Tanielian, T., Jaycox, L. H., & Scott, M. M. (2008, April). *Understanding the impact of deployment on children and families: Findings from a pilot study of Operation Purple Camp participants.* National Military Family Association and RAND Health. Retrieved from http://www.rand.org/pubs/working_papers/WR566.html

Flake, E. M., Davis, B. E., Johnson, P. L., & Middleton, L. S. (2009). The psychosocial effects of deployment on military children. *Journal of Developmental & Behavioral Pediatrics, 30*(4), 271–278. doi:10.1097/DBP.0b013e3181aac6e4

Heady, H. R. (2007). *Rural veterans: A special concern for rural health advocates.* National Rural Health Association (Issue Paper). Retrieved from https://www.rural-healthweb.org/getattachment/Advocate/Policy-Documents/Archive-(ME)-(1)/0207Veterans.pdf.aspx?lang=en-US

Heady, H. R. (2011). Rural veterans: Invisible heroes, special people, special issues. *Journal of Rural Social Sciences, 26*(3), 1–13.

Hefling, K. (2009). More military children seeking mental care. *Marine Corps Times.* Springfield, VA: Army Times Publishing Company.

Park, N. (2011). Military children and families: Strengths and challenges during peace and war. *American Psychologist, 66*(1), 65–72. doi: 10.1037/a002124.

Sheppard, S. C., Malatras, J. W., & Israel, A. C. (2010). The impact of deployment on US military families. *American Psychologist, 65*(6), 599–609. doi:10.1037/a0020332

# CHAPTER 12

༓

# Domestic Violence Postdeployment

## The Case of the Martin Family

STEVEN M. HYER

## LEARNING OBJECTIVES

- Discuss a military response to domestic violence
- Research military resources for domestic violence
- Assess the impact of domestic violence trauma on a school-aged child
- Identify rural resources for military families

## MILITARY FAMILY SOCIAL WORK AND CHILD WELFARE

Military families cope with many stressors, chief among them are the numerous and long-term separations because of training and deployment. Each branch of the US military has social workers who help families cope with these stressors. In the US Air Force, family advocacy officers function in that capacity (Rubin, Weiss, & Coll, 2012).

A family advocacy officer is typically a uniformed military social worker who has the responsibility of providing clinical and administrative oversight of the Family Advocacy Program (FAP). FAP is a program created by the Department of Defense to prevent and intervene in all forms of maltreatment involving service members and their families. The family advocacy officer, along with other civilian licensed clinical social workers, conduct risk assessments for all known instances of maltreatment, which includes clinical interviews with each member of a family, not just the family members involved in an incident. Based upon the risk assessment, a safety plan is made with the family to prevent further maltreatment. This safety plan may include a military protection order (or a no-contact order) that would prevent the service member from contacting the alleged victim.

The family advocacy officer then takes the safety planning recommendations and requests assistance from the service member's chain of command in enforcing the safety plan. This phase of remediation may include having the service member vacate that individual's residence for a time, issuing a no-contact order, or providing other assistance from the member's unit. It is vital for the family advocacy officer to have a good working relationship with the service member's unit leadership as the latter can provide additional insight into the health and well-being of that service member and his or her family.

The family advocacy officer uses a number of evaluation components: the risk assessment of the family; collateral information gained from the military unit; the law enforcement report of the incident, along with photos (if applicable) in order to present the facts of an incident of family maltreatment to the Case Review Committee. This committee is an administrative board that, on a monthly basis, reviews all incidents of family maltreatment involving service members assigned to the installation. The board is composed of the family advocacy officer, law enforcement personnel, a military attorney, and members of the installation leadership to determine whether, based on the facts of the incident, that incident meets the standard necessary to be considered maltreatment based on research-based definitions of adult partner and/or child maltreatment. This board is an administrative forum only and runs independent of any military or civilian criminal proceedings connected with the case. It allows the military to make standardized and consistent determinations of those incidents that actually constitute maltreatment and to provide a launching point for the family to engage in intervention services with the FAP.

If the committee deems that the service member's incident constitutes maltreatment, then that individual is recommended to engage in treatment with FAP in order to resolve whatever conditions led to the current incident of family violence as well as to reduce any future risk of violence. Service members are never mandated into treatment by FAP, although the family advocacy officer may recommend that the unit commander order the member to participate in treatment if the risk for future violence is high. FAP has no authority over civilians to participate in treatment whether they are living on or off the installation. Civilians may be court-ordered to treatment, but a civilian judge would have to order such offenders to a civilian treatment provider.

FAP is the primary provider of all intervention services for family maltreatment. Intervention services provided by FAP may include individual, couples, or group therapy. Group therapy is generally provided in a single-gender format; similar to a batterer intervention program. However, FAP would generally not recommend a maltreatment offender to attend for 52 weeks due to the length of treatment. While the appropriate interventions and behavioral changes by the offender need sufficient time to take place, service members are also expected to maintain mission readiness to fulfill military duties on a moment's notice anywhere around the world. One full year of a service member's involvement in any behavioral health treatment may in the eyes of chain of command label that individual unfit for continued military service. Thus, treatment goals that can be accomplished using interventions over a shorter period of time (e.g., six months) are preferred in military settings.

If the service member needs mental health treatment and/or substance abuse treatment, in conjunction with a family violence intervention plan, these services would be available and integrated into the treatment plan. In addition, all family members may receive intervention both on and off the installation necessary to help their needs and accomplish treatment goals. If the offender is a civilian intimate partner or spouse of the service member, that person may receive individual therapy in FAP or be referred off the installation for treatment.

The ultimate goal of FAP intervention is to resolve current family maltreatment and reduce future maltreatment risk. Cases in FAP are closed as resolved if the alleged offender (military or civilian) completes the recommended goals in the treatment plan. Although it is not necessary for victims in maltreatment incidents to complete their intervention plan for cases to close as resolved, victims will generally also complete their treatment plans as well.

## COMMUNITY SOCIAL WORKER INVOLVEMENT

Civilian social workers working in the community can have many different opportunities to work with military families dealing with maltreatment. The most common role would be working in child protection services (CPS) for the state (Gibbs, Martin, Clinton-Sherrod, Walters, & Johnson, 2011).

CPS takes the assessment lead in all instances of child maltreatment involving military children and families. CPS social workers interview children on or off military installations to determine the nature of the allegation and assess risk. Occasionally these interviews are done in collaboration with FAP social workers. Once an initial risk assessment is complete, CPS coordinates safety planning with FAP and military leadership to ensure all family members are kept safe from future maltreatment. CPS social workers regularly communicate with the FAP social worker assigned to a maltreatment case and may be invited to FAP case-staffing meetings to discuss mutual cases.

School social workers may also have frequent contact with children from military families (School Social Work Association of American, n.d.). They can help children adjust to the frequent relocations associated with permanent change of stations of their service-member parent. They can assist the children to cope with family separations due to a parent's deployment, which can often last one year or longer (Lester et al., 2010). Similarly, they can help children find ways to develop a current social support network despite being "the new kid" in school who appears during the middle of the school year.

## CASE VIGNETTE

The family advocacy officer (a social worker) on a rural Texas Air Force base was assigned to an incident of intimate partner violence on the base involving Jacob Martin. Jacob was arrested for punching and restraining his wife during an argument. According to the police report, their 14-year-old daughter Megan tried to get Jacob to release her mother, but Jacob pushed her to the ground and threatened to kill her if she ever tried to break up their fight again. Their 10-year-old son Benjamin was hiding in his bedroom but reportedly heard the entire incident. Prior to the incident, Jacob's wife had stated she was moving with their two children to where her parents lived in rural Kentucky and that she wanted a divorce. Jacob had been drinking during the argument.

Jacob had returned from deployment to Afghanistan about one year prior to the incident. This was his third deployment as a member of Security Forces for the deployed installation. His job while deployed was to provide airfield and runway security. During his most recent deployment, he witnessed multiple incidents of incoming mortar and rocket attacks that injured and killed fellow service members as well as local civilians. In addition, he experienced traumatic brain injury from two different vehicle-borne improvised explosive devices that exploded near the gates of the installation. Although he continued to perform Security Forces duties during his first two deployments, Jacob denied any traumatic incidents as he provided security at installations that were relatively free of enemy attacks.

Jacob had difficulty falling asleep within the first few weeks upon his return home. During this same interval and for several months, Jacob began drinking larger quantities of alcohol, which, he claimed, helped him fall asleep. This pattern quickly progressed so that he consumed enough alcohol to "pass out" on his days off from work. Approximately six months after returning home, he began having nightmares about one to two times per week about his deployments. He would wake up from his nightmares screaming and shouting to take cover or giving orders for incoming vehicles to stop. One particular incident that frightened his wife had her waking up to find her husband on top of her in order to restrain her; he ordered that she not move or he would fire upon her.

As time passed, Jacob's wife would tell him that he needed to cut back on his drinking as this was not usual for him. She also commented that he spent too much time watching sports and rarely played video games with their son or helped their daughter with school projects. These comments usually led to verbal arguments. During them, Jacob occasionally shoved his wife, particularly when she confronted him about his drinking. For two months, his wife told him he needed to go talk to someone at the mental health clinic, but he refused, claiming that he was "doing fine." Moreover, he argued, "people who go to mental health get kicked out of the Air Force." Based upon Jacob's dramatic changes in behavior and his refusal to get help, his wife decided to leave him and take their two children to her parents. That episode resulted in the most recent argument and incident. With the assistance of the family advocacy officer, Jacob's wife Jennifer did go to stay with her parents in rural Kentucky and took the children with her. Both children have had a difficult time transitioning in their new school.

A school social worker has been assigned to help the youngest child, Benjamin. During the course of assessment, Benjamin discloses that his dad (Jacob Martin) "hasn't been the same" since this most recent deployment. Benjamin says that he is "always mad about something" and "will blow up over little things." He recounts a time just a few months ago when he left his remote-control car in the yard after his dad had told him to put it away following dinner. When Benjamin went to his room after dinner to play on his iPad and had not taken care of the car, his father burst through the door and screamed at him. He threatened him that if he did not go pick up his car right now, then he would get his gun and use the car for target practice. Then he grabbed Benjamin by the arm, picked him up off his bed, and threw him into the hallway. Benjamin said he went and got the car from the yard and came back to his room. He said he cried the rest of the night.

Benjamin says that his mother told him things were going to get better once his dad got home, but "they haven't for me." Benjamin was already behind in school and is barely meeting minimum fourth-grade standards at his new rural Kentucky school. Benjamin finds that ever since the night of the incident, he is "always scared." He has had trouble sleeping and "can't make any friends" because he says that no one will talk to him. His teacher reported that Benjamin frequently seems tired during the school day and recently missed turning in a science project. Benjamin says that he is worried that his parents will get a divorce, that he will not see his father again for a long time, and that his father will get kicked out of the military.

Jennifer Martin has a high school education and has not been able to find a job in their small community. After speaking with Jennifer, the social worker informs her that they would still qualify for healthcare at the Army post, which is a 45-minute drive from their town. Service members on active duty and their family members qualify for medical services at military installation medical treatment facilities (MTFs) regardless of where they are stationed. Service members in the Guard or Reserve, however, have stricter guidelines about where and when they can receive medical treatment at a MTF.

After calling the FAP at the Army post, the family advocacy officer, Captain Stiller tells the social worker about a local pediatrician that accepts military health insurance. He also says that there is a therapist nearby who has experience working with military children. Captain Stiller says that Jacob Martin was involved in batterers' treatment at their previous base and that he just started cognitive processing therapy for his new diagnosis of PTSD. Jacob is still not able to "arm up" in his Security Forces job and has been assigned to administrative duties in the unit. He is concerned that he might be facing jail time depending on the outcome of his court martial trial next month. Domestic violence can be considered cause for court martial.

## Practice Application

Most military bases in the United States are located in or near rural communities. These bases provide housing for many soldiers, sailors, marines, and airmen and their families, including children. Child welfare workers in these rural communities where bases are located frequently must provide services on bases in order to complete investigations or offer services. It is important for these workers to understand how to interface with the military family advocacy officers (social workers) in order to provide the best care possible for the family and to assist the military to keep a ready and mentally healthy force. In many instances, the military can provide good resources such as domestic violence assistance for the family. In the case of this family, the child welfare, mental health, and military social workers coordinated efforts to help all members of the family. Depending on the outcome of the court martial in this case, the coordination might include increasing the safety perimeter for the family as Jacob might become violent again if he loses his military career. Using the strengths of all levels of intervention, micro, meso, and macro, and by using relationship building, the child welfare worker can help these military children and their mother try to be safer. At the same time, their father can get help to become sober and stop incidents of explosive rage. If the children and mother are safe and the father is no longer drinking and raging, there may, indeed, be hope for this family.

## DISCUSSION QUESTIONS

1. What potential interventions are needed for Benjamin at this time?
2. What might be some of Benjamin's strengths?
3. Say you are the social worker for Benjamin. How could Benjamin inform you about the functioning of the other family members, especially his older sister Megan?
4. Based on the information Benjamin tells you, should you file a suspected child maltreatment report with your state's child protection team?
5. Discuss the potential impact of this family's move to rural Kentucky. What sorts of services might there be? What sorts of supports?
6. Discuss the possible array of both civilian and military community services that can assist this family. Consider rural areas with, and without, a nearby military base.

## LEARNING ACTIVITIES

1. Military and Civilian Social Worker Role Play
   a. Role play phone calls or other interactions between military and civilian social workers. Discuss tasks and roles of each professional involved. Discuss how organizational and community structures might impact the communication.

2. Filing a Child Protective Services Complaint
   a. Role play a reporting phone call to CPS in a rural village. What information is necessary? Discuss the relative merits of reporting anonymously versus reporting with the full knowledge of the family involved. If time permits, have learners fill out a form to report the information using only observational and likely factual content.
3. Research Family Violence Resources for Military Families
   a. Have learners research the family violence resources at www.militaryonesource.mil
4. Course Assignment: Assessment Paper
   a. Have participants perform an assessment of Benjamin in his family and community settings. What is his diagnosis? What are the biopsychosocial considerations? Then, have them construct a genogram, ecomap, and case plan for him. Be sure to include the youth and his family in the case plan formulation.

## SUGGESTED READING

General military resources: www.militaryonesource.mil

## REFERENCES

Gibbs, D. A., Martin, S. L., Clinton-Sherrod, M., Walters, J. L. H., & Johnson, R. E. (2011, May). *Child maltreatment within military families* (Report No. RB-0002-1105). Research Triangle Park: NC: RTI Press. doi:10.3768/rtipress.2011. rb.0002.1105

Lester, P., Peterson, K., Reeves, J., Knauss, L., Glover, D., Mogil, C., Duan, N., Beardslee, W. (2010). The long war and parent combat deployments effects on military children and at-home spouses. *Journal of the American Academy of Child and Adolescent Psychiatry, 49,* 310–320. doi:10.1016/j.jaac.2010.01.003

Rubin, A., Weiss, E. L., & Coll, J. E. (2012). *Handbook of military social work.* Hoboken, NJ: Wiley.

School Social Work Association of America. (n.d.). *Resources for military families.* Retrieved from http://www.sswaa.org/?page=678

# CHAPTER 13

⬥

# Child Welfare

## *Two Kingdoms Collide*

### SUSIE T. CASHWELL

Amish Country. A friendly goat greets visitors to an Amish country farm. The family makes cheese from goat milk to sell at a local market.
David G. Riebschleger

## LEARNING OBJECTIVES

- Articulate the interaction of faith and child welfare services
- Apply social capital theory to case interventions
- Demonstrate ecological theory as it relates to case assessment

## BACKGROUND INFORMATION ON AMISH COMMUNITIES

This chapter explores a unique subculture of America that is entirely located in rural areas. The Amish are a religious sect found primarily in Pennsylvania, Ohio, and Indiana, though there are over 500 settlements across 31 states with over 300,000 Amish individuals. Of these 380,000 over 60% live in these three states identified (Young Center, n.d.). The Amish speak Pennsylvania Dutch, a language derived from German, Dutch, and English.

The religion itself dates to the Reformation when the Protestant movement split from the Catholic Church. The Amish belonged to the Anabaptist movement but departed from the teachings of the Catholic Church, as well as Martin Luther (Donnermeyer & Friedrich, 2002, Holmes & Block, 2013; Petrovich, 2013). The Amish faith aims to restore an apostolic Christianity missing from the world, and, to that end, the faithful live apart from and, as it were, in defiance to the bustling and familiar that lie just beyond their pale. As is true of many religious sectarians, the Amish have been affected by the ways and practices of the modern world and interpret Scripture rigorously to support their clearly demarcated two-kingdom view: that is, there is God's spiritual kingdom and then there is man's worldly kingdom filled with temptations and corrupting influences. Today, there are old-order Amish, new order Amish, and Amish Mennonites, each with similarities and differences.

The *Ordnung* governs Amish life. *Ordnung* refers to "discipline" and "community." "In sociological terms, the Ordnung consists of the norms by which the baptized members of the Amish live on a daily basis" (Donnermeyer & Friedrich, 2002, p. 9). The Ordnung is adapted by each district and is based on a community's interpretation (Tharpe, 2007). Each member votes on the Ordnung as males and females have equality in the church; however, the Amish still adhere to traditional patriarchal roles. The Ordnung also places restrictions on clothes, technology, community relationships, and relationship with outsiders.

The average American, to be sure, does not easily understand the Amish. Amish people reject many ways of mainstream American culture including the use of technological mainstays such as telephones, electricity, and automobiles. Sometimes they will use a telephone, if an emergency arises, but to do so they travel to the home of an Englisher (non-Amish individual) or use a payphone in the area. More conservative Amish sects reject the use of automobiles outright, though others allow it for travel as long as it has a non-Amish driver. Whereas average number of children in a typical American family ranges from two to three (US Census Bureau, 2012), the average number of children in an Amish family ranges from six to nine (Donnermeyer & Friedrich, 2002; Fischel, 2012; Holbreich et al., 2012).

While mainstream American culture values ambition, capitalism, and individualism, the Amish are governed by the value of Gelassenhelt, which literally means yielding to the will of God with a calm spirit (Fischel, 2012). Individualism is the opposite of Gelassenhelt. In turn, the well-being of the community outweighs the well-being of the individual. Obedience and humility are, therefore, prized. The Amish consider themselves a Plain people with a simple way of life, which separates them from the world. Dolls are made with no faces, jewelry is forbidden, and personal photographs are not allowed.

Part of the two-kingdom worldview entails the separation of church and state. Although the Amish attend school, they do so generally in Amish schools and only for a short time. In *Wisconsin v. Yoder*, 406 U.S. 205, 235-36[1972]), the US Supreme Court ruled that the Amish had a right to end compulsory education after the eighth grade or at the age of 14 (Fischel, 2012). The Amish pay taxes to the government but refuse benefits from the Social Security system or any other governmental system (Holmes & Block, 2013). While the Amish utilize traditional healthcare systems, as religious conscientious objectors they perform no military service.

Two important concepts vital to understanding the Amish and child welfare, as influenced by the two-kingdom worldview, are *Rumspringa* and shunning. Rumspringa is a period when Amish youth between 16 and 18 are allowed to experience the non-Amish world. In that interval, they may indulge in the practices of the worldly kingdom (e.g., drive cars, wear traditional American clothes, and use cell phones). After this trial period is over, it is expected that the teen will either accept the Amish way of life or leave the family.

Shunning is a "systematic isolation from the community, including members from his or her own family" (Fischel, 2012, p. 112). The strictest form of shunning is known as *Streng Meidung*. This level of shunning forbids any member of the church from eating at the same table as the member who has been shunned. Members in good standing can have no interaction at all with the shunned member. If one member of a married couple is shunned, then limited communication may occur between the two spouses. However, they may share a marital bed. If an Amish member commits a crime such as child abuse, members of the Amish community do not report it to the state child welfare agency; instead, the offender is approached by a deacon or bishop and is expected to repent and seek forgiveness, which demands a public confession (Miller, 2007). Once the person confesses and is forgiven, the matter is forgotten; nothing is reported to the authorities. If someone is not repentant or refuses to seek forgiveness, then that person is shunned. In those cases, the matter may or may not be reported.

## CASE VIGNETTE

Caseworker Bryan Smith from the local child welfare protection office responded to a call from the local child abuse hotline about a possible case of sexual abuse. He learned that the child in question, Katie Burkholder, was a 10-year-old Amish girl. Her 18-year-old cousin Ruth Iben, a person no longer a part of the Amish community, had placed the call to the hotline. Ruth reported that Katie told her that she was being raped by two of her maternal uncles, Mark and Joshua Yoder. Ruth revealed to the hotline caseworker that Katie had told her that her mother (Ruth) told Katie that it was probably Katie's own fault that Mark and Joshua would not leave her alone. Her mother reportedly said that all Katie needed to do was to just "pray harder" to get them to stop.

Katie appeared to be an active, healthy child who attended the district one-room schoolhouse. She said she loved to play with her dolls and chase the cats. She seemed bright educationally and enjoyed playing with her schoolmates. She had also reached all of her developmental milestones.

Ruth reported that Katie was not supposed to be talking to her, but they still tried to meet at the vegetable stand once every two weeks. Neither Ruth nor Katie was bound by the ban since Ruth left before entering the church, and Katie had not yet joined the church. The two became close when Ruth babysat Katie when the latter was younger. Katie's parents, nevertheless, forbade her contact with Ruth since Ruth was not a member of the church and could only be, therefore, a bad influence. Katie referred to her meetings with Ruth as "our little secret."

When Bryan went to investigate this allegation and met Katie, she reported that the abusive actions had happened several times. She said the first time was when she was playing with her doll in the barn and her uncle Mark Perry, 23, asked her to take off her dress. She said she told him "no," but he demanded that she respect him because he was an elder of the church. When she complied by taking off her dress, he and his brother Joshua Perry, 17, then removed their pants. According to Katie, Mark "put his finger down there." She pointed to her vaginal region. She also described what could only be construed as her performing oral sex on both men. She told Bryan that Mark put his penis in her while Joshua watched. As a result, she bled from her vagina. Frightened because of what had happened, she told her mother, who grew immediately angry and scolded her for "not praying enough."

During the hotline conversation, Ruth also revealed that the incident had been reported to the bishop. Katie's father Eli Burkholder was a deacon in the district and assisted the bishop with disciplinary actions. After consulting with Mark and Joshua and recommending prayer, Bishop Frank and Deacon Eli instructed them that they needed to repent and seek restoration. Although a deacon is typically the one who reprimands, in this case the bishop handled the matter directly. According to Ruth, Katie reported that even though the young men confessed their transgressions, their bad behavior continued. When meeting with Bryan, Katie implored him, "Please don't tell. I don't want to be put under the ban." She indicated that her parents told her she would be in trouble and the community would shun her if she told again. Although Katie tried to tell her mother again, her mother would not hear of it and was dismissive, saying "What is in the past stays in the past."

Bryan was a child protective services worker in Katie's Ohio County that contained a large Amish population. He understood the community well and knew of the bishop. The bishop had served that district for 20 years and was well respected in the English community. Six months prior to the Katie incident, an English farmer's barn burned and the Amish community, led by the bishop, hosted a barn raising at the farm to help the English family in need. While clear lines separated the Amish from the English in the region, the Amish were regarded as valued member of the community, both for their kindness as well as for the economic gains of the tourism they attracted. Visitors often found great appeal in Amish-owned and -operated stores that sold Amish food and crafts, including quilts and wood furniture. The stores formed a row and were next to each other.

Katie's aunt, Miriam Miller, owned the quilt shop and was the bishop's sister. Katie helped quilt for the store. While she did not regularly go to the store, she could be counted on for one or two days per month. She said she enjoyed going to the shop to play with her cousin. Katie stated they played "chase cats!" Mark and Joshua were skilled furniture craftsmen and worked next door to the quilt shop at the furniture store along with members of Katie's family. As a result, Katie would see them at the store at least once a week.

Most of the children in the area attended the schoolhouse Katie did; that school served Amish and a few English students. Katie's favorite subject was reading. She liked it when they read aloud from Scripture, though she did not like math. She identified several other children as friends—even though all of them were close family members. She reported, "Ruth is my best friend, but she doesn't go to school here anymore."

Around the time Katie reported that Mark and Joshua were "touching" her, Katie began having to see the local doctor several times for a urinary tract infection that did not seem to get better. Other than that, Katie would only see the doctor for her wellness checkups. None of the Amish children received vaccinations, even though the Ordnung did not strictly prohibit them. The Amish families very simply saw no purpose in them.

Bryan visited Katie's family and found out that her parents, Eli and Hannah, had been married for 16 years. They had five children with one on the way. Katie's oldest brother, Jacob, 15, would begin Rumspinga in the fall, but he also declared that he intended to be baptized into the church as soon as possible. He reportedly had no desire to partake in English ways. Katie was the second born, followed by Abram, 8, Ruth, 6, and Sarah, 2.

As with many Amish families, Katie had many relatives. Most of them lived in her small, rural community. A couple of families had moved to other settlements within the district, but only one had moved out of the district. Very few members of her extended family actually left the church. When asked, Katie's mother, Hannah, denied having been molested but did admit to having had nightmares as a child. During the interview she frequently told Bryan, "What is in the past stays in the past."

She also reported that her two younger brothers were still unmarried, though that would soon change for her brother Mark as his upcoming marriage to Sarah Miller had been published at the last church service. Hannah mentioned she did not attend church on the day of publication announcement because she had to prepare a large feast to honor the intended. As she continued, Hannah did disclose a couple of things about Mark from his past. She said he liked to play with fire and, when he was six, he killed her puppy. Still, she dismissed those incidents by telling Bryan, "He is the way he is. Leave it in the past."

Joshua, 17, was currently on his Rumspringa and was taking full advantage of it. He had not declared whether he would be joining the church, perhaps because, like his brother, he was enjoying his "freedom." Joshua was unbaptized in the church and therefore not subject to excommunication or shunning. He had an old car that he used to race the horse and buggies. Just two weeks beforehand, the local sheriff had to bring him home because of his drunk and disorderly conduct. With the money he earned from his woodworking, he enjoyed many of the "English ways," according to Hannah.

Ruth, it turns out, was the daughter of Eli's oldest sister, Mary. Both Ruth and her twin brother refused baptism into the church. Ruth reported to Bryan that an older brother and an uncle had raped her over the course of many years. She said that once those incidents were reported to the bishop, both the brother and the uncle made public confessions, and that was that. Ruth said she has never had any mental health or trauma treatment. Bryan needed to make a plan for Katie's safety, permanency, and well-being. He also needed to consider that uniqueness of this particular Amish group and family.

## Practice Application

In certain parts of the United States such as Ohio, Indiana, Pennsylvania, and Kentucky, there are large Amish communities that are long-standing stable communities in those states. Child welfare workers that work near these communities must be familiar with the customs of these communities not only to assess risk but also to be able to use the vast strengths of the community to assist children and families. In this case, Bryan, the child welfare worker, used his knowledge of local customs, including some of the language, to understand the context around which Katie suffered trauma at the hands of her cousins. He needs to use cultural humility in order to discuss the molestation with Katie's parents and ensure that despite their customs Katie is safe and well cared for. Bryan uses his social capital and also his trauma lens to begin to assist Katie and her family. Because Bryan is not part of the Amish community, he will need to be cognizant of dual relationships. For example, he might purchase food at the Amish farm market. He will have to understand the pull of Amish culture for Katie to recant her story in order to facilitate the cohesion of the group, and he will have to understand the role of women and girls in that society. In this instance, Bryan will have to be able to determine if her parents can, and will, keep her safe from her cousins.

## DISCUSSION QUESTIONS

1. Using the information in the chapter, decide if you would remove the child or children from the family if they refused to stay away from Mark and Joshua because "what is in the past stays in the past."
2. Discuss gender considerations regarding sending a male child protection worker to investigate this sexual abuse allegation.
3. Using the National Association of Social Workers Code of Ethics, identify ethical dilemmas associated with this case. Discuss the application of an ethical dilemma decision-making model.

## LEARNING ACTIVITIES

1. Debating Competing Rights: Freedom of Religion versus Child Protection
   a. Under the First Amendment to the Constitution of the United States, the government can do nothing to impede the expression of a person's religion or religious practices. It states specifically, "Congress shall make no law respecting an establishment of religion, or prohibiting the free exercise thereof; or abridging the freedom of speech, or of the press; or the right of the people peaceably to assemble, and to petition the government for a redress of grievances." Divide the class into two groups, A and B, and carry out a debate. Group A will defend the right of the government to intervene in Katie's case. Group B will defend the right of the church to manage the situation as an expression of its religious practices.

2. Safety Planning Exercise, with Attention to Social Capital
   a. Using the theory of social capital, develop a safety plan for Katie and her younger siblings.

3. Course Assignment: Eco-System Assessment
   a. Prepare a biopsychosocial assessment that includes a genogram, eco map, and sexual abuse risk assessment. Be sure to consider micro, meso, and macro levels of assessment and possible intervention. Consider what rural community contexts may be important.

4. Assignment: Presentation on Amish Culture
   a. Create a PowerPoint on the role of the Amish culture on social work with children in rural communities. This can be done individually or in a group format. This is easily adaptable to an online learning format. Include elements of rural environments.

5. Assignment: Ethics Paper
   a. Write a three- to five-page paper resolving an ethical dilemma based on this case study. Assign learners to use the National Association of Social Workers Code of Ethics and a decision-making model to supplement the materials in this chapter.

## SUGGESTED READING

### DOCUMENTARIES

*The Amish.* (2012). Directed by D. Belton. American Experience. [DVD]. A documentary about contemporary Amish faith and life and how the Amish have thrived in North America; 120 min.

*The Amish: A people of preservation.* (1996). PBS documentary. Heritage Productions. [DVD]. A documentary about the Amish of Lancaster County; 56 min.

*The Amish: Back roads to heaven.* (2007). Directed by B. Buller. Buller Films LLC. [DVD]. A documentary focusing on the Amish of Lancaster County, Pa.; 45 min.

*The Amish: How they survive.* (2005). Directed by B. Buller. Buller Films LLC. [DVD]. A documentary focusing on the Amish of Holmes County, Ohio; 49 min.

## INTERPRETATIVE FILM

*Amish grace.* (2010). Directed by G. Champion. Twentieth Century Fox Entertainment. [DVD]. Based on *Amish Grace: How Forgiveness Transcended Tragedy*; 88 min.

*Expecting Amish.* (2014). Directed by R. Gabia. Check Entertainment. [DVD]. A young Amish girl leaves on Rumspringa. She is forced to choose between the Plain life and the English life; 88 min.

*Saving Sarah Cain.* (2007). Directed by M. Landon. Fox Home Entertainment. [DVD]. A young woman who has left her Amish family returns to attend her sister's funeral only to discover that she is now the guardian of her sister's five children; 103 min.

*The radicals.* (1990/2004). Directed by R. V. Carrera. SIBRO Films. [DVD]. A powerful portrayal of the early Anabaptists in the 16th century; 99 min.

*Witness.* (1985). Directed by P. Weir. Paramount Pictures. [DVD]. A big-city cop on the lam hides out on an Amish farm, where he and a young widow are attracted to each other; 112 min.

## WEBSITES

Clinic for Special Children: https://clinicforspecialchildren.org/about/

DDC Clinic: Center for Special Needs Children. *Amish partnership*: http://ddcclinic.org/research/amishpartnership.html

National Geographic Channel. *Amish: Out of order facts:* http://channel.nationalgeographic.com/amish-out-of-order/articles/amish-out-of-order-facts/ on 7/14/2016.

Religious Tolerance. *The Amish: History, beliefs, practices, conflicts, etc.:* http://www.religioustolerance.org/amish.htm

Young Center. *Amish studies:* http://groups.etown.edu/amishstudies/ on 7/12/2016.

## BOOKS

Hurst, C. W., & McConnell, D. L. (2010). *An Amish paradox: Diversity and change in the world's largest Amish community.* Baltimore, MD: John Hopkins University Press.

Kaybill, D. B., Johnson-Weiner, K, & Nolt, S. M (2013). *The Amish.* Baltimore, MD: John Hopkins University Press.

# REFERENCES

Donnermeyer, J. F., & Friedrich, L. (2002). Amish society: An overview reconsidered. *Journal of Multicultural Nursing & Health, 8*(3), 6–14. Retrieved from http://db17.linccweb.org/login?url=http://search.proquest.com.db17.linccweb.org/docview/220297959?accountid=4036

Fischel, W. A. (2012). Do Amish one-room schools make the grade? The Dubious Data of *Wisconsin v Yoder. University of Chicago Law Review, 79*(1), 107–129.

Holbreich, M., Genuneit, J., Weber, J., Braun-Fahrländer, C., Waser, M., & von Mutius, E. (2012). Amish children living in northern Indiana have a very low prevalence of allergic sensitization. *Journal of Allergy and Clinical Immunology, 129*(6), 1671–1673. doi:http://dx.doi.org.db17.linccweb.org/10.1016/j.jaci.2012.03.016

Holmes, D., & Block, W. E. (2013). Amish in the 21st century. *Religion & Theology, 20*(3–4), 371–383. doi:10.1163/15743012-12341269

Kasdorf, J. S. (2007). Top pasture: "Amish forgiveness," silence, and the West Nickel Mines school shooting. *Cross Currents, 57*(3), 328–347.

Miller, W. F. (2007). Negotiating with modernity: Amish dispute resolution. *Ohio State Journal on Dispute Resolution, 22*(2), 477–526.

Petrovich, C.G. (2013). Spiritual theology in an Amish key: Theology, scripture, and praxis. *Journal of Spiritual Formation & Soul Care, 6*(2), 229–254.

Tharp, B. M. (2007). Valued Amish possessions: Expanding material culture and consumption. *Journal of American Culture, 30*(1), 38–53. doi:10.1111/j.1542-734X.2007.00463.x

US Census Bureau. (2012). Household and families: 2010. Retrieved from http://www.census.gov/prod/cen2010/briefs/c2010br-14.pdf

Young Center (n.d.). *Amish studies.* Retrieved from https://groups.etown.edu/amishstudies/

## CHAPTER 14

ᕼᐧᕼ

# Coming Out in Rural America

## *The Case of Emilio Hernandez*

RICHARD BRANDON-FRIEDMAN AND GAIL FOLARON

### LEARNING OBJECTIVES

- List the possible risks and benefits to "coming out" as a LGTBQ+ person
- Identify two or more possible complications of coming out in a small, rural community
- Explore various cultural perspectives that may challenge the integrity of the family, including rural social networks, the impact of religion, and the role of ethnic heritage
- Give an example of a time that a client's presenting problems are different from those that initially appear

### INTRODUCTION

Sexual minority youth experience victimization at significantly higher rates than their heterosexual peers. Within the school environment, 74% of sexual minority youth reported being harassed due to their sexual orientation and 56% felt unsafe attending school (Kosciw, Greytak, Palmer, & Boesen, 2014). These youth are also more likely to be physically abused by their parents and to be sexually abused (Friedman et al., 2011). Further, sexual minority Latina/o and Asian American youth experience higher levels of physical abuse than their White sexual minority peers, while Latina/o and African American youth are more likely to experience sexual abuse (Balsam, Lehavot, Beadnell, & Circo, 2010). Perhaps as a result of a traumatic history of abuse, sexual minority youth experience higher rates of mental health and substance use disorders, suicide ideation and attempts, and deliberate self-harm than their heterosexual peers (King et al., 2008). Another significant concern is homelessness and child welfare system involvement, as sexual minority youth are heavily overrepresented in both populations (Courtney, Maes Nino, & Peters, 2014). In fact, sexual minority youth make up as much as 40% of the homeless youth population, and as many as 55% of sexual minority youth that were homeless reported the primary reason for their homelessness was being forced out or running away because of their sexual orientation (Choi, Wilson, Shelton, & Gates, 2015).

To fully understand the experience of sexual minority youth, it is important to recognize the process through which they develop their sexual identity. The two most prominent models of homosexual (note: the early models of identity development only referenced "homosexuals") identity development and coming out were presented by Cass (1979) and Troiden (1988). Cass theorized six stages, *identity confusion*, in which the individual recognizes that his or her sexual feelings may be homosexual; *identity comparison*, in which the individual compares himself or herself to heterosexual others and begins to realize that he or she probably is homosexual; *identity tolerance*, in which the individual seeks out others that identify as homosexual but retains a public presentation of heterosexuality; *identity acceptance*, in which the individual begins to incorporate a positive image of himself or herself as a homosexual and may begin to disclose this to others; *identity pride*, whereby the individual feels a sense of loyalty and pride toward other homosexuals and is comfortable disclosing his or her sexuality to others; and finally, *identity synthesis*, in which the individual maintains his or her homosexual identity but no longer places it at the forefront of his or her sense of self.

Troiden (1988) developed a slightly different model detailing four stages: *sensitization*, a time prior to puberty in which prehomosexual feelings or experiences lead to feelings of being different but lack interpretation at the time; *identity confusion*, during which time the individual begins to personalize the concept of homosexuality and feels intense turmoil and uncertainty as the emerging identity is at odds with societal norms and preconceived ideas of the individual's future; *identity assumption*, the time in which the individual comes to tolerate and then accept his or her identification as a homosexual and to present this self to trusted others; and finally, *commitment*, the time in which the individual fully accepts and commits to an identity as a homosexual and fully integrates this identification into a positive sense of self. This model highlighted the sense of confusion and turmoil that may be present in an individual as he or she struggles with the acceptance of an identity that is often stigmatized and has many negative associations. It also emphasizes how societal expectations and events can influence this process by either aiding its progression or hindering it.

As can be seen from these models, the process of forming a sexual minority identity and revealing that identity to others relies on an inter-action between intra- and interpersonal factors. Internal factors that have negative effects on the process include internalized homonegativ-ity (the internalization of negative societal attitudes to homosexuality), moral conflicts that arise based on religious or moralistic teachings that homosexuality is wrong, and confusion or fear about what it means to be a sexual minority and what that means for a person's future. Even though these are internal factors, they are heavily influenced by the social envi-ronment in which the people live and the thoughts and behaviors of those around them.

For sexual minority youth, it is important that they receive a variety of social and familial supports, as each contributes to positive sexual minor-ity identity formation in a different manner. In terms of community sup-ports, research has indicated that gay-straight alliances, sexual minority community centers, supportive youth groups, and even a small network of supportive peers can significantly reduce the intrapersonal and social difficulties many sexual minority youth experience and increase their progress toward the development of a positive sexual identity (Asakura, 2010; Brandon-Friedman & Kim, 2016; Walls, Wisneski, & Kane, 2013). Family supports are protective factors against internalization of negative societal messaging regarding sexual minorities and suicidality as well as a willingness for youth to disclose their sexual identity to others. Family rejection contributes to reductions in psychosocial functioning (Bregman, Malik, Page, Makynen, & Lindahl, 2013; Eisenberg & Resnick, 2006; Shilo & Savaya, 2011). These difficulties are especially problematic among Latino men, who report higher levels of negative familial reactions to their com-ing out during adolescence (Connally, Wedemeyer, & Smith, 2013; Ryan, Huebner, Diaz, & Sanchez, 2009).

The support of family members and close peers is highly important for sexual minorities who live in rural areas, as they lack access to the com-munity-based supports often available to youth in larger urban areas. The increased interactions between familial social circles among families in rural areas can also contribute to difficulties, as individuals in smaller com-munities are much more aware of occurrences in others' homes than in

larger communities. Finally, rural communities tend to be more conservative, and even the professionals in social service agencies may harbor negative attitudes toward sexual minority individuals. Perhaps as a result of
all of these factors, sexual minorities in rural communities report harsher
social climates, increased stigma, and higher levels of discrimination (Cohn
& Hastings, 2010; Sandman, Fye, Hof, & Dinsmore, 2014; Swank, Frost, &
Fahs, 2012).

The following case vignette takes the reader into to a rural, Hispanic,
Catholic home in which both Emilio, a 17-year-old high school student, and
his family are struggling with his sexual orientation, experimentation, and
coming out process. As the case progresses, the school social worker and
the Department of Child Services become involved, and the word of family troubles spreads throughout the rural community. The challenges faced
by Emilio and his family are explored, the importance of social capital in a
rural community is demonstrated, and efforts of professionals to intervene
become evident. See chapter two for a discussion of social capital.

## CASE VIGNETTE

After getting into a fight on the way into school, Emilio Martinez, a
17-year-old student of Hispanic ethnicity, was sent to the office of Tracy
Rodriguez, the school social worker at a small middle school and high
school in a rural Southern town. Emilio was no stranger to Tracy. He was
frequently willing to volunteer when she needed assistance and was active
in the drama club. This was the first time he had been sent into her office
for negative behaviors.

When Emilio arrived at her office, Tracy immediately became concerned
due to Emilio's disheveled appearance and dress. He was wearing long
sleeves and his collar pulled up, an odd choice of clothing for a hot April
day. Tracy noticed that Emilio had bruises and abrasions; it appeared that
he was using clothing to cover up injuries.

Because Emilio knew Tracy and there appeared to be a crisis, she
did not engage in small talk. Rather, she jumped into the incident that
brought him into her office. Tracy asked what happened but Emilio
looked puzzled and did not say anything. Tracy had been trained in
trauma-informed care. She wondered if Emilio were reliving a painful
event. She decided to slow down and explore what happened. First, she
asked Emilio what was going on before the fight. Then she asked about his
actions once the fight commenced. In response to the "before" question,
Emilio shrugged. He said he really was not sure what happened, but he

noted that as he was coming into school, someone called him "a fag," and he just "lost it." He added, "I don't really remember what happened next. What I do remember is lying on the ground with blood coming out of my nose. The principal was standing over me."

Tracy asked about his other bruises that were obviously older than the recent fight. Emilio said that he had gotten into a fight a couple of days before with someone in the neighborhood. Since she knew that Emilio seemed to be well-adjusted with many friends, she was surprised to see that he had gotten into a physical fight that resulted in bruises.

While Emilio was telling his story, she noticed that he kept glancing at a poster she had on her wall that read, "This is a safe and inclusive place for lesbian, gay, bisexual, transgender, and allied youth." After Emilio finished his story of the fight, she said, "You said this fight started after someone called you a fag. You know Emilio, I'm not here to judge you. I'm here to support you in whatever situation you may be facing right now." He nodded and looked down. Tearfully, Emilio told Tracy that things had not been going well at home lately, and a couple of nights ago he and his father had gotten into a fight.

He then recounted the events escalated after his father overheard him talking about wanting to date a male classmate. Realizing that he had just "come out" to Tracy, Emilio initially looked terrified and began to backtrack, saying that it was all a misunderstanding. He mumbled something and then said, "No offense but I am old enough to protect myself so I don't really need any help. Thank you." Tracy acknowledged the difficulty that Emilio was likely having in dealing with questions about his sexual identity and reassured him that her office was a safe space.

After a few minutes of silence, Emilio described what had happened with his father. He had been discussing a crush on a male classmate with his "girlfriend" over the phone when his father, Mario Martinez, overheard him and became very angry. He said that his father took the phone away from Emilio and hit him across the face. Mario reportedly told Emilio that what he was thinking was immoral and dirty. He allegedly told him that if he acted on these feelings he would be an embarrassment to the family and "ruin the family's reputation" in the town and church. He then ordered Emilio to go to his room.

Over the next two hours Emilio said he could hear Mario pacing and screaming at his mother, blaming her for being "too soft" with Emilio. Emilio said that his father was also "ranting" about "teaching him [Emilio] a lesson he would not forget," saying his past actions had clearly not been enough. Remembering the previous times he had been hit for doing things he did that his father thought were "maricón" (sissy), and fearing what would come next, Emilio thought about running away. Before he could put his plan into action, however, Mario returned to try to "talk reason." He demanded that Emilio state that he was straight. Emilio said that when he refused to do so, "my father hit me in the face with my phone."

When asked about his girlfriend, Emilio explained that Amy was really his best friend and that, after he came out to her a year ago, they devised a plan that she would act as his girlfriend; that way his father and classmates would think he was heterosexual. Emilio noted that this strategy appeared to be working with his friends and family until now. His father now knew he was lying about having a girlfriend. Emilio then told Tracy he had spent the last couple of nights camped out in Amy's backyard shed, saying he was afraid of what would happen if he returned home. Emilio then looked down again and mumbled that he just wanted all of this "to be over," that he could not deal with his life anymore.

Faced with the realization that Emilio had been physically abused by his father and was possibly suicidal, Tracy faced the dilemma of reporting the situation to child protective services (CPS). She regretted not starting her meeting with Emilio with a discussion of the limits of confidentiality rather than assuming the problem was only a fight with a classmate. She also reflected on her statement that her office was a safe place. In this particular small community, Tracy knew there were few places that people might feel comfortable discussing their sexuality.

Tracy was aware of a recent survey of adults in the county about their attitudes toward homosexuality. The newspaper reported that fewer than 35% of the population claimed to know a gay, lesbian, or bisexual person. She was also aware that the values in the county were very conservative with strong support for gun rights, pro-life positions, and marriage between a man and a woman. In this rural environment, it was as hard to be different as it was to keep a secret. Even though Emilio had grown up with the majority of the students in the school, bullying did happen and people were ostracized. Tracy felt that given Emilio's popular social position he would likely become accepted within the school and community again, but in the meantime it might be very difficult for him. Similarly, reporting the abuse to CPS could lead to shunning of Emilio's whole family as it was possible that students, teachers, family members, and others might hear about the incident and ask questions about what happened. If this occurred, Emilio's sexuality might be revealed before he was ready to disclose it. Tracy, however, was legally responsible for reporting the alleged abuse.

Expressing her concern for his safety, Tracy informed Emilio that due to his bruises, the lack of a place to sleep, and his hints of suicide, she would need to contact CPS. Emilio begged Tracy not to call, saying that if she did everyone would know there were problems in his family, that people would figure out he was gay, and that it would ruin his life and that of his family. Tracy acknowledged his fears but noted her responsibility to help protect him. After much discussion, Emilio resigned himself to the fact that CPS would be involved and told Tracy to make the call. After the phone call, Tracy allowed Emilio to stay in her office until the CPS assessment worker arrived.

When recounting his story to the CPS worker, Emilio stated that while his father was "beating me," he was using gay slurs and lecturing him on the evils of sin and on his responsibilities as the only male to set an example for his two sisters. His father said he was going to make him a man and, if he had to, "to beat the gay out him." After he had reportedly beaten Emilio, Mario left the room and told Emilio that he would give him until morning to "rethink" things. Emilio reported that his father had hit him hard enough in the past to leave bruises but "never to this extent."

Emilio admitted that he was sometimes fearful of his father. Even while relating the story, Emilio made reference to his family's status in the community and about not wanting to harm his father's reputation by letting people know what happened at home. He also acknowledged that his sisters had been present throughout the incident and that they seemed frightened. One sister tried to intervene but was forced to leave the room.

Since it was the end of the school day and evident to the CPS worker that Emilio needed substitute housing for at least the night, the worker transported Emilio to the Family Support Center, which was located in a small house near the center of town. While walking to the door of the center, a friend saw Emilio and called out to him. Recognizing the awkwardness of the situation, the CPS worker loudly stated her appreciation for Emilio "helping her out with work on the house." Once inside, Emilio became argumentative, mumbling about how this situation was going to destroy his family and asked the CPS worker to just take him home and forget the whole situation. The CPS worker assured Emilio that she had worked in small communities her whole career and that efforts would be made to protect his family's privacy.

After Emilio was settled in, the CPS worker went to Emilio's home to meet with his parents. During the interview, she was informed that Emilio's parents immigrated to the United States 20 years ago and both were now citizens. "It was quite a struggle," Mr. Hernandez said. "We took odd jobs and worked long hours. We sent money back home to support our parents. We finally settled in this community and joined the local Catholic Church. The church is everything." Mr. Hernandez added, "We both volunteer down at the church. It has been a great support for us. We get so much more than we give."

The CPS worker recognized Mr. Hernandez as the supervisor of a local contracting company and Emilio's mother, Rosa, as a server at a local restaurant. Mr. Hernandez told her that he was concerned because it took a lot of hard work to be accepted as an American citizen, to build a future and establish close ties within the community. Referring to the incident, Mario said he had lost his temper and felt bad about what happened but that homosexuality was sinful and could not be accepted in his family.

The next day the CPS worker met with Emilio at the shelter. She found that he was having a hard time adjusting to it and that he was feeling alone and depressed. Throughout the interview he stated he was sure that he had lost his family for good and that he was never going to be able to have a relationship with them again. He noted the shame that his father felt and how much his mother had cried through the whole ordeal. Emilio expressed feelings of having let down his family and having betrayed them. He refused to discuss the physical altercation with his father, denying anything had happened and returning to his story of a fight in the neighborhood. When pressed about the incident and his relationship with his father, he became upset and seemed to "check out" mentally. The CPS worker arranged to get Emilio back to school the next day to relieve some of Emilio's preoccupations and normalize his routines.

During the interview, Emilio stated that his sisters called to say his parents had decided to obtain counseling services for the family at their church. Emilio expressed anxiety about obtaining mental health services within the church, saying that he did not want to talk with anyone about his family anymore or about his sexuality. He would rather be left alone. Emilio was also concerned about his reputation in school. The news of his having entered the shelter had spread quickly, and Amy had texted that there were rumors circulating that he was kicked out of his home and that he was a "fag."

Recognizing the importance of Amy in Emilio's life, the CPS worker obtained the necessary permissions and releases to schedule a meeting with her. Amy reported that she and Emilio had been friends since grade school and that their parents were close. Early in high school Emilio had disclosed to her that he thought he had a crush on a male friend and that he was finding himself attracted to other males. Amy said that Emilio was very confused and upset about these feelings and had been trying to change them. When discussing Emilio's family, Amy said she had concerns about Emilio because his family was so religious and his father put a lot of pressure on him to be a "man." She stated Emilio had told her that his father had threatened to kick him out if he refused to change his sinful thinking.

Amy reported that early in his junior year Emilio told her he tried having sex with a female classmate. She said Emilio felt humiliated by the experience and he said that the found it was not enjoyable. She noted that Emilio has been bullied at school in the past few months, with some calling him gay and taunting him. Concerned about the amount of gossip in the town and the difficult relationship between Emilio and his father, she and Emilio had agreed to "date" until he could move out.

Amy and Emilio had tried to find some support groups for gay teens online but, in the end, Emilio felt somewhat hopeless, as the people he met online seemed so different from him. He had told her that many of the other teens lived in larger cities and were unable to understand what a small community was like. She also stated that she and Emilio had found a youth group for gay teens, but they were not able to drive the two hours it would take to get there.

The next afternoon the CPS worker met with Emilio's parents to discuss the incident in more detail. Emilio's father was angry when she arrived at the house, questioning her position and why she and her agency felt they could judge him and his family. He told her that his father had whipped him when he was a kid and that he turned out fine. Agencies like CPS, he argued, say they are "protecting" kids but are really just making them weak. He said Emilio was a perfect example—he needed to be taught to be a man, but instead people were questioning his role as a father. He also said that he was not about to let CPS destroy his reputation in the community.

Over the course of the meeting, the CPS worker was able to calm Mario down and focus him on Emilio's needs. Once he was calmer, Mario began to speak of the shame that Emilio was bringing upon the family. He stated that despite what he saw in the media, being gay is not natural and is a sin. He explained that in Hispanic culture and in his church homosexuality is not okay and that his family would be shunned from their community, church, and friends. He kept saying that Emilio needs to recognize the shame he would bring on his family and to get his act together. He then said that if Emilio would not stop acting gay, he was not sure that Emilio could come home. The CPS worker noted that Mario's demeanor varied between angry and somewhat sorrowful. She could tell that Mario deeply loved his family and it seemed like he may be doing what he felt best for them.

When asked about her views, Rosa, Emilio's mother, began by defending Mario, saying how much he loved Emilio and his family and how good of a father he was. She explained that she had tried to talk to Emilio before and that Mario had tried so many things, but Emilio just would not listen. She stated that she did not think Mario was dangerous, just "a little hot-headed sometimes." When prompted about her feelings regarding Emilio's sexuality, Rosa began to cry softly. She said that she could not think about Emilio doing such unnatural things and she did not think she would be able to handle his sickness. She then began to talk about how "people like that" get ill and die of AIDS and that she did not want that for her son. She stated that she and Mario had had such high hopes for Emilio. He would soon be off to college and eventually get married. She said that she knew Mario loved his family very much and that he had hoped his son would carry on the family name and give them grandkids. She expressed regret that this would never happen now. Then she also began to question aloud how the family could possibly remain in the town once people knew about Emilio.

At that point, Mario began to get angry. He gestured to his wife to stop talking and asked the CPS worker what she would do if her son put her family through this. He stated that he could not accept that his son was hurting his wife this much. He then stated that Emilio's sisters had been mocked at school that day, with peers talking about Emilio being gay. Mario stated that Emilio's youngest sister had even tried to come home early because of it. He stated that he had always loved Emilio but that it was crazy that Emilio would do this to all of them. He then ruefully remarked that perhaps if he had done more, earlier, Emilio would not be like this.

The CPS worker explained that she could see that both parents loved Emilio very much and that she was going to work with them to be able to get him home. The CPS worker explained that the goal of the department was to work with the family to ensure Emilio's safety and to return him to the family's home as soon as possible. For the time being, however, she was going to recommend that Emilio stay in the shelter. She then scheduled a time for a family team meeting (FTM). She suggested that the family consider anyone who might help them with their struggles and bring those people to the meeting. Rosa suggested that it might help to have Amy and her family there, but Mario shook his head. He said, "This is very personal—we don't want to air our dirty laundry out in the community. Besides, hasn't Amy done enough? She lied to my face as much as my own son did. And who knows what her parents already know."

The interview with Emilio's sister, Gina, was brief but private. The CPS worker sat with her in her bedroom while Gina explained that Emilio and her father have had a somewhat troubled past. "I think it is because in some ways they are so much alike," she said. "They tend to get on each other's nerves." She said this was not the first time there were confrontations between the two. She added, "My father believes strongly in family, Catholicism, and machismo. The worst confrontations come when he sees Emilio acting like a sissy." She also stated that she felt her father might have felt deceived by what had gone on between Emilio and Amy, which was hard for him since he liked Amy's family so much.

On the day of the team meeting, Mario arrived early with his wife and the local priest, Father Gregory. Emilio began the FTM by apologizing to his mother and father "for everything." He stated that he wanted to come home and then he would try to do better and be what his father and mother wanted him to be. Emilio's father nodded approvingly throughout this part of the interview. At this point, Emilio's mother spoke up, saying that she just wanted Emilio home and that they would find a way to make things work. Mario suggested that Emilio go to counseling with Father Gregory. Emilio started to cry and stated that as much as he wanted to be back with his family, he wanted them to know that he could not change from being gay.

Emilio said he would not go to Father Gregory for counseling because he did not feel comfortable with him. Emilio had seen Father Gregory once before at his father's insistence. During that meeting, the priest told Emilio that it was okay to be gay but not okay to act upon it. He reminded Emilio that if he acted upon his urges he would be sinning against God and would no longer be welcome to receive the sacraments of the Church.

Mario scolded Emilio for disrespecting Father Gregory and demanded he apologize to him. The CPS worker noticed that Emilio's whole demeanor had changed during this exchange and that he had flinched as Mario yelled and seemed to shrink back in his chair. The CPS worker felt it was time to take a break and took Emilio to another room to talk to him. Emilio refused to talk to her and only repeated that he "never wanted all this to happen." Emilio then sat down in a corner and refused to go back into the room with his family. The CPS worker could hear Mario and Rosa arguing as Father Gregory attempted to talk to them.

The CPS worker returned to the meeting room, stating that Emilio would be returning when he was ready. Mario was still agitated and told the CPS worker that this was exactly why she should stay out of their family's business—how were they supposed to raise a "good son" when she was letting Emilio get away with disrespecting Father Gregory? Father Gregory then spoke up. He said that he had been doing some reflection and that he thought it might be best for Emilio to remain out of the home for some more time. The CPS worker noted that Mario gave significant weight to what Father Gregory said, so she asked Father Gregory about individual and family counseling. She noted that the department could work with the family to get Emilio counseling elsewhere, which she thought might be best for the time being. Mario began to object, saying he did not want people in the town talking about Emilio going to a therapist, but Father Gregory stated that he agreed it might be best if he continued to meet with Mario and Rosa while Emilio saw someone with whom he felt more comfortable. With this approval from Father Gregory, Mario relaxed and consented to that arrangement.

It was determined that Mario and Rosa would meet twice weekly with Father Gregory and that Emilio would remain at the shelter. The CPS worker then provided the family with a list of resources that a coworker had compiled regarding local agencies, websites, and books that might be helpful for a family dealing with a child's sexual orientation. She also agreed to speak with the social workers at both Emilio's school and the school Emilio's sisters attend to address the bullying. Another FTM was set for two weeks later.

At the beginning of the next FTM, the CPS worker stated that Emilio was approaching the limit of his time at the shelter and a decision on his placement was required. Mario volunteered that he wanted to apologize for some of his actions in the last meeting. He noted that he had become too agitated and would control himself better this time. He then said that he and Rosa had been meeting with Father Gregory as planned and that they had also met twice with Emilio's therapist, Shane Brannon. He noted that despite his initial hesitation, he had found the meetings with the therapist to be beneficial.

When prompted about Emilio's returning home, Mario stated that he and Rosa had discussed it and that they wanted him back. He said that he had been doing a lot of thinking and that he wanted to make things work out. Emilio would be starting college in a few months, and both Rosa and he wanted to share the last few months together before he left as a family. There would be a few ground rules, however. Mario said there would be no "gay talk," that he did not want to see Amy, and that he would monitor Emilio's friends.

When asked if he was okay with returning home, Emilio expressed some concerns, saying he did not want to feel trapped in his own home but that he would try it. He stated that he was beginning to understand that things would not return to the way they were but that he should be with his family. He repeated that he could not change who he was but that he wanted to try to help his family understand. He also noted he only had a one more month of school and, after summer, he would move out.

The CPS worker suggested that a safety plan be created for any issues that might arise upon Emilio's return to home. Shane suggested that the family should not talk about his being gay and that that should be reserved for therapy; everyone agreed. Shane noted that he had some continuing concerns about Emilio's interactions with Mario and Emilio's stress level when the two were together and that he felt there needed to be an agreement about how to deal with conflict. A plan was arranged whereby Emilio could go to his room and be alone when needed and that Mario would not follow or harass him. The CPS worker noted that there continued to be some clear tension between Emilio and his family but that there at least seemed to be an agreement as to how Emilio could return to the home safely.

## Practice Application

In this case, Emilio and his family confront the coming out process. While this process is developmental, it involves many deeply held cultural and religious beliefs that can rock the stability of youth and families and can put youth in danger of being physically or emotionally abused or bullied. In this case, Emilio's family needed the help of the priest who had cultural capital and the school and mental health social workers to help them to at least partially alleviate a crisis. LGBTQ youth need to be able to receive support and empowerment, as many times they cannot get it from their families. In small towns and rural communities where the private can become public so easily, youth need to know that they will be safe with their disclosures and be able to receive competent assistance from the professional community.

## DISCUSSION QUESTIONS

1. In addition to being struck and yelled at by his father, Emilio was facing rejection from his church, peers, and community. How might this type of isolation compound the impact of the trauma experienced in the home?
2. How might Emilio's history of abuse affect his feeling of self and relationships with others?
3. How might Emilio be progressing in moving through the stages of minority sexual identify as proposed by (a) Cass (1979) and (b) Troiden (1988)?
4. How might the rural context matter in addressing this immediate crisis? the long-term situation? What are positive and negative possibilities of rural cultural context that may apply?
5. What supports could be put into place to help Emilio and his family?
6. Who has the most social capital (see chapter 2 for discussion) that can be used to improve the situation for Emilio and his family?

7. How has the CPS worker utilized the social capital of members of the family and community already, and how might she continue to use it in the future?

8. What protective factors could be built into the safety plan to ensure that Emilio is safe during the summer months before he leaves for college?

9. How might the trauma Emilio has experienced affect his psychosocial development?

10. What are your hunches about the impact of Emilio's religious and ethnic culture on his experiences of trauma?

11. How might Emilio's trauma be differently experienced if he lived in a large city rather than a rural environment?

12. While much of the focus in this situation is necessarily on the needs of Emilio, others in this scenario have also experienced loss. Who are they? How might those losses affect their relationships moving forward?

13. How may this case vignette demonstrate cultural intersectionality? What factors may be considered intersectional for Emilio?

## LEARNING ACTIVITIES

1. Safety Planning Exercise
   a. Write a safety plan for the family that addresses the needs of all family members. Include activities to be considered or avoided, resources or supports to be included, and time lines for completion. What is the backup plan if the safety plan does not work as expected?

2. Assessment Outreach Decisions
   a. Do you agree with Tracy's activities in engaging and intervening with Emilio, including her usage of Emilio's relationship with Amy? What would you have done the same? What would you have done differently? rationales? ties to rural considerations?

3. Family Team Meeting Video Exercise
   a. Review the video *Child and Family Team Meetings* at https://www.youtube.com/watch?v=GEEEdzhel50 to learn about family engagement and teaming.

4. Conduct a Family Team Meeting Role Play
   a. Role play a child and family team meeting with the goals of ensuring Emilio's safety, determining a good permanency plan for Emilio, and enhancing the well-being of the both Emilio and the family. If Emilio cannot stay at home, develop a plan to keep the family connected in a positive way.

## SUGGESTED READING

Annes, A., & Redlin, M. (2012). Coming out and coming back: Rural gay migration and the city. *Journal of Rural Studies, 28*(1), 56–68. doi:10.1016/j.jrurstud.2011.08.005

D'Augelli, A. R. (2006). Coming out, visibility, and creating change: Empowering lesbian, gay, and bisexual people in a rural university community. *American Journal of Community Psychology, 37*(3), 203–210. doi:10.1007/s10464-006-9043-9046.

Eldridge, V. L., Mack, L., & Swank, E. (2006). Explaining comfort with homosexuality in rural America. *Journal of Homosexuality, 51*(2), 39–56. doi:10.1300/J082v51n02_03

Mathy, R. M., Carol, H. M., & Schillace, M. (2008). The impact of community size on lesbian and bisexual women's psychosexual development: Child maltreatment, suicide attempts, and self-disclosure. *Journal of Psychology & Human Sexuality, 15*(2–3), 47–71. doi: 10.1300/J056v15n02_04

Pace, N. J. (2004). Gay, rural, and coming out: A case study of one school's experience. *The Rural Educator, 25*(3), 14–18.

Poon, C. S., & Saewyc, E. M. (2009). Out yonder: Sexual-minority adolescents in rural communities in British Columbia. *American Journal of Public Health, 99*(1), 118–124. doi:10.2105/AJPH.2007.122945

## REFERENCES

Asakura, K. (2010). Queer youth space: A protective factor for sexual minority youth. *Smith College Studies in Social Work, 80*(4), 361–376.

Balsam, K. F., Lehavot, K., Beadnell, B., & Circo, E. (2010). Childhood abuse and mental health indicators among ethnically diverse lesbian, gay, and bisexual adults. *Journal of Consulting and Clinical Psychology, 78*(4), 459–468. doi:10.1037/a0018661

Brandon-Friedman, R. A., & Kim, H. W. (2016). Using social support levels to predict sexual identity development among college students who identify as a sexual minority. *Journal of Gay & Lesbian Social Services, 28*(4), 1–25. doi:10.1080/10538720.2016.1221784

Bregman, H. R., Malik, N. M., Page, M. J., Makynen, E., & Lindahl, K. M. (2013). Identity profiles in lesbian, gay, and bisexual youth: The role of family influences. *Journal of Youth & Adolescence, 42*(3), 417–430. doi:10.1007/s10964-012-9798-z

Cass, V. C. (1979). Homosexual identity formation: A theoretical model. *Journal of Homosexuality, 4*(3), 219–235. doi:10.1300/J082v04n03_01

Choi, S. K., Wilson, B. D. M., Shelton, J., & Gates, G. J. (2015). *Serving our youth 2015: The needs and experience of lesbian, gay, bisexual, transgender, and questioning youth experiencing homelessness.* Los Angeles, CA: Williams Institute, UCLA School of Law and True Colors Fund.

Cohn, T. J., & Hastings, S. L. (2010). Resilience among rural lesbian youth. *Journal of Lesbian Studies, 14*(1), 71–79.

Connally, D., Wedemeyer, R., & Smith, S. J. (2013). Cultural practice considerations: The coming out process for Mexican Americans along the rural US-Mexico border. *Contemporary Rural Social Work, 5*, 42–64.

Courtney, M. E., Maes Nino, C., & Peters, E. (2014). *System pathways into youth homelessness.* Winnipeg, Canada. Retrieved from http://www.spcw.mb.ca/files/8614/0735/0794/SystemPathways-SPCW-2014.pdf

Eisenberg, M. E., & Resnick, M. D. (2006). Suicidality among gay, lesbian and bisexual youth: The role of protective factors. *Journal of Adolescent Health, 39*(5), 662–668. doi:10.1016/j.jadohealth.2006.04.024

Friedman, M. S., Marshal, M. P., Guadamuz, T. E., Wei, C., Wong, C. F., Saewyc, E. M., & Stall, R. (2011). A meta-analysis of disparities in childhood sexual abuse, parental physical abuse, and peer vicitimization among sexual minority and sexual nonminority individuals. *American Journal of Public Health, 101*(8), 1481–1494. doi:10.2105/AJPH.2009.190009

King, M., Semlyen, J., Tai, S. S., Killaspy, H., Osborn, D., Popelyuk, D., & Nazareth, I. (2008). A systematic review of mental disorder, suicide, and deliberate self harm in lesbian, gay and bisexual people. *BMC Psychiatry, 80*(70). doi:10.1186/1471-244X-8-70

Kosciw, J. G., Greytak, E. A., Palmer, N. A., & Boesen, M. J. (2014). *The 2013 National School Climate Survey: The experiences of lesbian, gay, bisexual and transgender youth in our nation's schools.* New York, NY: Gay, Lesbian & Straight Education Network.

Ryan, C., Huebner, D., Diaz, R. M., & Sanchez, J. (2009). Family rejection as a predictor of negative health outcomes in white and Latino lesbian, gay, and bisexual young adults. *Pediatrics, 123*(1), 346–352. doi:10.1542/peds.2007-3524

Sandman, G. R., Fye, M. A., Hof, D. D., & Dinsmore, J. A. (2014). From awareness to action: Becoming and LGBT advocate in a conservative rural community. *VISTAS Online*, Article 66.

Shilo, G., & Savaya, R. (2011). Effects of family and friend support on LGB youths' mental health and sexual orientation milestones. *Family Relations, 60*(3), 318–330. doi:10.1111/j.1741-3729.2011.00648.x

Swank, E., Frost, D. M., & Fahs, B. (2012). Rural location and exposure to minority stress among sexual minorities in the United States. *Psychology and Sexuality, 3*(3), 226–243. doi:10.1080/19419899.2012.700026

Troiden, R. R. (1988). *Gay and lesbian identity: A sociological analysis.* Dix Hills, NY: General Hall.

Walls, N. E., Wisneski, H., & Kane, S. B. (2013). School climate, individual support or both? Gay-straight alliances and the mental health of sexual minority youth. *School Social Work Journal, 37*(2), 88–111. doi:10.1177/0044118X09334957

## CHAPTER 15

✧

# Technology and Child Welfare Practice

## *Lessons from Montana*

### CHARLIE WELLENSTEIN

Wolf Pack Country. The name of the school mascot is a wolf. Children are highly valued
among rural people. Schools are often centers of local culture events.
David G. Riebschleger

## LEARNING OBJECTIVES

• Describe potential uses and abuses of technology in child welfare settings
• Give an example of ethical and nonethical use of technology in social work
• Identify the differences between personal and professional behavior with respect to technology use

## INTRODUCTION

Technology and social media have started to enter the profession of child welfare. As technology advances, there are questions left unanswered regarding its use in child protective services (CPS), especially as the child welfare profession attempts to reach rural and underserved areas (Center for Advanced Studies in Child Welfare, 2011). This case presentation and suggested classroom activities hope to bring forth questions, ethical dilemmas, and possible resolutions.

Technology is being pioneered in the health and social work professions as a means to communicate efficiently with clients. An article in *The New York Times* (Fowler, 2012) described the use of texting by a pediatrician as an effective means of reaching teenage patients (who might otherwise ignore her) with needed medication monitoring and follow-up. Also, recent technological innovations such as the Crisis Text Line have been hailed as an effective means to immediately and effectively reach at-risk youth (Gregory, 2015). Several years ago, the quarterly journal *Child Welfare 360* (2011) dedicated an issue to the use of technology and social media in child welfare practice. Included among the articles that appeared was one that looked at the use of Facebook for foster children to find and connect with extended biological family-members.

Social work education has also embraced the use of technology, especially in rural areas and for students whose personal circumstances do not allow them to attend on-campus classes (Reamer, 2013). Hillman and Weichman (2016) describe those regions that lack higher education opportunities "educational deserts." They also note that minorities (American Indian and Hispanic people) are disproportionally overrepresented in these deserts.

A rural state like Montana fits this "educational desert" and long-distance descriptions. With a population that includes seven American Indian reservations, Montana is a state of approximately 1 million spread over 145,000 square miles (US Census, 2015). Most of the population and its flagship universities are in the western third of the state. To give a sense of the distances Montana involves, consider that it is a shorter drive to Seattle from the University of Montana than it is to reach the eastern edge of Montana. Given this profile, it is easy to appreciate the importance of technology and social media may hold for the state.

Technology and social media, however, are not without possible harms. These harms focus mostly on privacy issues and the efficacy of communication with clients. For example, *The Wall Street Journal* (Hoffman, 2012) detailed an account of a young adult who revealed to a "private" group on Facebook that he was gay. Only subsequently did he discover how easy it was for the "public" to access the postings of his "private" group. This example demonstrates that there is the both confusion and uncertainty about the boundaries between one's personal life and public.

Reamer (2012) presents other possible harms that can occur from the blurred boundaries that technology can occasion in the worker-client relationship. Yet there is scant discussion of the possible harms of using technology and social media as a means of discourse and support *between professionals*. Although the National Association of Social Workers (NASW, 2008) Code of Ethics mentions the protection of a client's confidentiality vis-à-vis technology, it does not discuss social media, nor does it indicate a prescriptive approach to its use either with clients or among professional colleagues.

One of the few sources about social media and professional sharing is found in a student magazine published by the American Psychological Association with the eye-catching, intriguing title of "Beware the Overshare: Can't Resist Tweeting and Blogging About Your Workday? If So, You May Be Compromising Confidentiality" (Chamberlin, 2014). There are few publications than can keep up with the advancement of technology and social media use. For those social workers in the field of child welfare, technology and social media force the question of how technology and social media are best used as a means of professional discourse and support, as well as client intervention.

## CASE VIGNETTE

Jenny Richards was a BSW student in her last semester of her practicum with child protective services in a frontier region of northwest Montana. Throughout her academic career, she was an exemplary student both in her classes and at the agency. Her colleagues at her practicum-site reported that they liked and respected her; her field instructor mentioned that she would be "an asset to child protective services" when she graduated.

Jenny was also one of the social work school's Child Welfare Scholars. As a scholar, she received a monthly stipend and was contractually required to be employed after graduation at CPS in return for the stipend. Chances were good that she would be employed in a rural area of the state in a two- to four-person office.

One month from her graduation, her faculty advisor discovered that Jenny had been on Facebook posting comments about her practicum with other employees of CPS (her advisor was shown the comments by another student). The comments were responses to other employees' complaints and dissatisfaction with the agency, including employee turnover, and parents/clients who were problematic. Clients were not mentioned by name, nor were there direct references to specific cases. However, the comments regarding clients could easily have applied to any case, so the assumption could be made that they referenced a specific individual.

The faculty advisor met with Jenny and advised her not to use Facebook as a means of discussing work; she also informed Jenny that she had contacted her agency supervisor. Jenny countered that her comments were not during working hours or intended for public viewing. Jenny also stated that she was using Facebook as a means of support and that her doing so was in accord with the recommendation she had heard repeatedly in her social work classrooms about the importance of developing a network of support. She said this was especially needed as she prepared to move to an isolated rural office. She noted that technology was often used as a means of teaching online courses and used innovatively to reach out to both clients and colleagues in rural settings. Jenny likened using Facebook to meeting with fellow workers for a cup of coffee to vent and debrief; this was consistent with a support network. Furthermore, she claimed the faculty advisor had overstepped her bounds by contacting the agency supervisor and did not know how younger workers use technology. From this conversation the faculty advisor and Jenny were left with questions about the possible harms and benefits of social media.

## Practice Application

These days some people seem to use social media for everything from obtaining training and new information to seeking support from others. While this is not necessarily wrong, it can be dangerous practice when workers do not pay close enough attention to confidentiality. Even when they think they are disguising the particulars of a case, workers can inadvertently disclose material that is meant to be confidential. Child welfare workers must be ever vigilant about confidentiality and find other means of support as they practice in a stressful field.

## DISCUSSION QUESTIONS

1. Are there limits to when a faculty member or supervisor can interfere with a student's or employee's personal activities? When does a person's professional life end and his or her personal life begin?
2. What is the role of social media in the field of child welfare? Should it be viewed as a productive means of support?
3. Should any conversation on social media regarding professional work be seen as an open door for any member of both the profession and public to view? For example, should social workers treat each posted comment as being possibly viewed by clients, defense attorneys, legislators, or the media?
4. Did Jenny violate any ethical standards through her comments to employees at CPS? What are the possible harms and benefits of using social media? Are there special considerations for rural social workers?
5. Should the faculty advisor notify Jenny's CPS supervisor that CPS workers in addition to Jenny were participants in the Facebook discussion?
6. Is it possible for a child welfare agency to develop policy defining the acceptable use of technology/social media by its employees and interns? What would an effective policy look like?
7. What aspects of the NASW Code of Ethics apply to this situation?
8. If you were a client whose family is mentioned on the social media site, how would you feel, and what might you think about viewing the comments online?
9. Is there a "generation gap" regarding technology between faculty and CPS supervisors and new employees?

## LEARNING ACTIVITIES

1. Use of Technology in Crisis Counseling: Individual Learning with Class Exercise
   a. Learners should watch the TED Talk on the Crisis Text Line (http://www.ted.com/talks/nancy_lublin_texting_that_saves_lives)
   b. Role play using two groups in class. One group will role play youth that are in crisis; the other group will be text line counselors. The

text line helpers should give the clients their cell phone numbers. Clients then should text the counselors indicating a crisis they are experiencing. The first text should be one brief phrase (e.g., "I am scared"; My boyfriend will not stop yelling") and the helpers should attempt to respond via text using social work skills: opened-ended questions, reflection, and empathy. Then bring the group together and debrief what was and was not effective, especially if this can be an effective intervention in rural communities. Also, discuss the ethical challenges of using a text line.

2.  Social Media as a Means of Support: A Class Exercise

a.  Find or develop a vignette that contains either a supervisor of a youth services agency who promotes a workplace that is extremely harsh, disorganized, or dismissive of the workers. It can also be a vignette where a youth dies (either from abuse or suicide) while in the care of a youth services agency. Divide into two groups in class.

b.  Each group will role play employees of that agency who are meeting as a means of support. One of the groups should meet face to face and the other group should role-play that they are in a rural state/ community and the only way to meet is through social media (e.g. Facebook). The two groups should meet for 15 minutes.

c.  Then bring the groups together and debrief about the possible benefits and harms of each type of meeting and what standards or suggestions should occur in a workplace to ensure ethical care of both clients' confidentiality and worker well-being. Also, the discussion can focus on how workers who are isolated in rural comminutes can find effective and ethical support through social media.

## REFERENCES

Center for Advanced Studies in Child Welfare. (2011). Child welfare and technology. *Child Welfare 360*. Retrieved from http://cascw.umn.edu/wp-content/uploads/2013/12/CW360_2011.pdf

Chamberlin, J. (2014, January). Beware the overshare: Can't resist tweeting and blogging about your workday? If so, you may be compromising confidentiality. *GradPSYCH Magazine*, p. 18. American Psychological Association. Retrieved from http://www.apa.org/gradpsych/2014/01/overshare.aspx

Fowler, G. A. (2012, October 13). When the most personal secrets get outed on Facebook. *Wall Street Journal*. Retrieved from http://www.wsj.com/article_email/SB10000872396390444165804578008740578200224-lMyQjAxMTAyMDEwMjAxODI3Wj.html

Gregory, A. (2015, February 9). R U there. *New Yorker Magazine*. Retrieved from http://www.newyorker.com/magazine/2015/02/09/r-u

Hillman, N., & Weichman, T. (2016). Education deserts: The continued significance of "place" in the twenty-first century. *Viewpoints: Voices from the field*. Washington, DC: American Council on Education.

Hoffman, J. (2012, October 8). Texting the teenage patient. *New York Times*. http://well.blogs.nytimes.com/2012/10/08/texting-the-teenage-patient/?_r=0

National Association of Social Workers. (2008). *Code of ethics*. Washington, DC: NASW Press.

Reamer, F. (2012). *Boundary issues and dual relationships in the human services*. New York, NY: Columbia University.

Reamer, F. (2013). Distance and online social work education: Novel ethical challenges. *Journal of Teaching in Social Work, 33*, 369–384. doi:10.1080/08841233.2013.828669

US Census Bureau. (2015). *Montana quick facts from the U.S. Census Bureau*. Retrieved from https://www.census.gov/quickfacts/table/PST045216/30

# CHAPTER 16

∿

# Foster Care Stigma and Ethical Boundary Violations in the Rural Child Welfare Workplace

### ANGELIQUE DAY

## LEARNING OBJECTIVES

- Describe the phenomenon of living in a "goldfish bowl" in rural areas
- Identify the laws and administrative procedures for protecting the rights of foster children to confidentiality
- Identify how the new worker in this vignette was retraumatized "by the system"
- List ways to build a supportive environment for colleagues and supervisees

## FOSTER CARE STIGMA AND BOUNDARIES

Child welfare workforce recruitment and retention are particularly needed in rural areas as the loss of a single worker can significantly decrease and disrupt child welfare services. One strategy for building and retaining child welfare workers is to generate "homegrown" providers (Belanger & Stone, 2008). This means that a person who grew up in a rural area is more likely to continue to live and work in a rural area. They may be more acclimated to the "informal" nature of many rural areas, including what some call "living in a goldfish bowl." This means that other people in the community may know a good deal about the child welfare worker as a person and as a professional (Pugh, 2007). The "goldfish bowl," however, can be an advantage in that, when one becomes an "insider" in a rural community, it can help with accessing resources (Riebschleger, 2007). Nevertheless, having other community members know a lot about the personal life of a child welfare worker can also create potential boundary issues, especially if there is not proactive and continuing attention to professional boundaries. The National Association of Social Workers (NASW; 2012) Code of Ethics strongly emphasizes that social workers have responsibilities to clientele, colleagues, and worksite organizations and a commitment to social justice.

When considering how to build a stronger rural child welfare workforce, it is possible that former foster youth who enter the child welfare workforce may be able to understand stigma and trauma associated with abuse and neglect experiences and services (Kaplan, Skolnik, & Turnbull, 2009). Such individuals may in fact become strong advocates for children and families as their experiences within the "system" may indeed have attuned them to what is needed in providing more sensitive and trauma-informed services, as well as building more child- and family-responsive policies. Some may argue that former foster youth engaged in child welfare services are more likely to experience the sorts of "triggers" that provoke reliving trauma. But as larger numbers of child welfare agencies attempt to move toward "trauma-informed" services and evidence-based "supportive supervision," it is possible that this more inclusive organizational change can contribute to child welfare workers who report feeling less impacted by primary or secondary trauma (Conners-Burrow et al., 2013). Consistent with the NASW (2012) Code of Ethics, the case vignette illustrates the need for organizational and individual oversight of social work ethics within a rural child welfare agency.

## CASE VIGNETTE

### Ready to Go

Four months after I graduated with my MSW degree in May 2005, I got the call I was waiting for, the job I had trained so hard to achieve, when the human resources department at a department of human services in a Midwest state offered me a position as a children's services specialist in a rural county. Children's services specialists focus on one of three areas: protective services, foster care, or adoption. The position I was offered would focus exclusively on child protective services work. Since most of my childhood was spent in a rural county, I thought that my familiarity with the state's small towns and the outdoors would help with my transition to the area.

## Foster Child Stigma?

Excited to share the news with friends and mentors who supported me through my studies, I was cautioned. "Angelique," they asked, "are you sure this is what you want to do? Will it bring back unconscious and unresolved issues from your past?" It was true that I was a victim of child abuse and neglect. In fact, my family had been investigated for abuse and neglect allegations five times before I was removed from the home when I was 11 years of age and placed in foster care. But, honestly, I also wondered whether there was some larger issue at stake in their counsel that went beyond their concerns for me as a person. Is there such as thing as foster care placement stigma? Could it be possible that the field of child welfare carried with it some social distancing or, at least, reasons to be cautious in sharing that one was a survivor of abuse and neglect and the foster care system?

## Coming Out

During my MSW training, I told a few professors about my childhood years in foster care. This disclosure was met with supportive and empowering words of encouragement. For example, some said that my personal experience gave me unique experiences that would be an asset to the field. Further, I grew up in an area where "everybody knew everybody." The culture that obtained was high in interpersonal disclosure because it was part-and-parcel of who a person was. For example, when people in the northernmost part of the state meet someone new, they begin to identify that person by family or other community people linkages. So someone might ask, "Are you related to Sally Day?" Or they might inquire, "Do you live near the Green family that runs the Hunt Club?" Sharing information about oneself was pretty normal where I grew up. Even if you did not share, those asking probably knew the answer already.

Expecting that my foster care alumni status would be an asset to the field and knowing the value attached to rural sharing, I volunteered my personal history with my employer and my colleagues. However, the warmth and support I had received in academic settings when I told my "story" earned a mixed response from my child welfare colleagues. Some were reassuring; others were silent and unreadable. I instantly felt vulnerable, rather than empowered. Nor was I prepared for what would happen next.

## What Happened Next

I begin by explaining how I discovered that I had been "looked up" in the system. My job required me to use an office computer to access the state database to research the case history of any family that was referred to me for investigation. CPS workers have access to a statewide data system (the Social Work Service System) that allows them to track the history of families who have been investigated for abuse and neglect in the past. This allows workers an opportunity to assess the level of risk children may face for exposure to abuse and neglect in the present and the future. This tracking system was first implemented in many states, in 1974 under the initial passage of the Child Abuse Prevention and Treatment Act (CAPTA). Under the provisions of CAPTA, among its other requirements, states were required to have a system in place to receive and respond to allegations of child abuse and neglect in order to be qualify for federal funds to support child welfare programming (Committee on Ways and Means, US House of Representatives, 2012).

When I opened the system, I noticed that my name appeared in the recent search list at the top of the database site. Out of curiosity I clicked on the link and was mortified to see that my family's CPS history appeared on the screen. There it was—every address where I had ever lived, my birthday, Social Security number, the names of my parents and siblings and their personal identifying information, the date and county of each investigation, my date of removal, and more. Included were numerous incidents of abuse and neglect that I did not even remember. When I asked my supervisor why my name popped up in the search, she said somewhat nonchalantly, "Someone in the office must have looked you up." She then said, "Don't worry about it, I am in the system too because I am a foster parent." "Besides," she emphasized, "everyone in this little burg knows all about the people living here. That's the way it is. You'll get used to it."

I was stunned by this reaction. As a new hire, then only weeks into my new position, I felt powerless as to how to deal with the situation. I also felt violated. I could not imagine how being a registered foster parent in the system was even marginally similar to being in the system as a victim of abuse and neglect and whose degree of personal information was so accessible to those privy to the means of access. I then made the decision to contact the county of origin for my own foster care file in order to obtain my child welfare records. I figured if my colleagues had access to my personal information, I should at least have the right to know what had been formally documented about me.

I learned from this inquiry that the information I sought was protected and that certain things were required before I could gain access to my records. Worth noting, CAPTA requires that a state preserve the confidentiality of all child abuse and neglect reports and records in order to protect the rights of the child and the child's parents or guardians (Section 106(b)(2)(B)(viii) of CAPTA). CAPTA, however, does allow the state to share confidential records information with certain individuals:

- Individuals who are the subject of a report (Section 106(b)(2)(B)(viii)(I));
- A grand jury or court, when necessary to determine an issue before the court or grand jury (Section 106(b)(2)(B)(viii)(V)); and
- Other entities or classes of individuals who are authorized by statute to receive information pursuant to a legitimate state purpose (Section 106(b)(2)(B)(viii)(VI)). (Children's Bureau, 2012)

I clearly had rights under the federal law, and my colleagues' inquiry into my records did not fit under the provisions of CAPTA. Not only was I protected under federal law, the NASW (2012) Code of Ethics also provided guidance and direction to me as a social worker with access to protected information, which provides that

> Social workers should protect the confidentiality of clients' written and electronic records and other sensitive information. Social workers should take reasonable steps to ensure that clients' records are stored in a secure location and that clients' records are not available to others who are not authorized to have access. (NASW, 2012, 1.07 Privacy and Confidentiality, Section L)

My colleagues' system inquiry, in short, had been conducted without good cause. To gain access to my own records, I was required to write a formal letter to the state Department of Human Services, sign the letter, and provide a copy of my driver's license so that my signature could be verified to confirm the authenticity of the request. However, any public child welfare worker at any county in the state could simply look up my file at will without cause or prior consent from me. Most of us, in taking jobs, assume the existence of an implicit trust among those with whom we work. We also assume a level of professionalism neither casual nor arbitrary. As a new hire, I assumed my colleagues knew more than I did. I assumed that I must be wrong and they must be right. Due to my inability to trust my coworkers, and the lack of support from my supervisor to address this breach of confidentiality, I decided, after some time passed, to halt my investigation into the colleague-perpetrator who accessed my records. Eight months after accepting my new position, I left it. The simple truth is that I could not shake the lack of trust I had in my colleagues.

The NASW (2012) Code of Ethics articulates standards that the social work profession can use to assess whether social workers have engaged in unethical conduct. NASW has formal procedures to adjudicate ethical complaints filed against its members. The problem—and it is a significant one—is that many child welfare workers are not social workers and they are not members of NASW. Thus they are not bound by the NASW Code of Ethics. Very few child protective service workers in my county had either a BSW or MSW. My colleagues, instead, were anthropology, criminal justice, business, and education majors, some of whom were unable to secure employment in their fields of study. However, all of them would be expected to comply with the federal CAPT regulations.

## Practice Application

The importance of adhering to values and ethics in child welfare cannot be overstated. A sizeable portion of the workforce in child welfare are people who have been traumatized, some of whom were former foster children or had involvement with child welfare when they were growing up. Confidentiality is extremely important when providing services to families and when working with coworkers, whether it is in a supervisory capacity or as a colleague. Maintaining appropriate boundaries and confidentially is especially important when working in rural communities particularly, because gossip spreads so quickly in small and rural towns. Pay attention to how you want your colleagues to treat you and be that colleague to others. Finally, be prepared to advocate for confidentiality and rights within child welfare practice. This situation clearly needed to be addressed in the agency from training, compliance, and ethical standpoints. We need to do what we can to contribute to a healthier, more supportive child welfare workplace.

## DISCUSSION QUESTIONS

1. Multidisciplinary teams have members who work under different codes of ethics. How are these codes similar? How do they differ? What

protections do clients and coworkers have who work (or are served) in multidisciplinary team environments?

2. Should foster care alumni who choose to work in child welfare services be discouraged to disclose their status as a former ward of the court to their employer/professional colleagues?

3. If you were the child welfare supervisor in this case study, what steps would you have taken to address the concerns of your new hire?

4. What were the responsibilities of the author's other social work colleagues who saw the file on the system? What might they do or not do?

5. How might this case show evidence of a lack of a trauma-informed child welfare system? To what extent does the case evidence system induce retraumatization?

6. What rural cultural considerations were mentioned or implicit in this vignette? What might they mean? What others are you familiar with?

7. To what extent may the rural/urban binary affect, or not affect, specific child welfare agency practices?

8. To what extent may former foster care alumni be an asset to child welfare practice and policy? How? Rationales?

9. What other kinds of ethical challenges arise in child welfare practice? How are they tied to NASW professional standards?

## LEARNING ACTIVITIES

1. Supervisory Responses Role Play
   a. In groups of two people, role play the worker's conversation with her supervisor about finding her foster care files posted on the office computer network.
   b. At the end of the role play, take a few minutes to talk about what each person was feeling and thinking during the conversation.

2. Foster Care Stigma: Class Discussion
   a. What is foster care stigma? How does it show up? What perpetuates it? To what extent might the child welfare system (policies, agencies, employees) play a role in continuing foster care stigma? Be sure to include informal conversations or apparent assumptions about foster youth and foster families.
   b. What role can the child welfare system and workers play in decreasing foster care stigma? What are specific strategies to accomplish this? Brainstorm and share ideas for foster care stigma reduction.

3. Ethical Issues Analysis
   a. Look up the professional code of ethics of your profession. Social workers or social work students should go to socialworkers.org and locate the NASW Code of Ethics. Read through the ethical code. Which specific ethical areas may have been violated in this case vignette?

## SUGGESTED READING

Child Welfare Information Gateway. *Youth perspectives on foster care:* https://www.childwelfare.gov/topics/systemwide/youth/resourcesforyouth/youthperspectives/. Numerous resources on increasing youth voice in foster care services.

Gletow, D. (2015, August 11). We care do better than this: The Foster Care Bill of Rights. *The Huffington Post.* http://www.huffingtonpost.com/danielle-gletow/we-can-do-better-than-thi_3_b_7967762.html

Zimet, M. (2014, September 29). *Foster care "stigma" is felt by youth, perpetuated by professionals.* Retrieved from https://chronicleofsocialchange.org/blogger-co-op/changing-perceptions-in-foster

## REFERENCES

Belanger, K., & Stone, W. (2008). The social services divide: Service availability and accessibility in rural versus urban counties and impact on child welfare outcomes. *Child Welfare, 87*(4), 101–124. Retrieved from http://www.ncbi.nlm.nih.gov/pubmed/19391469

Children's Bureau. (2012). *Child welfare policy manual. 2.1A.1 CAPTA, Assurances and Requirements, Access to Child Abuse and Neglect Information, Confidentiality.* Retrieved from http://www.acf.hhs.gov/cwpm/programs/cb/laws_policies/laws/cwpm/policy_dsp.jsp?citID=6

Committee on Ways and Means, US House of Representatives. (2012). Chapter 11: Child welfare. In *Green Book.* Retrieved from http://greenbook.waysandmeans.house.gov/2012-green-book/chapter-11-child-welfare/introduction-and-overview

Conners-Burrow, N. A., Kramer, T. L., Sigel, B. A., Helpenstill, K., Sievers, C., & McKelvey, L. (2013). Trauma-informed care training in a child welfare system: Moving it to the front line. *Children and Youth Services Review, 35*(11), 1830–1835. http://dx.doi.org/10.1016/j.childyouth.2013.08.013

Kaplan, S. J., Skolnik, L., & Turnbull, A. (2009). Enhancing the empowerment of youth in foster care: Supportive services. *Child Welfare, 88,* 133–161.

National Association of Social Workers. (2012). *Code of ethics.* Washington, DC: Author. Retrieved from socialworkers.org

Pugh, R. (2007). Dual relationships: Personal and professional boundaries in rural social work. *British Journal of Social Work, 37,* 1405–1423. http://dx.doi.org/10.1093/bjsw/bcl088

Riebschleger, J. (2007). Social workers' suggestions for effective rural practice. *Families in Society: The Journal of Contemporary Social Services, 88*(2), 203–213. doi:10.1606/1044-3894.3618

# CHAPTER 17

∽

# Rural Relationship, Resources, and Rhythms

## A Child Welfare Training Program Learns about Workforce Development for (and From) Rural and Tribal Child Welfare Workers

### KATHARINE CAHN AND MICHELLE WARDEN

## LEARNING OBJECTIVES

- Discuss building an integrated and adaptive workforce development system to meet needs of rural, tribal, and frontier child welfare settings
- Identify customize training methods that fit rural and/or tribal child welfare pacing and relational worldviews
- Describe training and coaching child welfare workers to recognize the resourcefulness of rural and tribal communities
- List two or more unique community dynamics of serving as a rural or tribal child welfare worker

## BACKGROUND INFORMATION

### Rural Social Work

It can be difficult to recruit, and especially to retain, rural health and human professionals such as social workers, psychologists, counselors, nurses,

physicians, and educators. Many of these kinds of providers can access programs such as the National Health Services Corps that offer educational
loan payback incentives for working in rural areas. The work can be quite
rewarding in feeling like one can make difference in people's lives, experiencing respect from others for one's work, experiencing flexibility in work-
style, enjoying beautiful scenery, and building new networks of friends
and colleagues. At the same time, one may need to travel great distances
on poor roads (or no roads) to deliver services. Technological connections
may or may not work and this can, indeed, matter when one is among the
very few in the nation who does not have telephone or Internet services
(Belanger & Stone, 2008). There are likely to be less formal resources in
rural areas (Belanger, Price-Mayo, & Espinosa, 2008). The margins between
professional and personal practice require vigilance but sensible adapta-
tion; this can be challenging (Bosch & Boisen, 2011). People will know
about you professionally and personally. It can be a bit of a "goldfish bowl"
experience. Not everyone will appreciate the rural lifestyle. Those who grew
up in rural areas are more likely to live in a rural area as professional services provider, but this is certainly not a requirement for successful rural
practice (Mackie, 2007, 2011).

Child welfare workers face their own additional challenges in negotiating systems of care toward rehabilitative treatment models for children and
families and trying to do this within a tort-based legal system that tends
to use a more punitive base. There is a lot to know in order to be a competent child welfare worker, and much of the work in frontier rural areas
may not allow much access to supportive supervision. For example, child
welfare workers will need to know how to build social and cultural capital
in rural areas and how to identify and use informal resources (Riebschleger,
Norris, Pierce, Pond, & Cummings, 2015). A strength-based approach is
critically important but can feel difficult at first when dealing with families
with a plethora of challenges. One needs to be able to understand every
person, family, community, and region as unique and use their unique features within tailored intervention plans (Templeman & Mitchell, 2001).
One must learn the values, customs, and histories of the people. One can
ask: "How do they communicate? What do they care about? Who should
I connect with and how? How can I listen best? What are the strengths
of this person, family, and community?" The child welfare worker is likely
to need to understand that many rural people are more likely to value
"insider" (Gemeinshaft) perspectives and relationships more than logical,
technology-driven "outsider" (Gesellshaft) perspectives (Tönnies, 1887).

One of the avenues for trying to build a stronger and more resilient child
welfare workforce involves partnerships between educational institutions

and local people from child welfare and tribal agencies to better the ways that professionals, such as social workers, are prepared to deliver services. This chapter takes the reader on a journey of the lessons learned by university grant recipients as they aim to help build a child welfare workforce development project in rural frontier Alaska and parts of Oregon. The lessons are shared in a series of four vignettes that are also called case studies; these terms are used interchangeably.

## A Workforce Development Project

Workforce development is an important part of rural social work as it presents unique challenges and opportunities (Portland State University, 2007). Programs to develop a skilled workforce for child welfare (including professional education and in-service or preservice training) are typically offered by universities or agency-based training academies. These programs are likely to be located in metro-population centers or perhaps near the state capitol where state agency central offices tend to be located. As readers of this book already know, "location matters." The urban location and staffing of many child welfare training and education programs can impact the culture of the program. Specifically, training methods, training content, examples used in training, and the background and cadence of those providing the training will likely "tilt toward" an urban mindset or culture. This reflex can lead to the marginalization of the experience of rural, frontier, and nonurban tribal child welfare workers, and perhaps fail to prepare them well for practice in a rural or tribal context. The case studies that follow are designed to expand the programmatic thinking of those involved with child welfare workforce development, with the goal of improving the preparation for those providing child welfare services in a rural or tribal context.

The case studies are loosely adapted and drawn from the experiences of an urban-based state university implementing a five-year training grant from the US Children's Bureau to address the unique training needs of rural and tribal child welfare practitioners in the Pacific Northwest. Both authors worked for this grant-funded program, one as the principal investigator (PI) and the other as a lead curriculum developer and trainer. The PI comes from an urban background, and some stories reflect her lessons learned. The trainer comes from a rural and Indigenous background, with rural child welfare practice experience. She contributed elements of the curriculum and developed case studies that draw on her practice experience.

The grant-funded training program was delivered in specific areas of two states: (a) a frontier region in Alaska served by (and serving) both

Alaskan native and non-native people and (b) several rural and frontier areas of Oregon, which were home to tribal child welfare programs as well as rural child welfare offices. However, lessons learned from this five-year grant echo and confirm lessons learned by rural and tribal social workers across the nation. For this chapter, the case studies have been expanded or adapted to include themes learned in many settings. They are meant to be used for illustration and to inform training or educational program development, not to describe actual events or people.

The four vignettes, or case studies, reflect specific understandings gleaned about: (a) how to deliver training; (b) how to see resources and understand the unique role of a culturally- and community-embedded child welfare worker; (c) how to design the pace of training to meet the diversity of pacing found in rural and tribal cultures; and (d) how to cultivate the kinds of relationship needed in shaping child welfare practice in rural, tribal, and frontier areas.

## FOUR VIGNETTES

### Vignette 1: How to Cover the Distance (Hint: Online Learning Is Not a "One-Size-Fits-All" Solution)

Due to distance and the often small populations of a given rural place, the costs of in-person training in rural areas can be steep, sometimes even prohibitively so. Online learning has been used with varying degrees of success to overcome the challenges of travel and time away from home and office (Raymond, 1988). However, educators and trainers should not idealize distance or online learning methods as one-size-fits-all. Indeed, the highly relational character of rural and tribal cultures may call for increased attention to in-person approaches. A training or educational program should use varied approaches that take into account the dynamics of relationship and challenges of web access.

"Are you kidding me?" The training director (Nan Woods) said, with a map of Alaska in one hand and the draft of a grant proposal budget worksheet she was developing in the other. "It costs $3,000 round-trip to fly one person in from the villages for a week of training? And it's a nine-hour drive each way with two overnights for a rural child welfare worker to attend a one-day meeting here at the university? I want to get my training out to a lot of rural workers, but the travel budget alone is going to break the bank! How can we have impact on enough people to write a competitive grant with those prices?"

"Maybe we should build an online or distance-instruction platform," said Adam Lake, the new distance learning specialist. "People wouldn't have to fly so far, travel in bad weather, or leave the office short-staffed for so long. They could just do training at their desks."

"Great idea," said Nan. "That will make the budget work, and we can try some of these new online tools you've been talking about." Soon, the grant proposal was sent off to the funder.

Four months later, the training team was excited to hear their proposal had been funded. They looked forward to exploring this new way to meet training needs of child welfare workers in rural, tribal, and frontier areas. Marina Bell, an experienced rural child welfare worker and new member of the training team, was invited to serve on the advisory committee for the new grant-funded rural training. She had grown up and was raising her family in a small timber town in the Pacific Cascades. She loved her town for its beauty and the way everyone knew everyone. She didn't mind the hour-long commute to her new job as a child welfare trainer; in fact, she enjoyed making a difference with new workers across the state. That made the drive worthwhile. She looked forward to sharing her rural understanding, as well as her tribal heritage, with training participants and project advisors.

At the first meeting, she heard Adam talk about the exciting new online tools he hoped to bring. He had just completed a degree in online learning and was eager to use some of the new approaches he'd learned. He talked about webinars with embedded videos, chat rooms, video feeds from all learners, and other special ways to link up via the web. Many around the room expressed enthusiasm.

But Marina was more cautious. "How is that ever going to work?" she thought to herself. "Living in a rural area, I can't even get Internet in my house some of the time." But she kept her own counsel. After all, she was new, and it would be rude to speak up before you knew people better. At least, that's how people did it where she came from. You didn't talk just to hear yourself talk.

A year later, Adam met with the advisory team again to report the results of his assessment of the capacity for web-based learning in the rural and frontier implementation sites. There had been a lot of surprises. For example, he was dismayed to find that very few of the rural and frontier areas where they would be training had steady Internet access; at that time, many of them only had dial-up. Despite days and weeks spent working on these technical issues, he could find no fix that would work.

"Listen" said one rural educator. "Why don't you use the technology we use to reach rural and village students? It's called POT!"

Adam was fascinated. What was this new technology?

The educator laughed and said: "It stands for 'Plain Old Telephone.'"

Adam realized that, once again, he had missed the joke. That seemed to happen a lot around the tribal and rural members of the advisory committee; they always seemed to be pulling his leg a little or knocking him down a peg. However, he wanted to reach as many as possible, so he laughed along and asked to learn more about how this "low-tech" POT approach worked.

The rural educator shared how students in their program demonstrated such skills as effective listening over the phone or on conference calls with other students from rural areas. One child welfare supervisor from a remote town in Alaska said that she was in that program and liked it. She was able keep her job as a child welfare supervisor near home while still working toward her degree. And she used the skills she learned every day. The village representatives suggested sending handouts by email in advance and setting up a telephone call-in line in case the webinar didn't work that day. They recommended making things as simple as possible to accommodate slower Internet—thus no embedded videos or fancy graphics.

At the same time the project explored online learning, the rural training needs assessment showed that rural staff didn't want training to be entirely by distance learning or web-based methods. They asked that at least some of their training be delivered in person, even though it meant arranging schedules and case coverage while they were gone. They explained their day-to-day work consisted of many hours on the road by themselves, that they worked in offices with very few people, and that, often, they were on their own. For them, training was a chance to get to know other rural child welfare workers and would reduce their sense of isolation. Learning in a relational context and learning from stories worked well for them. For a change, they said, they'd like to be in a room with all rural people. They noted that child welfare services were delivered in a community context, not just by formal agencies, so it was helpful to have learning experiences that offered cross-training opportunities to bring natural and professional supports along together. Relationship-building across formal and natural supports was something they wanted from their trainings.

Though the distance learning specialist was sorry not to be able to use all the fancy new equipment he'd mastered, he and the training program director adapted, and a much more relational, in-person training program was offered within driving or flying distance of the offices served at a time of year where travel was reliable. Sometimes, trainers flew in to work with whole communities, including the child welfare staff, community partners, village elders, and others important to their work. Follow-up coaching and site-specific sharing were provided by telephone conference calls. When online training (such as webinars) was used, it was accompanied by phone conference-call lines and emailed handouts to assure that everyone had access to the material.

## Vignette 2: Resource Rich, or Resource Poor? What Families Need Can Be Right Under Their Noses—They Just Need to Be Able to See It

An important competency of child welfare practice is understanding resources. Child welfare training often includes teaching workers how to tap evidence-based or promising services that will best meet the child's needs for safety, well-being, and permanence. The complaint about "lack of resources" is often used to characterize the challenge of working in rural areas. However, rural workers told the training team that, while their communities might lack formal resources, they were rich in ways of keeping children safe and supporting strong families. You just have to know where to look. Training or education should prepare child welfare workers to see and value these resources. Two vignettes from the training program illustrate this point and show how trainers can empower rural child welfare workers to value the resources around them.

The training team was working with a group of elders and state workers, assembled in a circle. They hoped the circle would facilitate shared knowledge. This time Marina was facilitating the conversation, capturing answers on an easel and pad. "What are the resources you use to help your children and families?" she asked. The hands of state-employed child welfare workers shot up. She wrote their answers—"drug and alcohol treatment," "parenting classes," "anger management"—on the flip chart. Marina noticed that the elders were quiet, even withdrawn. She asked them what they would say.

"Oh, we don't have any of that," one grandmother replied.

"I find that hard to believe," Marina said respectfully. "You have been helping your families for thousands of years before contact with any kind of White people. What do you do when someone is in trouble?"

The woman visibly brightened, "Oh, we bring him to the Tea Man."

"Well, then, that's what you do," said Marina. "And does that work?"

"Sometimes," the grandmother said, only to reconsider, "Yes, very often it does."

Marina wrote" Tea Man, very often" on the flip chart. Then other elders started talking about working with youth who were getting into trouble. What they did was pair the youth up with an elder. The youth learned traditional ways, maybe hunting or subsistence fishing, and that kept them busy. By hearing these examples of traditional (but not formal) supports, the non-Indigenous workers in the room were able to gain information about how to keep children safe and how to carry cultural humility into their practice with tribal or Alaskan native villages. Honoring traditional wisdom and healing practices remain, after all, time-tested in tribal and Alaskan native child welfare work. "Culture heals," said one social worker.

Marina was able to recognize that wisdom because it was not too far from how things happened in her own rural hometown. Perhaps because of the bottom falling out of the timber industry, people in this mountain town had had a lot of struggles with addictions; the treatment programs that could help were far away and pricey. Thus they found their own solutions to recovery. For example, a man named Bill had been a dealer for a long time, but he got clean and sober, was active in his church, and had been serious in his recovery for more than 15 years. Marina knew that Bill was the person in town anyone went to if they were ready to get off drugs. They weren't going to drive 60 to 100 miles to find a drug treatment program; they'd go see Bill because that's who they trusted. And, Marina knew, if people relapsed, they relapsed, and went to see Bill some more. That's just the way it was. As a child welfare worker, Marina knew that a parent who "went to see Bill" was actively engaged in what she needed to do to keep her child safe, not slacking or being noncompliant. In her work interfacing with the courts on her cases, Marina realized she could help the judge understand that informal supports and many eyes and ears would help to assure safety of the child. There aren't too many secrets in a small town like mine, thought Marina. We do know how to keep children safe. Because of her sensitivity to this work, she was able to pass these best rural practices along to workers in the rural child welfare training.

### Vignette 3: Rural and Tribal Diversity. Varying the Pace of Training to Hear All Voices

Rural culture is not monolithic, and the cultural backgrounds brought into the room vary. In this training program, and in other rural areas, there may be cultural differences in communication styles and pacing between White workers or White agency culture and the Indigenous cultures of local tribes or villages. How can training incorporate all voices?

The training program had learned a lot about how to build trainings for rural and tribal workers. Finally, they were ready to launch the first session of the in-person training, called "In Celebration of Rural Practice." It was held at a beautiful rural retreat center, with a good off-season group rate. Rural state and tribal child welfare workers gathered after breakfast and the training began. Very quickly it became apparent that something was seriously wrong.

A tribal liaison pulled the training program director aside. "These state workers are so rude," she said. "They are noisy; they interrupt; they don't let us finish our sentences or get a word in edgewise. I don't know that I can advise the tribal participants to stay."

Concerned to hear this, the training director spoke to one of the non-native rural child welfare supervisors who seemed to have a lot of credibility with her peers. "Could you and your colleagues please be a little quieter?" she asked. "Could you try to make more room in the conversation for the Alaskan Native and American Indian participants to contribute?"

The rural supervisor responded, "The thing is we are just so glad to finally be with other rural workers that we can't help it if we laugh and joke around. We don't mean to be rude, but being quiet would defeat the whole purpose of being at this special training. We're having fun."

The training team met and came up with a plan. They asked the tribal liaison for permission to use a traditional practice called the talking circle to open the next day (Running Wolf & Pickard, 2003). A talking circle generally involves the arrangement of chairs in a room into a circle, the purpose of which allows each person in the room a designated time and space to share his or her experience without being interrupted. The talking circle took 90 minutes, and the training team cut other planned sections of the training to make room for it. In the end, the team members were glad they did. The level of trust, the depth of the personal stories, and the insights that arose made for a powerful learning experience. So the talking circle enabled those to speak who would never interrupt another speaker and those who might speak too much to wait their turn and attend fully.

### Vignette 4: Relationship, Relationship, Relationship: The Unique Role of Rural and Tribal Workers

One overarching theme of the rural and tribal training grant involved the central importance of relationships and relationship skills in effective rural practice. In its finer distinctions, that theme includes establishing relationships, establishing credibility, staff recruitment and retention, and, of the utmost importance, the constant of multiple roles. The simple truth is that in rural or tribal areas, people are interrelated across multiple roles. Folks have to trust one another and figure out a way to live together; the luxury of anonymity common to urban environments has no place in rural areas.

Going home to another neighborhood, going elsewhere for grocery shopping, attending faith or cultural events someplace else, or coaching sports teams that are not local would be unimaginable in rural communities of the sort discussed in this chapter. That said, the National Association of Social Workers (2012) Code of Ethics cautions against having multiple relationships. For that reason, child welfare workers in rural or tribal areas walk a very fine line. Figuring out how to do this entails both strength and stress for rural and tribal child welfare workers; for trainees, learning to navigate the ethical balance between confidentiality and belonging is, at the very least, demanding. Furthermore, relational/personal attributes such as humility, personal integrity, and helpfulness are more highly valued than formal attributes—for instance, titles or degrees.

Just as the process of entering and remaining engaged in a rural community takes time and patience, the same holds true for workers who must establish their characters. Because of the place-specific social and cultural capital required in rural areas and the time involved in developing them, social workforce researchers have concluded that sometimes it may be more effective to "grow your own" staff (an oft-repeated imperative in training programs as well). Recruiting child welfare staff with established roots in the rural or Indigenous place and its culture also helps. The next case study addresses the content of training that aids in meeting these specific needs.

As she listened to the tribal and rural practitioners on the advisory group and in focus groups around the state, Nan realized that both the MSW program and her training programs at the university had been teaching child welfare workers in competencies related to *tasks* and *knowledge*. But what she was hearing in the focus groups stressed the *relationship* skills, interpersonal intelligence, and sensitivity needed for rural child welfare practice.

"Teach people how to enter this community if they aren't from here," said one rural supervisor. "Teach them the pacing of things. Tell them, don't get down to business right away . . . that's just rude. Wait to get a feel of what's going on in the room, and who's related to whom, and what's going on. Find the common ground."

Along the same lines, a tribal child welfare worker observed, "You just can't push the tribes or the tribal council around. Things will happen when they're supposed to happen." Nan wondered how she could teach that kind of patience or, for that matter, whether it could be taught.

Help came from a tribal social worker who talked about cultural humility. "Sure," she said, "I have a social work degree, but many of my fellow workers don't. They were picked for their jobs by the tribe for other reasons. I value my degree, but I don't flaunt it. In fact, people tease me about it. I make sure to be of service in concrete ways. I help at the potluck, show up at community gatherings, and respect the elders properly. I don't want people to think I've lost my appreciation of where I come from—or my manners, even though I once left my home for school and now sometimes have to remove someone's child or a cousin's child. It isn't easy. It seems as if their eyes are always on me, thinking maybe I'm not one of them anymore. I'm never off-duty." She offered to be a mentor to others wishing to work in tribal areas.

"You send us these new social workers with their fresh-out-of-graduate-school degrees, and they don't make it here," said one rural supervisor. "By the end of the first year, they can't wait to go back to the city and, quite frankly, they've burned so many bridges we're glad to see them go. We really need to grow our own. We need a way to get in-service training or social work education for people who live here, who know our families and are going to stay."

## Conclusions

Developing the rural or tribal child welfare workforce is both challenging and rewarding, with training solutions available that meet the challenges and tap the resources available in rural areas. The challenges of low population, lack of travel or communications infrastructure, lack of formal resources, and the need to cover great distances to attend an educational event are well documented. The vignettes provided in this section show that training delivery approaches, learning strategies, and content can be shaped to meet these approaches in ways to offer more effective workforce education and training programming for rural and tribal areas. But there are also strengths to draw from to meet the unique context of rural and tribal practice. The interdependence and creativity of rural communities, as well as the strong cultural ties and resilience of Indigenous communities, are resources that will enrich child welfare practice. These elements should be featured in training to enrich the experience for child welfare workers who practice in rural and tribal settings. A stable rural or tribal workforce is best built from people who are rooted in their communities and places, people who can learn and contextualize best practices to meet their community setting (Mathias & Benton, 2011). Rural practitioners should be included in training teams and university-based child welfare workforce development programs so that they can bring their perspective and sensitivity to all curricula and training approaches. In this way, staff working in rural and tribal child welfare settings will be served in training rooms where their practice is celebrated, even honored—not cheapened or thought of as "lacking," "less than," "intractable" or some other paternalistic qualifier.

## Practice Application

Developing the workforce for child welfare in the United States has been an ongoing effort since the 1980s. Counties and states have invested much time, effort, and money into ensuring that children and families have the best workers possible. Workers must learn to work in both urban and rural settings because every state has aspects of both and children are sometimes placed in foster homes all over the states. While most front-line workers only take the training and do not necessarily become the trainers, it is important for all workers to understand the training needs of the workforce in order to ensure that coworkers, new workers, and student interns in the agency are trained for competent practice in rural and urban settings.

# DISCUSSION QUESTIONS

1. Is online or in-person (group-based) training more effective for you (in terms of learning)? What is the difference between the two in your experience? Which one do you pay more attention to, and in which do you learn the most?
2. If safety, permanence, and well-being are the goals of all child welfare practice, wouldn't the competencies of training workers be the same for urban and rural areas? Why would they vary? What stays the same?
3. Would you rather work in a rural setting or an urban setting? Which kind of setting is more familiar to you?
4. How is the National Association of Social Workerse Code of Ethics mandate to avoid dual, or multiple, roles carried out in rural or close-knit tribal areas? How might a child welfare worker honor confidentiality or set boundaries?
5. When people from some cultures leave silence between sentences and others interrupt or talk over one another, how can these differences be accommodated in a classroom setting?

# LEARNING ACTIVITIES

1. Relationship Planning
   a. Training and workforce development programs need to draw on relational strengths and create relational opportunities. Learners can discuss relational opportunities. How will they stay in touch after graduation or after training ends?

2. Researching Cell and Internet Access in Rural Areas
   a. Ask participants to search cell phone and Internet coverage across the country. Where are the gaps? How can rural workers in the gap areas access learning?
3. Application of Rural Practice—Ethical Scenarios
   a. The competencies and ethical code for rural child welfare are the same as those for staff working in urban areas but require retranslating or adapting to the rural or tribal context. Discuss typical scenarios for workers in rural contexts.
4. Interview Assignment
   a. "Grow your own," or investing in the education and training of people who live in tribal or rural areas, may be more likely to succeed than asking urban culture people to adapt to rural or tribal ways. Survey or interview workers in your local child welfare office. Are they from the same rural areas they grew up in, or are they "transplants?" If from an urban or suburban area (a background size form of transplants), how did they learn to work in rural areas?

## SUGGESTED READING

Child Welfare Information Gateway: https://www.childwelfare.gov/topics/system-wide/diverse-populations/rural/. Resources on rural child welfare.
National Resource Center for Permanency and Family Connections: http://www.nrcpfc.org/is/rural-issues.html. Rural issues in child welfare.

## REFERENCES

Bosch, L. A., & Boisen, L. S. (2011). Dual relationships in rural areas. In L. Ginsberg (Ed.), *Social work in rural communities* (5th ed., pp. 111–123). Alexandria, VA: Council on Social Work Education.
Belanger, K., Price-Mayo, B., & Espinosa, D. (2008). The plight of rural child welfare: Meeting standards without services. *Journal of Public Child Welfare*, 1(4), 1–19. Retrieved from http://www.tandfonline.com/doi/pdf/10.1080/15548730802118181
Belanger, K., & Stone. W. (2008). The social services divide: Service availability and accessibility in rural versus urban counties and impact on child welfare outcomes. *Child Welfare*, 87, 101–124. Retrieved from http://www.tandfonline.com/doi/pdf/10.1080/15548730802118181.pdf
Mackie, P. F. E. (2007). Understanding the educational and demographic differences between rural and urban social workers. *The Journal of Baccalaureate Social Work*, 12, 114–128. doi:10.18084/1084-7219.12.2.114)
Mackie, P. F. E. (2011). Rural social work recruitment and retention challenges: Why is it difficult to fill rural social work positions? In L. Ginsberg (Ed.), *Social work*

*in rural communities* (5th ed., pp. 141–160). Alexandria, VA: Council on Social Work Education.

Mathias, C., & Benton, A. D. (2011). Social justice through the education of a rural and tribal child welfare workforce. *Journal of Public Child Welfare, 5*(2–3), 282–296 Retrieved from http://dx.doi.org/10.1080/15548732.2011.573756

National Association of Social Workers. (2012). *Code of ethics.* Washington, DC: Author. Retrieved from socialworkers.org

Portland State University. (2007, June). *Training for excellence in child welfare practice in rural Oregon and Alaska.* Retrieved from https://www.childwelfare.gov/topics/management/funding/funding-sources/federal-funding/cb-funding/cbreports/rural/portland/#tab=summary

Raymond, F. B. (1988, July). *Providing social work education and training in rural areas through interactive television.* Paper presented at the Annual National Institute on Social Work and Human Services in Rural Areas. Fort Collins, CO. Retrieved from http://files.eric.ed.gov/fulltext/ED309910.pdf

Riebschleger, J., Norris, D., Pierce, B., Pond, D., & Cummings, C. (2015). Preparing social work students for rural child welfare practice: Emerging competencies. *Journal of Social Work Education, 51*(Suppl. 2), S209–S224. doi10.1080/10437797.2015.1072422

Running Wolf, P., & Rickard, J.A. (2003). Talking circles: A Native American approach to experiential learning. *Journal of Multicultural Counseling and Development, 31,* 39–43. doi:10.1002/j.2161-1912.2003.tb00529.x

Templeman, S. B., & Mitchell, L. (2001). Challenging the one-size-fits-all myth: Findings and solutions from a statewide focus group of rural social workers. *Child Welfare, 81,* 757–772. Retrieved from http://www.cwla.org/child-welfare-journal/

Tönnies, F. (1887). *Gemeinschaft und Gesellschaft.* Leipzig: Fues's Verlag. Translated by Charles Price Loomis as *Community and Society* (East Lansing: Michigan State University Press, 1957), 31, 39–43.

# CHAPTER 18

∾

# Secondary Trauma Prevention
# in Rural Child Welfare

## *Professionals' Self-Care Strategies*

JOANNE RIEBSCHLEGER AND BARBARA J. PIERCE

Four generation family farm. The owners take pride in their well-kept four generation farm. Small family farms are becoming more rare in a global economy with large, corporate farms.
David G. Riebschleger

## LEARNING OBJECTIVES

- Give an example of how rural child welfare settings can contribute to professionals' work-related stress
- Identify four or more possible indicators of secondary trauma
- Make a list of at least four specific actions the reader can take to reduce workplace stress
- Describe the importance of developing and accessing multiple sources of social and workplace support
- Articulate two or more ways that working in rural areas can contribute to professionals' satisfaction with their professional and personal lives

## CHILD TRAUMA AND RESILIENCE

Today's child welfare practitioners are likely paying attention to the emotional, social, and physical (brain-related) impacts of child and family exposure to trauma situations or events. The National Child Traumatic Stress Network (n.d.) defines trauma events as "high risk situations such as school shootings, gang violence, terrorist attacks, natural disasters, serious accidents, sudden or violent losses of loved ones, and physical and sexual assaults" (p. 1). When a person's capacity to cope cannot keep up with stress associated with trauma events, he or she can experience stress symptoms.

Children exposed to severe and/or ongoing abuse and neglect episodes can react to these experiences much like a war veteran who has symptoms of posttraumatic stress disorder (PTSD). Children may have difficulties with sleeping, eating, paying attention, controlling their emotions, and toileting. They may develop stomachaches and headaches. They may have trouble paying attention. They may be extremely anxious in the present when exposed to a "trigger" for their past stress, such as a bedroom door squeaking in the night just as it did when a sexual predator entered their bedroom to abuse them. Traumatized children may experience brain development deficiencies and behavior problems, including acting out or being extremely withdrawn (Saxe, Ellis, & Brown, 2016). Child welfare workers and other community professionals are often engaged in trying to build more trauma-sensitive systems of care. This means that the professionals work together to try to avoid retraumatizing children. This can happen when children have to tell their abuse and neglect stories repeatedly and when children are frequently moved about from foster home to foster home, necessitating multiple school changes (Riebschleger, Day, & Dworsky, 2015).

It is important to remember, however, that children and families can be resilient even if exposed to severe and/or ongoing trauma events. Some children who receive support from one or a number of nurturing adults can grow up to be productive adults who have healthy families. Children who exhibit the strength to build on their talents also demonstrate stronger developmental outcomes, which may include playing a sport, drawing, painting, singing, writing, or simply communicating well with others. While it is not entirely clear why some children stay strong in stressful situations, plenty of evidence supports that they do.

## SECONDARY TRAUMA

Child welfare professionals can experience secondary trauma because of their association with children experiencing abuse and neglect. Secondary traumatic stress arises out of emotional labor. This means that engaging in highly charged emotional situations can be very stressful. Examples include investigating abuse and removing children from their homes. One of the most traumatizing can be the "dead baby run," which means that a worker has been called to a site, such as a hospital, to find a child killed by someone's abusive or neglectful actions. Child welfare professionals listen to a lot of severe abuse stories in their work. No matter how seasoned the professional, there are times when the stories are so awful that the worker has a physical and/or emotional stress reaction. And child welfare crises recognize no clock—evenings and weekends are equally in play (Tavormina & Clossey, 2015). It is not an easy thing to remove a child from his or her family, nor are the struggles that ensue about whether and where to place or not place a child.

Just as professionals can derive a great deal of satisfaction from their emotional labor, they can also experience additional stress when they realize that, despite their best efforts, children are sometimes retraumatized by the child welfare system. Children can be abused before, during, and after out-of-home care (Riebschleger et al., 2015). Abused children are sometimes court-ordered to return to a home that the caseworker may deem an abusive living situation. Foster parents may insist a child be removed from their home. Adoptions can fall apart. Clients wind up angry and hostile.

Child welfare workers can experience trauma symptoms such as changes in sleeping and eating. They may develop headaches and stomachaches. They may have difficulty making decisions and remembering things. They may find they are re-experiencing, in dreams and/or in thoughts, feelings about traumatizing events. They may feel sad, angry, or have a sense of being "frozen" from emotions. They may find themselves turning to alcohol or cigarettes to calm themselves. They may withdraw from friends, family, and work colleagues. Professionals may appear uncaring and apathetic in working with people. Their work performance quality may fall. They may not seem to care about their work. They may suddenly believe they are ineffective. They may have trouble making decisions. These behaviors can be signs of traumatic stress, burnout, and compassion fatigue (Salloum, Kondrat, Johnco, & Olson, 2015). Sometimes the symptoms reach the stage of clinical diagnosis: PTSD, anxiety disorders, and depression.

## Rural Social Work Practice: Possible Stressors

It is possible that working in some rural areas, especially without sufficient support, can add to work-related stress. It is possible in frontier areas to be the only social worker for a hundred or more miles. Rural professionals sometimes report that they cover a large geographic territory to serve clients who may be living in severe poverty. They may have to serve their clients without access to nearby and sufficient community resources. They sometimes have more than one kind of job at the agency (foster care *and* protective services, for example). Rural child welfare workers may experience professional isolation when they do not have access to supportive peer or agency supervision (Daley, 2015). Simply put, they may not have anyone to talk to about their workplace-related stressors and sometimes feel as if they are always "on call."

## Worker Resilience

But all is not lost. The good news is that child welfare professionals are not destined to become "crispy critters"—a term used in some agency work-sites to refer to people experiencing stress and burnout. Like the children and families that they serve, child welfare workers can be resilient in the face of much stress. Rural social workers can, for example, set up a face-to-face or Skype/Zoom peer network for social and work-related support. They can find mentors and advisors, as well as cultural guides who help them access resources. They can work to build new resources where none exist. They can even seek professional help if the stress becomes too great.

One of the most important actions that child welfare professionals can undertake is to plan for and engage in self-care activities (Salloum, Kondrat, Johnco, & Olson, 2015). Care for traumatic stress must be a shared endeavor. Workers must learn to make and carry out their own self-care plans; supervisors must learn to assess and intervene with individual workers and their teams to encourage a positive work culture; and organizations must recognize that the nature of the work they do involves secondary traumatic stress and plan for a culture of positivity and care toward workers. It is important for workers to realize that clients can pick up on worker stress. One worker had this interaction with a preschooler:

> Ms. Stephanie, you go home and take a nap?
>
> No, friend. Ms. Stephanie wants to see another friend after I take you back.
>
> No, Ms. Stephanie. You go home and take a nap!
>
> I wish buddy, but I haven't seen all my friends yet today.
>
> Ugh. You go home and take a nap! I call my mommy and she tell her you take a nap! (personal communication, S. Dobbs, July 8, 2016)

Individuals must learn to build their own self-care plans. Self-care plans are not cookie-cutter formatted. People should know what causes stress and what relieves stress in their lives. If they do not, they need to learn to reflect upon these ideas and get in touch with their stress and stress relief. There are, in fact, many techniques to use "in the moment" when something stressful has just happened on the job: for example, taking a five-minute break, getting in touch with feelings, and consciously developing another way to think about or deal with the issue can be extremely helpful. This is a cognitive-behavioral technique that depends upon "reframing," which is also of use in general interviewing techniques and stating strengths. Workers have to learn the value of the broader perspective. Most families with whom child welfare workers work do well because interventions, in fact, do make a big difference in the lives of the children in those families. It is also very important for workers to understand that the majority of people in the world are good and caring people who do not abuse or neglect children. This perspective can help workers, particularly when they are parenting their own children and are inclined to overprotect them.

Workers can also make sure they are "leaving work at work" when they are not on call. This allows them the chance to gain "nourishment" from their own families to help sustain the work-life balance. Some workers exercise, while others are involved in community activities, their church, or sports with their own children. Some workers enjoy music as a relaxation activity; others may enjoy art or dance. No matter what, something is out there that helps.

Mindfulness techniques and yoga practice have also been demonstrated to be helpful in coping with stress. Another mindful technique for some people is prayer, as are breathing techniques. Still, whatever works requires consistency. Take vacation days and, if need be, use them as "mental health" days. Too often workers "plod through" when they should, instead, be taking a bit of time to get away and recharge their emotional batteries. Talk openly with family and friends about your feelings but not about case specifics, since we must always remember to protect confidentiality. Workers can also form close networks of colleagues, even if they live remotely. Skype and Zoom rooms are good for that. More than anything, seek supervision for secondary traumatic stress.

Supervisors must learn to assess secondary traumatic stress and discuss it with their teams. They must encourage self-care, breaks, vacations, flexible scheduling, or a team approach whenever possible (consistent, of course, with agency policies). Sometimes pairing up workers on a difficult case relieves the burden of having to bear it alone; one person suffers, two commiserate and support. Supervisors should institute weekly check-ins to find out how workers are holding up or even daily ones (e.g., a "buddy system" whereby you make sure your buddy goes to lunch or takes a break). Last and likely most important, supervisors must engage in clinical supervision to address the "slings and arrows" that frequently rain down upon child welfare workers.

Agencies, too, must bear some responsibility in helping workers with secondary traumatic stress. By encouraging a climate of positivity, celebrating successes, and providing support during difficult times, the agency can help workers with the emotional labor of love that they engage in every day. Policies that promote flexibility include job sharing, elasticity in scheduling hours, work-life balance, and access to employee assistance programs. In short, all must be done that can be done to promote a positive workplace culture. That way, workers want to stay and will do their utmost to provide the services children and their families need.

While practicing in rural areas can be stressful because of isolation or the "fishbowl" phenomenon, it can also be an enriching, positive experience. Social workers are respected members of the community who have high social capital for their ability to "get things done." Living in rural areas can provide for a wonderful lifestyle for the worker and his or her family. Rural areas often have safe schools, clean air, less traffic, easy parking, and, when you work at and invest the time, friendly relationships. It can be comforting when your pharmacist knows your family or when your neighbors are looking out for you in good times and bad.

## CASE VIGNETTE

Matilda Calhoun was a 34-year-old woman living in a small town of 4,000 people in California. She grew up in the area and had three children, ages 1, 6, and 10. Her partner was a local healthcare professional. The local people considered them "insiders" in the community, given Matilda's local upbringing and her partner's regular contributions to local health fairs, school activities, and nonprofit organizations. She and her partner knew many of their professional colleagues from shared community activities. Ms. Calhoun had worked for five years at the local community mental health clinic as a child and mental health therapist. Her responsibilities included working closely with the local child welfare workers and school system staff in cases that had multiagency involvement.

Ms. Calhoun recently began to work with six-year-old Sam and his mother Georgina Vernon. Sam was an only child. Ms. Vernon asked for services for her son Sam after his first-grade teacher, Ms. Marsh, had notified her that Sam was crying in school for "no reason," not paying attention to his class assignments, constantly fidgeting, not listening to teacher's directions, and staying by himself on the playground. Ms. Marsh was worried Sam might have ADHD. Ms. Vernon disputed that diagnosis and instead said of her son, "He seemed listless, not hyperactive, he just doesn't seem to have any energy." She said this behavior seemed to worsen after Sam returned from weekend visits with "the father." She noted that she and her husband were in the midst of an acrimonious divorce. When asked what other kinds of behaviors Sam was demonstrating, Ms. Vernon said that before visiting his father Sam would grow extremely anxious and insist that he did not want to go there. She also noted that Sam seemed to be having problems staying asleep; about twice a week he was waking up with nightmares. She said he wasn't eating much but that was par for him as he has "always been a slender boy."

Ms. Vernon indicated that she had taken Sam to the local primary-care provider who recommended he be assessed by a mental health professional. According to Ms. Vernon, this professional, Dr. Kumar, did not note any physical health problems except that Sam was slightly underweight for his age. She then called and made her son an appointment at the mental-health clinic (CMH). When Sam met with Ms. Calhoun, he was initially very quiet and reserved. He took a long time to go through the toy box in Ms. Calhoun's office and appeared to have a difficult time deciding what toys to play with. When he finally settled on Homer and Bart Simpson figures, he began to talk about school and his toys at his mothers' home.

Ms. Calhoun obtained a release of information (just to be safe) and called Sam's father, Patrick Vernon. When asked how Sam might be adjusting to the divorce, Mr. Vernon said that his wife "is trying to work against me." He disclosed that she had bipolar disorder and was prone to "crazy thinking." He remarked, "You can't believe a word she says."

In the second visit to the CMH clinic, Sam began to pretend he was "Bart." Bart began to beat up Homer, viciously kicking and hitting Homer while making angry fight sounds, "ARRGH . . . YOU . . . YOU . . . POW !" He continued to beat Homer over and over again for more than five minutes; after that catharsis, he seemed much calmer and at ease. He began to talk more openly about wanting to have more friends and feeling sad a lot. He refused to talk about anything that took place at his father's home. Nor would he explain what Bart was feeling and what made him so mad at Homer. When Ms. Vernon joined the session, she volunteered that she was on medications for bipolar disorder and had been stable and medication-compliant since Sam was born. While pregnant, however, she did not take her bipolar medications upon the advice of her obstetrician. "That was difficult," she reflected.

During the third visit, Bart continued to kick, slap, punch, and throw Homer to the ground. At one point, Homer began to mount Bart from the rear, which was followed by Bart's particularly aggressive attack on Homer. Again, Sam refused to tell Ms. Calhoun the nature of Bart's anger toward Homer or anything about his father's home. On the fourth visit, Sam told Ms. Calhoun that his father cautioned him never to tell "Miss C" (Patrick's name for Ms. Calhoun) anything about what happened when Sam stayed with him.

During the fifth visit, "Miss C" worked with Sam to find out the names of those people his father never put on the "forbidden list." Excluded from it was Ms. Marsh, Sam's teacher. So Ms. Calhoun and Sam figured out that it was okay for him to tell his teacher about what was going on at his father's house. Not too long thereafter, Ms. Calhoun received a call from Ms. Vernon who informed her that someone had filed a child protective services (CPS) complaint against her and that she didn't know what was going on. When the CPS people came to the house, she said, they asked a lot of questions about the divorce, Sam's father, Sam's behaviors, and her mental health. During that same period, Sam's father had filed for full custody of Sam. Relating this information to Ms. Calhoun deeply upset Ms. Vernon; she cried throughout the conversation. She said she was worried about losing custody of Sam because of her mental illness diagnosis. A few days later, Ms. Vernon called again, saying this time that CPS had asked the court to suspend Sam's visits with his father, pending a psychological evaluation of Sam and further investigation into the abuse/neglect charge. Ms. Vernon indicated that her father "has some money" and intended to pay for an attorney for her.

Sam saw a psychologist, Dr. Wilson, an African American woman, whose investigative specialty was sexual abuse. Her practice was in a city 100 miles to the south. The local CPS worker was now in touch with Ms. Calhoun and Sam's teacher (Ms. Marsh), who reported the sexual abuse. A sexual abuse investigation was currently underway. The child welfare worker, Mr. Hadden, said that the custody lawsuit was on hold. Ms. Calhoun continued to see Sam about every other week. He grew 2.5 inches in the three months following his time with Dr. Wilson. He spoke openly and at normal volume; he also made good eye contact. His teacher reported the welcome news that Sam was doing "above-grade-level work." Ms. Vernon said his nightmares had discontinued. Her only complaint was that he "has so much energy now" that she finds herself already exhausted by his bedtime, not hers. In sessions, Sam began to tell Ms. Calhoun that his father and his male friend Tommy would stick something in his "hiney" that went "whir, whir, whir." He said, "it hurt a lot. After they did that, they'd give me ice cream. Sometimes I ate it, sometimes I didn't, depending on how grumpy I was."

Mr. Vernon was charged with first-degree child abuse and went to trial. He pled not-guilty. Since Sam would possibly have to testify, Dr. Hadden, Ms. Calhoun, and Mr. Hadden worked with Sam on how to look only at Ms. Calhoun or Dr. Hadden in court—and *not* at his father. Prior to court, the prosecutor had everyone on the "plaintiff" side meet in a conference room. Dr. Wilson showed Ms. Calhoun pictures drawn by Sam before and after disclosure of sexual abuse. The "before" drawings had basic "tadpole" figures that looked to be drawn by a three-year-old. The only colors Sam used were red and black. The "after" drawings looked typical of a six-year-old as they depicted more solid figures with hair, shoes, and fingers. The postdisclosure pictures even had a sun in the top-right corner.

Ms. Calhoun was subpoenaed to attend the trial but was never called to testify. Dr. Hadden said that Dr. Wilson did a wonderful job of describing the sexual abuse and Sam's behaviors before and after disclosure. Sam did not have to testify during the trial. At the end of the trial, the jury returned a verdict of "not guilty." Within a week, Sam was ordered to begin visits every other week with his father.

Ms. Calhoun was so upset by the verdict that she could not stop crying. She slept poorly. She wondered if she should leave her job. She could not handle the idea that this young boy was soon to return to a home where he could expect a vibrator up the anus with no one there to protect him. Ms. Calhoun called Dr. Hadden who was also very upset. Out of frustration, she even called the family judge in the case, whom she had known for years. She wanted to know what happened and what might happen next. The judge said the law can be pretty rough on people, but that's the way it is. "However," he said, "I hate to say this but I did hear a jury member say aloud to another jury member, 'I wouldn't believe that Black woman from downstate . . . or that kid's crazy mother.'" Ms. Calhoun was not comforted by this disclosure. She wondered whether the outcome would have been different had she, a local white professional, been called to testify rather than the African American child sexual abuse specialist from "downstate." In the wake, she was sickened by a sense that something had gone entirely wrong.

Only months later did her nausea and pain begin to abate when she learned that, after the trial, Mr. Vernon no longer asked to have Sam visit. She recognized that losing his father was yet another "loss" for Sam and that he might imagine he was, somehow, at fault. She knew, finally, that much more work was to be done to deal with Sam's trauma—and her own.

### Practice Application

Working in child welfare whether in the private or public sector is very stressful work. It is also quite rewarding. Learning to accept that the social worker works in a context that includes many other professionals including the courts is important because social workers do not independently make all of the decisions. Social workers must realize that they must learn to work within the confines of the role and that is sometimes a hard lesson. This work also can and does produce secondary traumatic stress. Workers have to remember to be vigilant with their own self-care plan, seek supervision and support when necessary, and understand that their work despite being challenging is important and matters to the children and families they serve.

## DISCUSSION QUESTIONS

1. In the participant's experiences, what kinds of factors make for a stressful workplace in general? a happier workplace in general? How do these ideas tie to child welfare settings? to child welfare in rural settings?
2. Should the judge have told Ms. Calhoun about the jury member? Was this any kind of "dual relationship" situation, or was it professionally okay?

3. Are rural areas more racist? To what extent could this situation happen in an urban or a suburban setting?
4. What are some ways Ms. Calhoun can deal with her trauma symptoms?

## LEARNING ACTIVITIES

1. Stress Management Activity Planning
   a. The participants will read and complete the handouts in "Managing Stress as Child Welfare Caseworker" (see Suggested Readings). Have them talk about the handout on organizational, emotional, behavioral, and physical indicators of stress. Have each one complete the Caseworker Readiness Activity sheet. He or she will prepare a plan to engage in one activity that may help the particular person manage work and personal stress.
   b. Then review stress-reduction strategies and discuss what works for whom among class discussion volunteers.
2. System Analysis for Secondary Trauma
   a. The purpose of this exercise is to represent the need for reducing stress at many levels in the child welfare system and beyond. Ask participants to draw some kind of visual figure for micro, meso, and macro systems. One common way to show this is to have them draw a series of concentric circles spreading out from a smaller center. This will look like a halved onion.
   b. In the center, they are to consider a stressed child welfare professional who works in a rural setting. This is a micro system. In the middle circles, participants should label the medium-size systems surrounding the worker, such as small groups, peers, supervision, friends, and family. In the outer layers of the "onion," the participants should label the macro systems surrounding the micro and meso systems. Macro systems include large groups, neighborhoods, communities, organizations, institutions, and policies. The participants should label the layers with the best-fit macro systems for the stressed child welfare professional shown in the center of the figure.
   c. Ask small groups of participants to identify ways to reduce or prevent the level of stress for this worker (and others like him or her). Ask them to consider how a rural environment might increase and decrease stress levels for some people, and possibly the specific type of worker. If time permits, ask about possible interactions between personal and workplace-related stress.

## SUGGESTED READING

Children's Trauma Institute. (2011, September). *Resilience alliance: Promoting resilience and reducing secondary trauma among child welfare staff.* New York, NY: Author.

Collins, J. (2014, April). Emerging approaches in child welfare. *Children's Voice,* Series addressing secondary traumatic stress. Retrieved from www.cwla.org/addressing-secondary-traumatic-stress

LaLiberte, T., & Crudo, T. (Eds.). (2012, Spring). *CW 360: Secondary trauma and the child welfare workforce.* Center for Advanced Studies in Child Welfare. Minneapolis: University of Minnesota School of Social Work. Retrieved from http://cascw.umn.edu/wp-content/uploads/2013/12/CW360_2012.pdf

National Child Traumatic Stress Network: www.nctsnet.org. An abundance of resources at this site devoted to child welfare trauma.

North Carolina Division of Social Services and the Family and Children's Resource Program. (2014, July). Supporting child welfare worker resiliency. *Children's Services Practice Notes, 19*(3), 1. Retrieved from www.practicenotes.org/v19n3/resiliency.htm

Ohio Child Welfare Training Program and IHS. (n.d.). *Managing stress as a child welfare caseworker: Caseworker readiness activity.* Retrieved from http://www.ocwtp.net/PDFs/CW%20Readiness/Section%202/Managing%20Stress%20as%20a%20Child%20Welfare%20Caseworker.pdf

Siegfried, C. B. (2008, March). *Child welfare work and secondary traumatic stress.* Child Welfare Trauma Training Toolkit: Secondary Traumatic Stress. National Child Traumatic Stress Network. Retrieved from http://www.nctsnet.org/nctsn_assets/pdfs/CWT3_SHO_STS.pdf

Salloum, A., Kondrat, D. C., Johnco, C., & Olson, K. R. (2015). *The Trauma-Informed Self-Care Measure.* doi:10.1037/t40859-000

## REFERENCES

Daley, M. (2015). *Rural social work in the 21st century.* Chicago, IL: Lyceum.

National Child Traumatic Stress Network. (2005). *Understanding child traumatic stress.* Retrieved from http://www.nctsnet.org/sites/default/files/assets/pdfs/Understanding

Riebschleger, J., Day, A., & Dworsky, A. (2015). Foster care youths' stories of trauma before, during, and after placement: Using youth voices for building trauma-informed systems of care. *Journal of Aggression, Maltreatment, and Trauma, 24,* 339–360. doi:10.1080/10926771.2015.1009603

Saxe, G. N., Ellis, B. H., & Brown, A. D. (2016). *Trauma systems therapy for children and teens* (2nd ed.). New York, NY: Guilford Press.

Salloum, A., Kondrat, D. C., Johnco, C., & Olson, K. R. (2015). The role of self-care on compassion satisfaction, burnout, and secondary trauma among child welfare workers. *Child and Youth Services Review, 49,* 54–61. doi:10.1016/j.childyouth.2014.12.023

Tavormina, M., & Clossey, L. (2015). Exploring crisis and its effect on workers in child protective services. *Child & Family Social Work.* doi:10.1111.cfs.12209

# INDEX

Page references for figures are indicated by *f* and for tables by *t*.